Calvin and the
Rhetoric of Piety

COLUMBIA SERIES IN REFORMED THEOLOGY

The Columbia Series in Reformed Theology represents a joint commitment of Columbia Theological Seminary and Westminster John Knox Press to provide theological resources for the church today.
The Reformed tradition has always sought to discern what the living God revealed in scripture is saying and doing in every new time and situation. Volumes in this series examine significant individuals, events, and issues in the development of this tradition and explore their implications for contemporary Christian faith and life.
This series is addressed to scholars, pastors, and laypersons. The Editorial Board hopes that these volumes will contribute to the continuing reformation of the church.

EDITORIAL BOARD

Shirley Guthrie, Columbia Theological Seminary

George Stroup, Columbia Theological Seminary

Donald K. McKim, Memphis Theological Seminary

B. A. Gerrish, University of Chicago

Amy Plantinga Pauw,
Louisville Presbyterian Theological Seminary

Columbia Theological Seminary wishes to express its appreciation to the following churches for supporting this joint publishing venture:

First Presbyterian Church, Tupelo, Mississippi

First Presbyterian Church, Nashville, Tennessee

Trinity Presbyterian Church, Atlanta, Georgia

Spring Hill Presbyterian Church, Mobile, Alabama

St. Stephen Presbyterian Church, Fort Worth, Texas

COLUMBIA SERIES IN REFORMED THEOLOGY

Calvin and the
Rhetoric of Piety

SERENE JONES

 Westminster John Knox Press
Louisville, Kentucky

Grateful acknowledgment is made to Westminster John Knox Press for permission to reprint as an appendix portions from *Calvin: Institutes of the Christian Religion,* edited by John T. McNeill, translated by Ford Lewis Battles, The Library of Christian Classics, copyright © 1960.

Book and cover design by Drew Stevens

First edition

Published by Westminster John Knox Press
Louisville, Kentucky

This book is printed on acid-free paper that meets the American National Standards Institute Z39.48 standard. ⊚

PRINTED IN THE UNITED STATES OF AMERICA

95 96 97 98 99 00 01 02 03 04 — 10 9 8 7 6 5 4 3 2 1

Library of Congress Cataloging-in-Publication Data

Jones, Serene, date.
 Calvin and the rhetoric of piety / Serene Jones — 1st ed.
   p. cm. — (Columbia series in Reformed theology)
 Includes bibliographical references and index.
 ISBN 0-664-22070-3
 1. Calvin, Jean, 1509–1564—Literary art. 2. Calvin, Jean, 1509–1564—
Contributions in doctrine of Christian spirituality. 3. Spiritual life—
Reformed Church—History—16th century. 4. Reformed Church—
Doctrines—History—16th century. I. Title. II. Series.
BX9418.J72 1995
230′.42′092—dc20   95-9324

CONTENTS

PREFACE

As I have lived with the *Institutes* over the past several years, I have become increasingly aware of its capacity to surprise me. Each time I return to the text, I stumble upon words—an image or a turn of phrase—I had previously hurried past or missed. When I pause long enough to enter the play of these words, I inevitably end up winding through worlds of meaning where I meet unexpected people and visit unfamiliar textual lands. It still amazes me that such small groupings of ink marks on a page can both carry and yet hide so many voices and so many different places.

When I reflect on the history of this present book, I am also taken aback by the many people and lands that are both hidden and yet present in each of its small ink marks. To name them all would be impossible, particularly those voices that remain most hidden: the voices of countless students whose questions and insights constantly pushed me into unexpected territory; the struggles of union organizers and fellow workers at Yale upon whose labor these ink marks depend; the names of numerous friends at South Church and Center Church who helped me to understand the true sense of "piety"; and the many people whose unfamiliar accents have taught me to delight in the "strangeness" of Calvin's voice. From fields of Enid, Oklahoma, to temples of Madurai, South India; from the villages of Panay, Philippines, to the city streets of New Haven and Waterbury, Connecticut; from the inscribed voices on the shelves of Sterling Memorial Library to the unwritten whispers of those whose voices have been drowned out by louder powers; from all these places and people, I have drawn the voice of this text. While it is a voice for which I claim full responsibility, it is nonetheless a voice that has its own history.

I wish to thank David Kelsey and Kathryn Tanner for directing the doctoral thesis from which this book has sprung and for being lively colleagues in the years hence. I am privileged to have benefited from the inspiration and advice of George Lindbeck, Letty Russell, Cornel West, and the late Hans Frei. I am also thankful for the generous help of Edward Dowey, Elsie McKee, and Brian Armstrong. Thanks to all these colleagues, I have had the courage to write about Calvin from the perspective of a constructive theologian who takes history seriously but who cannot claim the expertise of a historian. Lisa Cartwright, Mary Renda, Nancy Schnogg, Beryl Satter, Mary Ann Foley, Joan Bryant, and Amy Plantinga Pauw deserve medals for the hours they spent with me discussing theory, theology, history, and writing. I thank John Leinenweber for his superb skills in Latin, and Wendy Boring, Toni Vahlsing, and Joseph Mangina for their careful textual work. Harry and Deb Townshend made it possible for me to bring all this together in the form of a book by offering the gift of Ragged Hill. Yale Divinity School and the Lilly Foundation have generously contributed to its production. Cynthia Thompson and Timothy Staveteig from Westminster John Knox have been tireless in their support, and Kalbryn McLean's editorial wit and precision ushered the text into its final form. Verity Jones, Kindy Jones, Cornelia Dinnean, and Lynne Huffer have spun the bonds that hold this text, as well as its author, together. The drive and faith of Sarah Jones and the theological acumen and boldness of Joe Jones grace every page I write. And finally, I dedicate this book to Shepard Parsons, the most powerful Christian rhetorician I know.

ABBREVIATIONS

Inst.   John Calvin. *Institutes of the Christian Religion.* Edited by J. T. McNeill, trans. Ford Lewis Battles. Library of Christian Classics, vols. 20, 21. Philadelphia: Westminster Press, 1960.

OC   *Ioannis Calvini opera quae supersunt omnia.* Edited by Wilhelm Baum, Edward Cunitz, and Edward Reutz. 59 vols. Brunsvigae: C. A. Schwetsche, 1863–1900.

OS   *Ioannis Calvini Opera Selecta.* Vol. 3 Edited by Peter Barth and Wilhelm Niesel. Munich, 1928.

INTRODUCTION

Over the course of the past five centuries, John Calvin has been the subject of a variety of biographical portraits. He has been depicted as the great religious reformer of Geneva, a man whose intellect and drive created a new understanding of Christian piety. Many of these portraits present him as a disciplined and doctrinaire "person of faith and service," a model supposedly worthy of imitation by Christians of every age. In addition to this image of Calvin as the ideal churchman, he has been depicted by intellectual and social historians as a compelling influence for change in European history. He has been portrayed both as the austere architect of the "work ethic," and its concomitant capitalist morality, and as the revolutionary ideologue of democratic individualism. Philosophically, he has been represented as the person behind Enlightenment empiricism, as well as Kant's epistemology and Schleiermacher's pietist methodology. Most recently, he has been rendered anew in "a sixteenth-century portrait" of the turbulent forces that marked the men and women of early modern history.[1]

Wandering down this hall of portraits, one cannot help but note the striking differences that mark each image. In each portrayal, the face of Calvin changes. It changes from "man of faith" to intellectual genius, from moral disciplinarian to revolutionary hero, from controlled arbiter of doctrine to fractured creature of a tumultuous age. The thoughtful gallery walker will recognize, no doubt, that this diversity represents not only the complexity of Calvin's life and writings but also the varied aesthetic sensibilities of the scholars who have described him.[2] Given the wealth of knowledge and creative skill invested in each of these biographical renderings, it may appear strange that one aspect of Calvin's rich legacy remains virtually unrepresented. What is missing is a picture of Calvin himself as an artist.

In the six chapters that follow, this portrait of Calvin will begin to emerge: a portrait of a sixteenth-century theologian engaged in the creative activity of artistic production. Unlike many of the previous portrayals of Calvin, this particular depiction draws its material not so much from

1

the life of Calvin as from his art. The art to which I refer is his theological writing, more specifically, the highly crafted literary text known as the *Institutes of the Christian Religion*.[3] Here, the reader finds Calvin, a master of both French and Latin eloquence, skillfully practicing his talent for sharp and enlivening prose. Here, one also discovers Calvin's theology unfolding as more than a straightforward summary of doctrine; it unfolds as carefully detailed and rich language, wrought by the pen of one of early modern Europe's most powerful rhetoricians.

It is not purely by accident or personal predilection that I have chosen to render a portrait of Calvin as an artist and to treat his theology as art. While it is true that one need only glance at Calvin's texts to appreciate his skill as a writer, there are clear historical reasons why this approach constitutes a much needed addition to the field of theological scholarship on Calvin.[4] During Calvin's lifetime, the French celebration of the classical arts reached its apex, and in his early years of schooling in France, Calvin received extensive training in what was considered to be the queen of these arts, the art of rhetoric. The term "art" was applied to the rhetorical enterprise because, like painting, sculpture, and architecture, it required that its practitioner consciously use in his or her production both creative energy and original insight. Furthermore, if crafted with true artistic genius, eloquent language had the capacity not only to persuade the intellect but also, like its sister arts, to affect the emotions and will of its audience. In each of these areas, Calvin's talent for shaping both the written and spoken word did not simply meet Renaissance standards but itself became a new standard by which the artistry of rhetoric was measured.

In order to study Calvin's theology as art, one must pay close attention to how the rhetorical tools of his trade, namely, words, are used. That, in short, is the principal task of this book: to attend to the subtleties and nuances of the linguistic texture of his prized work, the *Institutes*, and subsequently to develop a deeper appreciation of the rhetorical mechanisms that drive his theological/artistic project. This task needs a delight in detail and a patience for pondering the particular, since a deeper appreciation of Calvin's rhetoric requires dwelling on the significance of words, phrases, and images that the reader might normally pass over. The task also requires that one respect Calvin's intentions in constructing the text; the reader must not assume that intentionality can be quickly grasped or that meaning and intention are simply synonymous. To do this work, one must read slowly and with caution. One must continually ask probing questions about word choice and the play of various tropes while simultaneously charting the text's argument in all its twists, turns, and inconsistencies. In other words, one must learn to read Calvin's theology as a literary critic might read Rabelais or Montaigne.

Given the present array of methodological options available to students of literary criticism, however, it is not enough to say that one needs to read like a literary critic. The question remains: What kind of literary critic? The answer one gives to this question depends on one's interests in reading Calvin. As a Christian theologian, I approach the *Institutes* with a whole host of very particular critical interests. I am interested in such things as Calvin's use of scripture, his relation to previous theologians in the West, his conformity (or lack of conformity) to the major creeds and dogmas of the church, and most important, the usefulness of his theology in Reformed churches today. Hence, I am not approaching the text like a literary critic who has no explicitly stated theological agenda. I am coming to the text with the intention of interrogating its theology and, at the same time, attending to its literary texture. My approach thus remains constantly attentive to the theological rules that guide and structure Calvin's use of rhetoric. In this sense, I read as a literary critic with clear ecclesial interests.

The fact that I approach the text as a theologian, however, does not completely account for my choice of literary theories when I attend to the text's rhetorical dimensions. For this part of my analysis, I use a set of literary guidelines that would have been familiar to Calvin as a trained Renaissance writer. These guidelines follow the directions and insights offered by the great orators of classical Rome, Cicero and Quintilian. Using their texts as a guide, one can reconstruct a rough approximation of the rhetorical rules that influenced Calvin's own discursive constructions. For the Latin orators and for Calvin as well, the principal goal for crafting eloquent prose was that it be persuasive and capable of convincing and moving its audience toward desired ends and actions. In addition to this "prime directive," the practitioners and theorists of classical rhetoric offered copious advice on how to use the tools of language in the most persuasive manner. When this advice is compared with Calvin's writing, it helps one understand why Calvin might have chosen to use a certain word, phrase, or argument. Accordingly, the modern reader must also be constantly aware that Calvin was writing for particular audiences. His goal was to move them toward very specific kinds of Christian actions, beliefs, and dispositions. Furthermore, he accomplished this persuasion by drawing on a tradition containing more than the insights of scripture and the grammar of Christian doctrine.

As I work through Calvin's theology using the guidelines of classical rhetoric to uncover the subtleties of his art, the aesthetics of his project will be seen more clearly. While this task alone constitutes a needed contribution to Calvinist studies, it also has broader ramifications for the understanding of Calvin's life and work. History records that Calvin was a well-known public speaker, a widely published author, and in both roles, was able to persuade and win the allegiance of his many sixteenth-century followers. What has rarely been asked, however, is the seemingly mundane but critically important question concerning the actual practices he used to accomplish these ends. When one begins to attend to these practices—best described as rhetorical—it is possible to develop a richer, more complex appreciation for his success as pastor, prophet, preacher, political leader, and theologian.

For example, readings of Calvin's *Institutes* that only delineate the content of his doctrinal formulations often miss the equally important pastoral dimension of the text. But to appreciate the full import of his doctrines one cannot overlook this more practical dimension. For instance, in Calvin's discussion of Christian piety, the emotional and experiential nature of his language is quite evident. Clearly, laypersons and pastors of sixteenth-century Geneva were not converted or deeply moved by his treatment of *pietas* simply because it made propositional sense of what they considered to be a scriptural truth. They were also moved because Calvin's discussion of piety was cast in language, images, and metaphors that somehow spoke to complexities of their lives. It helped to give meaning to the linguistic and cultural milieu in which they carried on their daily tasks. Similarly, Calvin's notion of piety did not compel Genevan citizens to build hospitals and schools because his definition of it was philosophically rigorous. Rather, Calvin's discussion of the pious disposition led people to do such things because his rhetoric was crafted to encourage these forms of Christian social action. Thus, when Calvin's description of piety is explored in terms of its rhetoric, one discovers that Calvin's concern was not only to teach a truth about God but also to give depth and sustenance to the spiritual lives of his vast parish of readers.

When this persuasive dimension of Calvin's theology is sought, one can envision new modes of conversation between today's pastors and that seemingly distant and formidable character from Geneva. These conversations might include the sharing of insights on such practical issues as how one speaks to the terminally ill about evil and providence, how one phrases a discussion of unmerited grace in the midst of a church meeting where personal differences hamper public action, or how one moves a congregation to hope in the middle of a city where despair and violence rule the day. Although such relevance may not always be evident to the modern reader, Calvin directly confronts such questions on almost every page of the *Institutes*. The power of his confrontation partially results from the extreme care he took in his use of language. Hence, another central task of this book is to help make these aspects of Calvin's work more evident and therefore more useful to present-day practitioners of Christian rhetoric. If Calvin's text is as successful as I believe it is at addressing the kinds of issues raised above, then a rhetorical analysis can provide the basis for a thoughtful study of the ways in which aesthetics, social praxis, and propositional truth claims cohere in the production of theological discourse.

Another set of questions raised by a rhetorical analysis of the *Institutes* concerns the relationship between politics and theology. Students of Calvin's theology are well aware that he devotes a number of pages near the end of the *Institutes* to a discussion of the responsibilities the Christian has toward the civil state and its rulers, whether they are monarchs, aristocrats, tyrants, or democratic councils. These sections of the text have consequently become the primary sources for conversations about Calvin's understanding of the interaction between church and state. However, a rhetorical reading of earlier and more theologically substantive portions of the text suggests that an exploration of Calvin and politics need not be limited to these concluding chapters, but can be expanded to include discussions of doctrines that may at first glance appear to be decidedly nonpolitical. An attentive reading of the text's rhetoric allows one to see the pervasive politics of Calvin's doctrinal treatments because this kind of reading attempts to identify the ever-present contexts and character of his doctrines' audiences. In the highly conflicted terrain of sixteenth-century Europe, this audience included kings, nobles, French intellectuals, and Roman Catholic apologists, as well as Calvin's own faithful flock of students and colleagues. Thus, on every page of the *Institutes,* Calvin uses words that, by speaking to these multiple audiences, address the major political figures and ideologies of his age. When this dimension of Calvin's writings comes into view, one can see that for him, theological discourse cannot extricate itself from the power relations and broader social configurations of the culture to which it speaks. Here, once again, one discovers new ways to discuss the relevance of Calvin's work for our own time, a time in which defining the proper relation between politics and theology continues to be a source of great debate.

Because a rhetorical reading of the *Institutes* throws light on the pastoral and political character of Calvin's writings, this type of analysis also raises more general questions about the nature and function of theological language and Christian doctrine. For example, if one takes Calvin's *Institutes* as a model for Reformed dogmatics, then a question arises about how one is to understand the task of theology. Is theology's sole purpose to present propositional truth claims to which the Christian is called to offer intellectual assent? To judge by Calvin's work, it seems not. Is doctrine to be understood as a static compendium of abstract principles that transcend the vicissitudes of history and politics? Again, Calvin's example suggests that such a definition is certainly inadequate. The questions continue and become even more complex. How is one to understand the role of rhetoric in the formulation of doctrine? Are the words that convey doctrine only surface ornaments that refer to revelatory truths beyond language? Calvin's way of doing theology suggests that language is more than the mere ornamental adornment of truth. Then, is the language of Christian doctrine simply an expressive representation of human religious sentiments that are deeper than or prior to language? As I shall argue, Calvin also challenges this notion of doctrine as he constructs a theological rhetoric designed to mold Christian sentiments and experiences. And finally, how far into theological writings can one carry this metaphor of art and artist, of rhetoric and rhetorician? What happens if God is also imaged as an artist and orator, and God's revelatory word is literally understood as language or the material of representation? As I shall maintain, Calvin develops the metaphor of rhetoric in this manner but leaves room for studies such as this one to explore its possibilities.

The chapters ahead begin the task of looking at such questions and their answers in light of Calvin's creative approach to writing theology. In the opening chapter, the groundwork for a rhetorical analysis of his writing is laid by introducing the understanding of rhetoric held by humanists in sixteenth-century France. This first chapter begins with an overview of the young Calvin's educational history, highlighting the central role that rhetorical training played in his studies. It then outlines the conceptual parameters of rhetoric by summarizing Cicero and Quintilian's advice on constructing persuasive and eloquent orations. Next, it illustrates how Renaissance humanists reworked classical rhetoric to fit the needs of their time. A central component of this reworking is the notion that written prose, if truly eloquent, has the capacity to transform the disposition of its reading audience by inducing a "play of mind" that leads to specific actions that the author intends to elicit.

In order for this conception of rhetoric to be applied to the *Institutes*, one must also have at least a minimal grasp of the historical readership Calvin addressed. In chapter 2 I take up the task of describing, in very general terms, the character of these audiences. This discussion of audiences is not intended to be exhaustive. Historians have identified a number of international sixteenth-century readers whom I have chosen not to describe in order to keep this study focused and manageable. In determining which audiences to consider, I followed a principle of selection provided by three of Calvin's "prefatory letters" to the *Institutes*. On the basis of these letters, I identify several communities of readers that Calvin sought to address. With the help of contemporary historians, I then offer a short overview of the "needs and expectations" that Calvin might have considered as he crafted the rhetoric of the *Institutes* to speak to these communities. This chapter's discussion of Calvin's sixteenth-century readers also serves as an invitation for present-day readers to use their own historical imaginations as they encounter his rhetoric. On the basis of the information provided in chapter 2, readers are encouraged to imagine that they are Genevan Libertine opponents or staunch supporters of Calvin, a French king or a rebel French aristocrat, a rigorously philosophical Scholastic or an avant-garde humanist. Having taken on these roles, the present-day readers can then imagine how certain passages in the *Institutes* might sound to them. Given their social position, would they find the text nurturing or caustic, provocative or subversive? Would Calvin's words sound profoundly faithful or dangerously heretical?

The chances are that, depending on the audience one imagines, the meaning and persuasive effect of the text will appear quite different. In fact, there may be occasions on which one imagines the text generating multiple meanings and producing a variety of persuasive repercussions. This multiplicity, however, should not be interpreted as a problem but rather as a sign of both Calvin's rhetorical genius and the unceasing productivity of language. In the process of entering into this exercise, it is also important to remember that one's own modern cultural assumptions will inevitably be projected back onto these characters of the sixteenth century. Therefore, such an exercise in imagination will not be precise or historically neutral. However, what this approach does facilitate is a reading that is open to the rhetorical nuances of the text and its multiple meanings. The openness of this approach stands in contrast to many previous interpretations of Calvin that assume the text simply speaks to a uniform, universal, and ahistorical audience that is capable of grasping the one true meaning of doctrine despite the complexity of its language and the multiple agendas of its author.

In chapters 3 through 5, I use the background information of the previous chapters in a rhetorical analysis of the first three chapters of Book 1 of the *Institutes*. Each of these readings proposes a new interpretation of Calvin's theology. Each interpretation pays close attention to Calvin's language and to the effects it might have had upon his intended readers. And yet each reading is radically different from the others. This difference has to do partially with the shifting genres Calvin employs as he moves from one chapter of the *Institutes* to the next. In addition, the differences between these three readings result from shifting nuances in my own approach to the text. Given the complexity of Calvin's rhetoric, I have found it necessary to shift my analytic method in order to follow the text's constantly moving dimensions and meanings. This shifting allows each reading to accentuate a different level of the text's discourse and a different layer of its rhetorical significance.

For example, in chapter 3, I examine the first chapter of the *Institutes*, in which Calvin discusses how we come to know God: Is it by beginning with divine wisdom or self-knowledge? Here, my analysis focuses specifically on the logical progression of the text's argument. I identify several possible audiences and trace the ways in which his arguments engage each of these designated groups of readers.

In chapter 4, however, my emphasis shifts as I turn to Calvin's definition of *pietas* found in the second chapter of the *Institutes*. Here, the stress is not on the argument as much as it is on the attitude of praise Calvin is trying to inculcate in his readers. As I try to show, he encourages this attitude not through a precise form of reasoning but through rhetorical appeals designed to uplift and nurture the piety of his readers. When this dimension of his language is noted, one is able to appreciate more clearly Calvin's skill at shaping the Christian character of his readers.

In chapter 5, I turn to the third chapter of the *Institutes* where Calvin develops his well-known discussion of the *divinitatis sensus*, an awareness of divinity implanted in each person. Once again, the focus of my rhetorical analysis shifts as I explore how Calvin textually constructs a pagan "other" over and against which he defines the identity of his own community of faith. Here, then, the emphasis falls on Calvin's metaphorical logic of identity and the role his language plays in the crafting of an emergent social body.

These five chapters together try to portray Calvin as a rhetorical artist. The portrait is tentative because reading three chapters of the *Institutes* certainly does not provide sufficient material for a full portrait of Calvin's life and work as an artist of language. The three readings described above, however, do give one a sense of the colors and contours that could eventually fill in the rough sketch, though it may well be that this particular portrait must ever remain as unfinished and indeterminate as the language from which it is drawn. Yet even in its unfinished state, this picture looks quite different from previous portraits of Calvin. In chapter 3, I illustrate how it challenges the interpretation of Calvin's view of divine and self-knowledge found in the famous Barth-Brunner debates. In chapter 4, I develop a sketch of Calvin's notion of piety that is quite different from Paul Tillich's existentialist interpretation of Calvin's position. And finally, in chapter 5, I excavate the multiple ways in which the text contributes to the construction of new social identities, both real and imagined. It is through these comparative assessments that one begins to get a sense of the broader theological implications of using rhetoric as an approach for understanding Christian doctrine.

In the concluding chapter of the book, I explicitly turn to these broader ramifications and explore the more general and systematic theological questions raised by my analysis. The questions are complex. They concern such topics as the relation between theological discourse and its social contexts, the interplay between theology and the metaphorical character of meaning, theology and the ever-shifting power relations it negotiates, theology and the formation of Christian character, and the ethics of theological rhetoric with respect to an author's audiences and to the identities he or she constructs and then either validates or rejects. While it is true that the portrait I draw of Calvin's theology can serve as a starting point for sorting through these issues, these particular questions ultimately tell us as much about the portrait of late-twentieth-century theology as they do about sixteenth-century theology. And it may well be that this portrait of contemporary theology must finally remain even more unfinished and indeterminate than the face of that long-dead but still lively theologian from Geneva. If so, perhaps the portrait of Calvin should be smiling.

Note on editions, citations, and translations:
    In order to facilitate the reader's own close reading of Book 1, chapters 1, 2, and 3 of the 1559 *Institutes of the Christian Religion,* the full English text of these chapters is provided in this book's appendix. I suggest reading through it before beginning my chapters 3, 4, and 5. In addition to the appendix, both English and Latin versions of crucial texts are provided in the footnotes of each chapter. I hope that the reader will take full advantage of this material, for following the text in its original language, as well as in English translation, allows one to better appreciate the rhetorical flow of Calvin's language. The Latin text is taken from Book 1 of the *Institutio Christianae Religionis,* 1559, found in volume 3 of *Ioannis Calvini Opera Selecta,* ed. Peter Barth and Wilhelm Niesel (Munich: 1928), cited throughout as OS. The English translation is taken from the *Institutes of The Christian Religion* (1559), ed. J. T. McNeill, trans. Ford Lewis Battles, Library of Christian Classics, vols. 20, 21 (Philadelphia: Westminster Press, 1960), cited throughout as *Inst.* For Latin references to Calvin's other writings (sermons, commentaries, prefaces, etc.), I use *Ioannis Calvini opera quae supersunt omnia,* ed. Wilhelm Baum, Edward Cunitz, and Edward Reutz, 59 vols. (Brunsvigae: C. A. Schwetscke, 1863–1900), referred to throughout as OC.

NOTES

1. William Bouwsma, *John Calvin: A Sixteenth-Century Portrait* (New York: Oxford University Press, 1988).
    2. For an interesting discussion of the history of Calvin scholarship and its varied theoretical frameworks, see Benoit Girardin, *Rhétorique et théologique: Calvin, le Commentaire de l'Epitre aux Romains* (Paris: Editions Beauchesne, 1979).
    3. Calvin's skills as a literary artist are evidenced not only in his best-known work, the 1559 Latin edition of the *Institutes of the Christian Religion,* but also in the numerous sermons, tracts, treatises, commentaries, and letters he penned over the

years. In these works, Calvin demonstrates his facility for crafting eloquent prose both in Latin, the formal language of the sixteenth-century church and academy, and in French, his native tongue and the more popular medium of discourse in his day. In chapters 1 and 2, I will discuss some of these materials. However, chapters 3, 4, and 5 focus almost exclusively on the first three chapters of the 1559 *Institutes* with only occasional references to his other writings. The fact that I do not offer extensive analysis of works outside the '59 *Institutes* is not meant to suggest that these writings are any less interesting, from a rhetorical perspective, than the *Institutes*. Quite the contrary, these materials provide fertile ground for the type of rhetorical analysis I undertake in the present study.

4. As is often the case, early modern historians and literary theorists have already paved the way for the present work on Calvin's theology and the rhetorical tradition. To scholars such as Brian Armstrong, William Bouwsma, Quirinus Breen, Benoit Girardin, Francis Higman, and David Willis, I owe a great deal. Without their ground-breaking investigations of Calvin's humanism and his relation to Cicero and other classical orators, this work could not have been written.

1

CALVIN AND THE RHETORICAL TRADITION

The art of delivering a beautiful oration in an effective oratorical style is nothing else, Brutus, . . . than presenting the best thoughts in the choicest language.

Nihil enim est aliud, Brute, . . . pulchre et oratorie dicere nisi optimis sententiis verbisque lectissimis dicere.

Cicero

Doctrine stated generally does not move us.

Generalis enim doctrina minus afficit.

John Calvin

It is a midweek morning in the city of Geneva and through the high windows of the Great Hall in the downtown Academy come the sounds of the outside world, the urban bustle of horses' hooves and merchants' friendly shouts. Inside the hall a hush has just settled over an eager audience of hundreds. Every bench is full, and the crowd spills into the aisles. Among those gathered, one can pick out the restless, young ministerial students who will soon be sent on a perilous journey to underground churches in France. There are also older faces in the crowd, many of them international figures with names as distinguished as John Knox, Thomas Bodley (the Oxford librarian), and Nicolas Folion, the famous doctor from the Sorbonne.[1] Scattered here and there, couriers from the French royal courts sit poised, ready to absorb the morning lecture and then report to rebel aristocrats in their homeland. Many Genevan citizens have also turned out for this event: the most powerful political and religious leaders of the city fill the seats near the front while, interspersed with the larger crowd, lesser-known printers, textile producers, and local traders wait attentively. In the back sits the opposition. The atmosphere is electric.

As the hush falls, the lecturer appears and moves with familiarity and confidence to his position at the lectern. It is clear that he has been here before; in fact, he stands in this same position, before similar crowds, almost seven days a week. The year is 1561, and the assembled mass waits eagerly to hear the first words of the French-speaking reformer, John Calvin. He opens the sacred Scriptures and begins.

Why has this man attracted such a diverse and intent audience on a weekday morning? Why is it that in this Great Hall at the Academy of Geneva he has the ear of all of Europe? If one takes Calvin's sermons, commentaries, tracts, and theological works as an indication of how he might have addressed the crowd that day, one thing becomes clear: Calvin stood

11

before the assemblage as a writer and speaker of great skill and power. He knew how to capture the attention of his audience, how to hold them attentive to his words, how to appeal to their deepest fears and loftiest expectations, how to spin an argument of fine and simple beauty, how to move and compel them to action. In short, Calvin was able to fill that hall with spectators, students, and followers because of his renown as one of the grandest French orators of his time, a reputation that has since earned him the title "the founder of modern French eloquence."[2]

Although Calvin scholars have long acknowledged his skills as an orator and writer, it is only in recent years that this aspect of his formation as a theologian and political leader has received extended attention. Both historical and textual research have revealed that although Calvin may have exhibited a native ability for constructing persuasive discourse early in his life, these skills were, for the most part, the product of years of training in the classical rhetorical tradition. As skills he learned during his legal studies in Bourges, they were part and parcel of the intellectual repertoire he painstakingly mastered as a young student of the humanist movement in Paris. And when he left Paris, exiled in 1534, he took these skills with him into the foreign lands of his exile and the strange new world of theology.

In describing the years following his flight from France, Calvin's biographers recount the moving story of a life that continued to be fractured by political strife and yet held together by a singular theological vision. As one reads historical accounts of his struggles, his setbacks, his skillful political negotiations, and his final victory in the fight for power in Geneva, it is easy to imagine how these oratorical skills must have served him. Armed with weapons of eloquence and fortified by his training in the art of persuasion, Calvin was well prepared to manage these fracturing forces by stirring the allegiance of committed followers and responding to the attacks of his most formidable opponents. What these historical reconstructions of his tumultuous life rarely provide, however, is an account of how his rhetorical talents helped to shape his theological vision as well. While it does not take a wild leap of the imagination to assume that the skills that carried Calvin to the apex of political power also spilled over into his work as a theologian, systematic theologians of today are only now beginning to take this imaginative leap and read Calvin's theology in light of these rhetorical sensibilities. When this leap is taken, Calvin's theological writings suddenly appear as passionately engaged as that public lecture which attracted the crowd of hundreds. And in this context, new possibilities arise for interpreting the meaning of the doctrines espoused in his texts.

In the pages that follow, the reader will be introduced to these interpretive possibilities. However, to appreciate fully the depth and complexity of the marks left by the rhetorical tradition on Calvin's theology, one must first have a firm grasp of the tools with which he worked. Understanding the nature of these tools requires an overview of what Calvin actually learned about language and oration during his early years in France. How did he understand the character of effective writing? What would have constituted a text as truly eloquent and persuasive? By grappling with these questions and becoming familiar with the sixteenth-century discipline of rhetoric, one can engage in the imaginative enterprise of reading Calvin rhetorically. Hence, this study will begin by entering the world of Renaissance rhetoric.

THE WORLD OF RENAISSANCE RHETORIC

The dialogue between Christian theology and the discipline of classical rhetoric has a long history. Since the time of the early church, Christian apologists have turned to the ancient Roman and Greek orators for guidance in presenting persuasive accounts of the Christian message.[3] The depth of this influence is perhaps best illustrated in the writings of Augustine, who, after years of practice in the skills of eloquence, composed a body of theological literature known for its passion and beauty as well as its theological acumen. Similarly, during the High Middle Ages, theologians such as Abelard, Anselm, and Thomas structured their works around finely tuned rhetorical schemes designed to facilitate the teaching of "divine wisdom" and to "nurture the soul" in its journey toward God.[4] Thus, it was a long tradition of conversation between rhetoric and theology into which Calvin stepped. But by the time Calvin entered the dialogue in the sixteenth century, it had been cast in decidedly new terms.

The new terms of this conversation were first set in fourteenth-century Italy, following the recovery of a large body of classical texts on rhetoric, the most celebrated of which were the works of Cicero and Quintilian.[5] The flurry of scholarly excitement that these texts initially generated was immense. The source of this excitement, however, was not simply academic curiosity. The recovery of Cicero and Quintilian coincided with the emergence of powerful city-states in the Italian territories, and this rise created social needs that the texts of the ancient orators were well designed to serve. With the growth of these cities came a dramatic increase in administrative bureaucracies and juridical courts. At the same time, there appeared a new class of professional men and women whose vocation was that of managing the increasingly complicated institutional apparatuses of these territories. The most influential figures in this new class were a group of scholars and statespersons who held the title of "professional rhetoricians." Included in their ranks one finds such well-known figures as Coluccio Salutati, Leonardo Bruni, and in the fifteenth century, Lorenzo Valla.[6] Because of their skills as writers and effective negotiators, they were commissioned to compose foreign correspondence and to facilitate the contractual forms of the many treaties being forged between territorial bodies. They also performed similar duties in the papal administrations, particularly in the area of real estate acquisition and management. In addition to serving these instrumental functions, rhetoricians also took up the task of articulating a public ideology conducive to the smooth workings of these new institutional forms. In this enterprise, they found the writings of Cicero especially useful because he provided a conceptual framework in which notions of the public good and civic responsibility made practical sense. Thus, with the assistance of the esteemed orators of the classical era, these professional rhetoricians soon became the politicians of a new epoch in European history.

During the fifteenth and sixteenth centuries, these rhetoricians increasingly turned to the law courts of Italy and France as the most appropriate structure to house their administrative and adjudicatory responsibilities. And as the complexities of governing the interests of both nation and church grew, so did their legal duties.[7] The gradual but nonetheless radical shift from feudal economic arrangements to entrepreneurial and capitalist modes of production required the creation of a new language of commerce; and the rise of the new bourgeois class brought with it the need to redefine the basis of property rights. Furthermore, along with these shifting economic demands, the familial structure was undergoing redefinition, and a new language of contract was required to mediate the social relations that constituted the emerging nuclear family. In each of these instances, it was the lawyers whom society called upon to produce the language and laws needed to shape and regulate these still nascent social forms.[8]

Why were the tools of rhetoric considered effective guides for this emergent civil militia of lawyers? A partial answer lies in the fact that, unlike the rhetorically skilled arbiters of early modern Europe, previous generations of medieval lawyers had approached issues of social conflict as situations to be transcended rather than managed, and this transcendence was accomplished by appeal to ecclesial authority and "ultimate principles of justice." This approach, however, failed to provide adequate tools for adjudicating the growing number of legal disputes with particularities that could hardly have been imagined in the Middle Ages. In contrast, this new generation of rhetoricians/lawyers had become much more tolerant of conflict, in all its diversity, and viewed it as an inherent part of human society requiring careful management rather than transcendence.[9] The art of management drew upon skills similar to those needed for excellence in

oratory. As rhetoricians, these men and women had honed the skill of assessing a given situation in terms of the practical issues at stake and the
political interests involved. With this kind of skill, they were less likely to
search for universal principles and instead relied upon the practical wisdom of prudential judgment. Therefore, when it came to articulating a
novel set of discursive rules capable of regulating the expanding and
changing institutional forms of early modern Europe, the move from
rhetoric to law was natural. With prudential judgment as their guide,
lawyers set out to define an innovative "set of empirical, pragmatic and
secular attitudes" necessary for the orderly administration of the emergent polis.[10]

   Thus, in early–sixteenth-century France, a legal education had become
a practical necessity for anyone aspiring to a career in the administrative
affairs of either church or state. It was also highly valued by many who
never intended to practice law in the courts but nonetheless sought the
prestige afforded by a degree in jurisprudence.[11] In fact, it was not at all
unusual to find young students who, upon completing their legal studies,
turned away from the courts and followed vocational paths of a more
scholarly nature. More often than not, this path led them directly into the
exciting fray of a broad educational movement known as "humanism."[12]

   Although it is difficult to summarize briefly a movement as vast, internally complex, and conflicted as the humanism of France during this period, it is possible to identify a few of the most predominant features, features that appear in the works of humanists ranging from the famous
Erasmus of Rotterdam to the esteemed professor Guillaume Budé.[13] Like
their colleagues in the field of legal studies, humanists such as these academicians were very interested in the works of the classical era, particularly those composed by Roman rhetoricians. Inspired by the views of discourse promoted by Cicero and Quintilian, they sought to redefine the
norms of scholarly acumen in order to meet the needs of their age. In doing so, they became fascinated with the nature of language and its usefulness as a political tool. This interest in language and its persuasive power
led the humanists to devote considerable attention to such topics as the
value of the vernacular, the art of translation, the role of social context in
determining a word's meaning, and the playful extravagances of discursive ornamentation. As cultural philosophers, these same humanists also
took great delight in celebrating the enormous powers of the human intellect and rigorously encouraged innovative explorations in disciplines
as diverse as historical studies, astronomy, and the science of human
anatomy. Thus, in these shared features—their love of classical literature
and philosophy, their fascination with the rhetorical dimensions of language, and their high estimation of human knowledge and power—one

finds the humanists of sixteenth-century France representing, in its opulent form and optimistic temper, the grand spirit of the Renaissance in early modern Europe.

Such was the world of jurisprudence and humanism when Calvin entered the French intellectual scene in 1527.[14] After completing his secondary education in Montaigu, Calvin left Paris at the age of eighteen and, like many of the young men of his time, moved to Orleans to begin the study of Roman and French jurisprudence. After a year in Orleans, Calvin went to live in the nearby city of Bourges, where the Italian humanist Andreas Alciati was offering lectures in law.[15] Heralded as the premier reformer of juridical science, Alciati was trained, as were most Italian humanists, in the art of classical rhetoric. This skill not only made him an immensely popular and entertaining lecturer but also informed his analysis of legal texts. He encouraged his students to read Roman law by placing it in its original rhetorical framework. In this framework, the language of law was viewed as an active language, designed to move and convince audiences, designed to incorporate a multitude of underlying political agendas and to accommodate its audiences by adopting the most popular linguistic conventions of its time.

Intrigued by this new approach to analyzing and interpreting texts, Calvin soon began a thorough study of the works of both Cicero and Quintilian. In an acknowledgment of his growing mastery of the subject, he was asked to deliver lectures on rhetoric at a local Augustinian convent.[16] During this period, Calvin also began to work on what would become his first scholarly publication, a commentary on Seneca's *De clementia*.[17] The fact that Calvin chose to devote his energy to this particular enterprise suggests that, at this point in his career, he had elected not to pursue a legal career but instead had opted for a life of scholarship shaped by the methods and interests of French humanism. Unfortunately, the published work never received the degree of critical acclaim Calvin had anticipated. That it received little notice, however, was not due to any flaw in Calvin's analysis of Seneca's text. In fact, the work has since been described as a "perfect specimen of sixteenth-century classical scholarship" in that it exhibits the well-honed skills of an author practiced in the arts of philology, textual criticism, and translation, the three hallmarks of humanist scholarship.[18] This commentary thus serves as perhaps the best evidence that by 1532, Calvin had become an accomplished master in the ancient art of rhetoric and in its reconceptualization in the world of Renaissance humanism.

Despite his disappointment with the commentary's lackluster reception, Calvin returned to Paris in 1533 and immediately became embroiled in the controversy surrounding the place of humanism and reform in the university.[19] Through a series of political intrigues, the conservative Parisian academy's Faculty of Theology had convinced King Francis I, a former champion of educational reform, that many of their humanist colleagues were underground Lutherans and thus secretly harbored seditious intentions. Because of his close association with Nicolas Cop, the newly elected rector of the university and an outspoken proponent of humanism, Calvin was among the many people targeted by this conservative backlash.[20] Thus, following the famous Affair of the Placards in October of 1534, Calvin was forced to leave Paris in order to avoid imprisonment and possible execution.[21] Like many of his humanist friends, Calvin eventually took refuge in the city of Basel.

The intellectual scene in Basel presented Calvin with theological challenges that had been largely absent from his studies in France. The city itself was full of French exiles and the humanist spirit thus remained a lively one. But the rhetoric of radical ecclesiastical reform was even stronger, and Calvin soon became acquainted with some of the most famous and controversial figures of the Reformation, men such as his cousin, Pierre Olivétan; Simon Grynaeus, the Greek scholar; Wolfgang Capito, a colleague of Martin Bucer; Henri Bullinger, the powerful reformer who had succeeded Zwingli as the head of the Zurich church; and Pierre Viret and Guillaume Farel, former students of theology in Paris who had been following closely the reform of the French-speaking Cantons in Switzerland.[22] In the midst of the passionate conversations stimulated by these figures, Calvin turned to the study of scripture and Christian doctrine and, as in his former studies, approached these topics with a tenacious rigor. It was in this new environment that Calvin also began turning his own pen to the topic of theology and, among other things, undertook the composition of his 1536 *Institutes of the Christian Religion*.[23]

During this period of tumultuous upheaval and relocation, Calvin was transformed from a law student and humanist scholar of the highest caliber into an exiled theologian. Although many pages have since been devoted to analyzing the "conversion experience" that precipitated this change, it would be a mistake to assume that this shift in vocational direction amounted to a total renunciation of all that he had learned under the direction of his French and classical mentors. Given that there was nothing particularly religious about his work on Seneca or anything notably clerical about his appreciation of classical rhetoric, it is likely that Calvin was simply able to take the rhetorical skills he mastered during his humanist education and apply them to the theological tasks that now occupied his attention. Having thus looked at the historical context in which Calvin's understanding of rhetoric developed, I will now turn briefly to the theoretical underpinnings of this classical discipline.

RENAISSANCE RHETORIC'S THEORETICAL UNDERPINNINGS

Venturing into the conceptual world of this discipline called rhetoric may appear, at first glance, to be a rather daunting enterprise. This is particularly true for students and academicians well versed in the literary trends of today's scholarship. At present, many texts written in the fields of literature and cultural studies use the word "rhetoric" to describe the "ground-breaking" project undertaken in their pages. A trip to the local university bookstore will reveal lengthy volumes carrying titles such as "the rhetoric of reason," "colonialism and its rhetorics," "the rhetoric of feminism," or "philosophy as rhetoric." And in each of these texts, one will find the term "rhetoric" defined in a different manner. As a catch-all term, its current meanings seem to be almost endless in variety. It may simply refer to "language," or it may designate the varying functions language serves when deployed in diverse social contexts. Or yet again, it may be used to convey meanings that only the practiced connoisseur of a particular discipline would be able to appreciate or even comprehend.

Because of this array of definitions marking the territory of the discipline called rhetoric, it is crucial that one be precise about the intended use of the term in a given text. As the preceding analysis of the social function of rhetoric in the sixteenth century suggests, the definition I use here is one that comes as close as possible to the definition of rhetoric Calvin himself might have offered. Fortunately, it is fairly easy to describe the primary contours of the terrain covered by Calvin's definition. It does not require delving into the complicated and highly nuanced world of contemporary literary criticism. Rather, one needs only an overview of the clear, simply written, and concise little handbooks on the art of rhetoric composed by Calvin's favored orator Cicero. Used frequently in high school and college courses today, these handbooks are titled *De inventione, De oratore,* and *Orator.*[24]

In these texts, Cicero undertakes the task of teaching his students the basic skills needed to write and deliver eloquent speeches. Cicero begins by laying out the technical vocabulary associated with rhetoric. He first outlines three major types of oration or argument, each of which is defined according to its subject matter and context. These types are the panegyric or demonstrative (*demonstrativum*), used most often in public rituals; the forensic or judicial (*iudiciale*), used in a courtroom setting; and the deliberative (*deliberativum*), deployed primarily when speaking to the public on matters of civic responsibility.[25] In addition to these three forms of oration, Cicero provides a five-part framework that highlights particular skills the student needs to master in order to speak eloquently. First, there is the art of invention (*inventio*), a term that refers to the orator's capacity to construct effectively a thesis and its supporting arguments. This aspect of oration is frequently referred to simply as the speech's content. Second, there is the art of skillful arrangement (*collocatio*) or order. If an orator wants to persuade his audience, he must carefully organize his speech so that his listeners can easily follow him to a convincing conclusion.[26] Next, Cicero tells his students that memory (*memoria*) plays a crucial role in developing the skills of effective persuasion. While a speech may be carefully written prior to its presentation, a good rhetorician does not resort to the text but, having memorized it, addresses the audience directly.

Fourth, and perhaps most importantly, there are the skills associated with cultivating a persuasive style. Cicero calls these skills ornamentation or *elocutio*. In order to persuade effectively, Cicero explains that it is necessary to embellish one's speech with words, images, metaphors, sounds, and stories—all designed to resonate with a particular audience's expectations and experiences. Decorating one's discourse with these ornaments of language is a skill that may take years to perfect, but its fruits, Cicero tells his students, promise to be sweet and immensely satisfying. Finally, there is the art of delivery (*actio*). Excellence in this area demands that the orator present himself as a person of noble and virtuous intentions and as an expert in full command of the topic to be presented. Cicero also encourages his students to explore the delights of rhythm and intonation in order to embellish further the play of the spoken word.

The term coined in antiquity to describe a speech that fully exploits the wealth of resources available for constructing decorous discourse is *copia* (the closest English equivalent for this term is the notion of copiousness). Cicero considers a copious orator to be one who, having studied philosophy and history, is able to draw upon vast reserves of linguistic usage and choose the phrase, term, argument, or example best suited to the audience's sentiments.[27] Closely related to *copia* is the term *imitatio*, or imitation, which refers to the activity of mining and then using these resources. To describe the process whereby an orator makes copious use of the rhetoric deployed by previous authors and thereby imitates discursive gestures from the past, Quintilian offers the image of digestion.[28] As the metaphor suggests, *imitatio* entails more than simple linear repetition. An orator must take in or swallow the discourse from the past by fully absorbing its complexities and becoming acquainted with the intentions, personal character, and social background of the one from whom it originated. If the discourse is digested in this manner, the material is softened and then consumed so that eventually it becomes part of the one who has swallowed it. Thus, when an orator finally rearticulates the original argument or image, its meaning has become as much a part of the orator as it was of the original author. As part of the new orator's repertoire, such resources can be redeployed in a manner appropriate to a new social context.

It should be noted that in his discussion of such topics as *imitatio* and *copia,* Cicero was offering advice to students who anticipated serving the polis as politicians and public orators. Toward this end, Cicero was concerned primarily with the rhetorical quality of oral discourse. However, by the time humanists like Erasmus and Budé turned to Cicero for advice on discursive excellence, the revolutionary invention of the printing press had turned the written word into an increasingly important medium for public communications.[29] This change required that early modern rhetoricians rethink at least two of Cicero's technical observations about proper discursive form. First, Cicero had argued that the only form of rhetoric appropriate for the writing of published texts was the demonstrative form. However, given the variety of uses to which sixteenth-century texts were put, this new age of rhetoricians brought the forensic and the deliberative styles of presentation into the realm of the written word as well.[30] Second, Cicero had stated quite forcefully that once a person had chosen a particular style, he should not confuse his orations by incorporating strategies appropriate to other styles of writing; in other words, one discourse, one stylistic form. In contrast, French rhetoricians were known to have encouraged stylistic improvisations that blended together different forms and styles of writing. They encouraged this improvisation because, unlike a public speech, writing could be read in a variety of contexts and put to a variety of uses as a text traveled from one audience to another, each of which might demand a different form and style. Given that written texts could be much longer than public orations, the humanist rhetoricians could also construct sections requiring forensic rhetoric and then move on to develop other sections through a more deliberative or demonstrative style of discourse without severely disorienting the reader.

But to return to Cicero: Having familiarized his students with the basic vocabulary of oratorical skills, he then goes on to discuss a number of things that a rhetorician should keep in mind in the process of building a persuasive and decorous appeal. The simplest but perhaps most fundamental of the insights shared by Cicero is his understanding of language as an active social force. While Cicero never directly challenged the Platonic notion that language is a kind of static sign system through which mental ideas are represented, he believed that such a definition did not capture the full power and force of language. In addition to representing ideas, language, Cicero argues, is an active instrument; in short, it does things.[31] It does things to people's minds and hearts. And hence, it has the capacity, if properly manipulated, to transform states, to overthrow governments, to garner public support for policies, to win wars, and, at times, to destroy reputations and lives. Its uses are always multiple. It can be deployed "to prove, to please and to sway or persuade."[32] Cicero thus adds that, depending on the character of the artisan who wields it, language can serve as a constructive tool or as a destructive weapon. Consequently, trained rhetoricians carry a heavy responsibility; they control the discursive mechanism by which public sentiments are aroused and managed and the public order either maintained or threatened.

In an effort to ensure that his students not misuse this tool, Cicero offers further advice on the effective manipulation of language. He stresses first and foremost that when choosing a style and selecting linguistic ornaments, the orator should be aware of the needs, expectations, dispositions, and abilities of his audience. On the basis of this assessment, the orator is urged to accommodate (*accommodare*) his arguments and metaphors to meet the audience in their own context. As Cicero explains it, "the eloquence of orators has always been controlled by the good sense of the audience, since all who desire to win approval have regard to the goodwill of their auditors, and shape (*fingere*) and adapt (*accommodare*) themselves completely according to this and to their opinion and approval."[33] Moreover, in order to determine what will in fact win the approval of the audience, Cicero suggests that the orator consider a variety of environmental factors such as the time and place of the oration and the political interests and background of the audience. For this reason, Cicero's ideal orator is, by necessity, an avid student of popular culture.

In addition to noting these fluctuating factors, Cicero reminds his students that there are certain basic proclivities shared by all audiences, proclivities that an accommodative discourse must also address. For instance, although an audience will most certainly use its reason to test the adequacy of an argument, one's rhetoric should also cater to and entice the faculty of the will—a faculty often moved by the emotions. With regard to the faculty of reason, Cicero adds a cautionary note: Although arguments should be carefully and logically constructed, one must remember that the majority of persons encountered in a public oration do not have the philosopher's propensity for careful dialectics. Rather, most audiences are guided by a more ordinary form of "popular intelligence," and they are consequently more impressed by probability than by dialectical precision. Cicero also stresses in this context the fundamentally self-interested nature of persons and therefore encourages his students never to overlook the more selfish instincts of their audiences.

This notion of accommodation should not be interpreted, however, as permission for an orator to tell an audience what it wants to hear. Rather, Cicero believes that truly eloquent orations are most powerful when they succeed in persuading audiences to assent to positions they might not otherwise entertain. If one is to accomplish such a feat, Cicero teaches, the orator must be clear, from the beginning, as to the specific goals and purposes he intends his discourse to satisfy. Attaining clarity of purpose requires identifying the kind of appeal one wishes to make. If the purpose is to teach, then one must adopt a language suited to the purposes of pedagogy. If the purpose is to defend a controversial position or to ward off the attacks of one's opponents, then a forensic rhetoric would be more appropriate, be it apologetic or polemical in character. Likewise, if one intends to uplift and edify the audience, then a more effusive style of deliberative discourse may be considered the most effective form of address. Furthermore, if one's goal includes all three of the above agendas, then care must be taken to weave the three together in a convincing manner.[34] What is most important, however, is that one not lose sight of the intended goal in the process of constructing a well-accommodated appeal. If this should happen, then the orator has failed at his task, no matter how loudly the audience may applaud.

Determining one's rhetorical goal and then identifying the form of speech appropriate to it also requires that the orator consider purposes of a more lofty nature. According to Cicero, the central and overarching goal that should guide the reflections of all orators—be they involved in teaching, arguing, or praising—is that of serving the polis. Promoting the good of the state is best accomplished, he explains, by persuading one's audience to pursue actions that are virtuous and thereby contribute to the building of community. In order to determine what constitutes "the good of the state" and "virtuous action," rhetoricians are encouraged to turn to their colleagues, the philosophers, whose civic task rests in articulating the "truths" and "principles" around which the state should be structured. Cicero maintains that in his personal development as a rhetorician, the insights of academic philosophers played a crucial role. He states, "I confess that whatever ability I possess as an orator comes not from the workshops of the rhetoricians but from the spacious grounds of the academy."[35] He makes a similar concession in *De oratore:* "No one has ever succeeded in achieving splendor or excellence in oratory, I will not say merely without training in speaking (*dicendi doctrina*), but without taking all knowledge (*sapientia*) for his province as well."[36]

Having praised the philosophers for providing rhetoricians with the wisdom necessary to promote the good, Cicero quickly adds that philosophers fail at times to serve the state because they do not present their work in accessible and persuasive language. In his now famous quotation, Cicero summarizes this interdependence of philosophy and rhetoric: "I have been led by reason itself to hold this opinion first and foremost, that wisdom (*sapientia*) without eloquence (*eloquentia*) does too little for the good of states, but that eloquence without wisdom is generally highly disadvantageous and never helpful."[37] Thus, it is only when the philosopher and rhetorician work together that the art of eloquence is able to realize its most lofty goal, the shaping of an ideal Roman citizen.

Rhetoricians in early modern Europe were also cognizant of the importance of identifying the goal of one's oration or writing and of n losing sight of it in the process of forming decorous discourse. And, like Cicero, they agreed that the overarching goal of oration should not be simply gaining the applause of the crowd, but rather serving the good. However, the definition of "the good" had changed considerably since the time of Cicero. According to the Italian humanists of the fourteenth and fifteenth centuries, the good was best described as a conflation of Cicero's notion of "the good of the State" with the Christian notion of the good as "service and obedience to the divine wisdom of God." Using a language reminiscent of Augustine, Petrarch describes the goal of oration aimed at attaining divine wisdom as follows: Such an oration should persuade its recipients "to know themselves, to return the soul to itself [God], and to despise empty glory."[38] Virtuous discourse, then, had as its aim the care of the soul and its conversion to faith in God. Likewise, the discursive appeals of rhetoricians who functioned primarily in the law courts were designed to articulate the more practical dimensions of this faith as it applied to the activities of daily life. In this sense, the rhetoric of law dovetailed with the rhetoric of faith insofar as the latter turned its audience toward God while the former helped devoted Christians find their place as ideal Florentine citizens.

Both of these agendas were also shaped by another insight into the function of rhetoric, an insight that was to become one of the major hallmarks of early modern humanism. Best summarized by Petrarch, it was the conviction that "it is better to will the good than to know the truth."[39] As this statement suggests, Petrarch and his students believed that in the final analysis, virtuous action was more important than mere intellectual assent to the truths of divine wisdom and the principles of right reason. While this position did not amount to a full-scale rejection of the rigors of dialectical argumentation and its predilection for engaging the faculties of the intellect, it nevertheless sought to temper their place in the life of faith. Given this orientation, it is not surprising that many of Italy's and France's most skilled orators looked upon the medieval Scholastic tradition with great contempt. One of the strongest critics of Scholasticism was the great rhetorician Lorenzo Valla. Well known for his contentious spirit, Valla penned a number of tracts attacking a variety of "philosophers" whose ideas he regarded as not only philosophically untenable but antithetical to the Christian faith. Deeply immersed in the skeptical tradition, Valla contested the grounds upon which Scholastic dialecticians stood when they claimed to have achieved absolute certainty by means of logical argumentation. Similarly, he distrusted philosophers who generated volumes devoted to speculative metaphysics, all of which, he contended, had no immediate relation to the practical affairs of daily life.[40]

This emphasis upon constructing discourse capable of helping persons actually "will the good" led many Renaissance rhetoricians to focus on developing a virtuous disposition in their readers. How was this crafting of a person's disposition to be accomplished? How were orators to train the faculties of reason and the will to know and desire God and to seek the good? How was one to "teach virtue"? According to rhetoricians like Petrarch, such training did not consist in simply telling reason and the will what they should know and do. Rather, it was a slow process that transpired as the reader, in working through a text, began to follow the habits of thinking and willing embodied in the movement of the text itself.[41] In other words, textual rhetoric was designed to simulate the very disposition its author intended to nurture. In this way, the reader's disposition was transformed by the underlying, often unidentified, educative agenda of a given discourse. By imitating the text's deliberative processes, the reader learned such things as the emotive state appropriate to virtuous action, the type of practical reason required to make decisions of a virtuous nature, and the habits of willing that led to faithful living.

Petrarch summarizes this educative view of rhetoric when he states that

> useful teachers of virtue are those whose first and last intention is to make hearer and reader good, those who do not merely teach what virtue and vice are and hammer into our heads the brilliant name of one and the grim name of the other, but sow in our hearts love of the best and eager desire for it, and at the same time hatred of the worst and how to flee from it.[42]

In order to "sow in the heart" (*pectoribus inserere*) love of God and the desire to do the good, the subsequent rhetoricians of Calvin's era developed rhetorical strategies that avoided the useless tactic of simply "hammering it into the reader's head" (*auribus* [lit., ears] *instrepere*). These strategies were often difficult for the reader to detect and varied widely according to the type of text an author chose to write.

As today's critics have become increasingly interested in this practical, action-oriented dimension of sixteenth-century literature, they have begun to evaluate the functions of texts from this period in new ways. In order to identify the "disposition-forming" or "virtue-shaping" dimensions of a literary text's rhetoric, modern interpreters have attempted to trace the "play of mind" that a text elicits.[43] The notion of a "play of mind" is broadly understood to include the variety of mental and emotional activities through which the text leads its readers. At times, a text may require its readers to take an unprecedented conceptual leap aimed at not only opening up new intellectual possibilities but also evoking unprecedented affective reactions. At other times, the text may challenge its readers by deploying a startling metaphor or an unusual juxtaposition of images that forces them to perceive their world in a new way. The text may also re-orient its readers' disposition by asking them to assume unfamiliar char-acter roles in the hope that they may begin to experience previously for-eign emotional states. In reading Calvin's theology through the lens of sixteenth-century rhetoric, these particular characteristics of writing—as well as many other "plays of mind" that Calvin is especially skilled at ma-nipulating—will serve a crucial role in my analysis.

Having worked through a brief definition of what Calvin would have understood as the "art of eloquence," I shall now turn to his writings and explore the nature of his own unique use of this richly textured discipline called rhetoric.

CALVIN'S USE OF RHETORIC

When Calvin left France in 1534, he left behind more than his friends and colleagues. He left behind a way of life, one that he had carefully cho-sen and energetically engaged in until the French Parlement forced him into permanent exile. It was a life devoted to the study of the writings of the classical Roman era and its grand orators. As far as Calvin's biogra-phers have determined, after leaving France, he never returned to the learned halls of humanist scholarship in the French Academy; he never again secluded himself in the purely academic world of Cicero and Seneca, the world of Roman law, history, politics, and philosophy. His travels, both geographic and intellectual, took him elsewhere. From Basel, he traveled to Geneva for a short period and then returned to German lands, having been thrown out of the Swiss city, to pastor a small French congregation in Strasbourg. From Strasbourg, he soon traveled back to Geneva, where he was to stay until his death in 1564.

During this thirty-year period, Calvin became an increasingly prolific writer. Although he is best known for his 1559 Latin edition of the *Insti-tutes*, he produced volumes of biblical commentary as well as numerous sermons, theological treatises, and widely published polemical tracts. While it is highly unlikely that Calvin had Cicero's *Orator* open on the desk as he penned these works—he probably had open the Bible and the writings of Augustine—his style of writing suggests that the discipline of rhetoric continued to influence his work at a variety of levels, even as the French halls of humanism became an increasingly distant memory. This influence, however, was not one of strict dependence on the categories and schemes discussed by Cicero and elaborated by the French human-ists. Calvin's use of rhetoric was much more creative; he refined and often stretched the rhetorical rules he was taught in law school. And the result is a style of presentation that is quite original. In fact, as one scholar has noted, Calvin's preference for a lucid and concise style in both Latin and French, void of unnecessary rhetorical flourishes or distracting ornamentation, constituted a certain "sober literary aesthetic" that differed significantly from the style adopted by his French contemporaries.[44] As such, his style marked a new period in the evolution of the French language, one that would be recognized only later when it was taken up by such figures as Montaigne, Descartes, and Pascal.[45]

It would be possible, if not also extremely fruitful, to analyze any one of Calvin's works in terms of this rhetorical style and form. Calvin scholars have already begun this process by rhetorically evaluating his earliest theological writings in Strasbourg, his 1536 edition of the *Institutes*, and his French polemical tracts.[46] Similarly, several authors have taken particular interest in the role played by rhetoric in the construction of the 1559 *Institutes*, the text that will be the primary focus of my attention as well.[47] Given that the 1559 *Institutes* not only represents the crowning achievement of Calvin's career but also stands as the founding model of Reformed systematics—if it can be properly called either "Reformed" or "systematic"—it provides the best starting point for a rhetorical reading of Calvin by a modern-day scholar with systematic theological interests. It also serves as an interesting arena for assessing Calvin's use of rhetoric because its length and the complexity of its arguments required Calvin to draw upon a wide spectrum of oratorical forms and styles. At times, he deploys the kind of homiletic exhortations found in his sermons. At other times, he launches into the caustic rhetoric that fills his polemical tracts. Likewise, he frequently writes with the more pedagogical temper reflected in his commentaries. The *Institutes* thus provides one with a text that is both rich in rhetorical subtleties and full of interpretive possibilities.

Where does one begin the task of tracing the specific ways in which his rhetorical training influenced this particular work? I shall start by looking at Calvin's understanding of the nature and function of theology. When Calvin reflects upon the theological task that he has undertaken in the *Institutes*, he offers his reader several comments that suggest rhetorical eloquence plays an important role. "The theologian's task," he explains, "is not to divert the ears with chatter but to strengthen consciences by teaching things true, sure, and profitable (*utilia*)."[48] What, for Calvin, constitutes profitable or useful knowledge? On this point, he is unequivocal. It is "this recognition of him [God] which consists more in living experience (*vivus sensus*) than in vain and high-flown speculation (*speculatio*)."[49] Making the same observation with even more force, he remarks, "We are called to a knowledge of God: not that knowledge which, content with empty speculation (*speculatio*), merely flits in the brain, but that which will be sound (*solida*) and fruitful (*fructuosa*) if we duly perceive it, and if it takes root in the heart."[50] On the basis of these comments, it appears that for Calvin, the theologian's task is inherently practical; it involves teaching persons "truths" that lead to faith. And this faith is not based upon high-flown speculation but rather is rooted in the heart and manifest in the activities of daily living.

How does Calvin explain the concrete ways in which the theologian nurtures such a faith in his audience? First and foremost, Calvin directs the reader to scripture, where faith is schooled in the knowledge of God and the discipline of true piety. "In the reading of Scripture, we ought ceaselessly to endeavor to seek out and meditate upon those things which make for edification (*aedificatio*)."[51] The emphasis here is on the dispositional orientation that proper reading should elicit; it should aim at edification. However, scripture cannot accomplish such a feat on its own: it requires the assistance of the Spirit. As Calvin describes it,

> the testimony of the Spirit is more excellent than all reason . . . the Word will not find acceptance in men's hearts before it is sealed by the inward testimony of the Spirit. The same Spirit, therefore, who has spoken through the mouths of the prophets must penetrate into our hearts to persuade (*persuadere*) us that they faithfully proclaim what had been divinely commanded.[52]

Using the notion of persuasion once again, Calvin further explains that scripture will only lead to edification if, through the Spirit, "we are persuaded beyond a doubt that God is its Author."[53]

The persuasive role played by scripture and the Holy Spirit, however, does not undercut the critically important role played by theologians, particularly when they utilize their own persuasive skills as rhetoricians. In his *Commentary on First Corinthians*, Calvin explains that eloquence and rhetorical excellence are "noble gifts that men [should] put to good use," and when put to the service of the Word, "they come from the Holy Spirit."[54] Thus, for Calvin, the eloquence of scripture, the power of the Spirit, and the rhetorical finesse of the theologian must work together to persuade and move the hearts of the faithful. The force of this particular point should not be missed: in order for faith to be nurtured by doctrine, in order for hearts to be moved by the truth of divine wisdom, the theologian must construct discourse capable of teaching, convincing, delighting, encouraging, and challenging the reader "to know God and to do his will." For this task, the tools of rhetoric are essential because they are, in short, the tools of persuasion.[55]

In addition to understanding the persuasive dimension of theology, Calvin, like Cicero, recognizes that language is not inherently persuasive, that not all discursive forms are able to move their readers. Just as Cicero criticizes philosophers who know the truth but lack the rhetorical skill to teach it to their students, Calvin confesses that "doctrine stated generally does not move us."[56] In this statement, Calvin acknowledges that some doctrinal formulations, even though they may be true, nonetheless fall short of their persuasive goal because the language in which they are clothed lacks the passion and eloquence necessary for moving the hearts and souls of the audience. Who were the theologians who engaged in such unproductive activities? Calvin himself most likely had in mind those "dreadful" Scholastic theologians who could string together logically coherent propositions concerning the content of divine wisdom but who failed to move the heart or edify the soul. Such Scholastic theologians, according to Calvin, belong to that group of persons who "occupy minds with idle chatter" and teach doctrine that "merely flits in the brain doing nothing." On the basis of these remarks and others like them scattered throughout the *Institutes,* it appears that Calvin shared the humanist Lorenzo Valla's suspicion of dialectics and its Scholastic practitioners. Like Valla, Calvin believed that good theology is practically useful and therefore eloquent theology. Thus, rather than flitting around the brain, eloquent theology is able to "persuade us that God is the fountain of every good, and that we must seek nothing elsewhere than in him," and moves us to "honor and adore" him.[57]

Calvin also follows Cicero's advice concerning the necessarily accommodative character of well-constructed rhetoric. He acknowledges that doctrines that "move" are doctrines that accommodate the linguistic and social expectations of the reader. In the *Institutes,* Calvin mentions the importance of accommodation (*accommodare*) several times.[58] When he describes God's revelatory activity, Calvin depicts God as the Grand Orator who speaks to a rather dim-witted audience and thus uses a language that is clear and comprehensible to the simplest of minds. The most accessible form of this accommodating speech comes to us in the beauty of creation. In the splendor of the skies and the glory of the earth, God "renders himself near and familiar to us, and in some manner communicates himself."[59] Likewise, Calvin describes scripture as accommodated to our limited understanding. For instance, in his description of the process by which Moses wrote the creation narratives, Calvin explains that "Moses, accommodating himself to the rudeness of common folk, mentions in the history of Creation no other works of God than those which show themselves to our own eyes."[60] This statement is especially illuminating in that it portrays the accommodating Spirit of God working through the brilliantly accommodative rhetoric of a human being.

According to Calvin (like Petrarch), when the language of theology is appropriately accommodated to the needs of its audience, it should actually "make the reader good." And as the previous discussion suggests, this process of making the audience good does not consist solely in telling them what they should believe; rather, it requires that the theologian construct a discourse that will transform the disposition of the audience as they read through a given text. Calvin's constant reference to the specific kind of disposition he intended each section of the *Institutes* to nurture attests to the level of seriousness with which he viewed the "disposition-forming" character of his own writing. The consistency with which Calvin refers to these dispositions is indeed remarkable; hardly a page goes by without his noting the affective state he wants his remarks to elicit. And the dispositions he names are quite diverse. For example, he explains that the doctrine of creation should function "not only to arouse (*excitare*) us to the worship of God, but also to awaken (*expergefacere*) and encourage (*erigere*) us to the hope (*spes*) of future life."[61] In addition to encouraging hope of future life, his discussion of knowing God's presence in creation serves another function as well: "This knowledge is especially useful (*utilis*) . . . [because] once the beginning of the universe is known, God's eternity may shine forth more clearly, and we may be more rapt in wonder at it."[62] Building on this and similar points, Calvin stresses the fact that these dispositions are not merely intellectual but affective. The task of doctrine is to help persons "recognize that God has destined all things for our good and salvation but at the same time to feel his power and grace in ourselves and in the great benefits he has conferred upon us, and so bestir ourselves to trust (*fiducia*), invoke (*invocatio*), praise (*laus*), and love (*amor*) him."[63]

When Calvin describes the state he intends his doctrine to inculcate, he adds that a single doctrine may simultaneously serve two entirely different functions. An instance of this blending of functions appears in his discussion of the doctrine of providence. Referring to the psalmists whose writings bear witness to the providential rule of God in creation, Calvin makes the following observation:

> By setting forth examples of this sort, the prophet [writing in the Psalms] shows that what are thought to be chance occurrences are just so many proofs of heavenly providence, especially of fatherly kindness. And hence ground for rejoicing is given to the godly, while as for the wicked and the reprobate, their mouths are stopped.[64]

Thus, for the godly, the dispositional response elicited by this doctrine is joy, whereas for the reprobate the intended reaction is feeling judged and silenced.

Calvin did not believe, however, that simply naming the disposition suffices to induce it in the reader. Quite to the contrary, he typically identifies the disposition associated with a particular doctrine only after he has already taken the reader through a process of reading which itself produces that disposition. And this is where his real skills as a rhetorician come to the fore; this is where one finds him drawing most heavily upon the advice of Cicero and reworking this advice to his own advantage. As I shall show in the following chapters, when Calvin intends to make his readership feel judged, challenged, or scolded, he uses the classical form of forensic rhetoric, the rhetoric of defense and attack. His arguments become sharp-edged, his language becomes caustic, and the reader is overwhelmed by the force of his polemic. On the opposite side of the spectrum, when Calvin wants to uplift and nurture his readers, he employs the classical panegyric or demonstrative form. In these sections, his language becomes sermonic. He exploits the powers of rhythm and rhyme as he either gently rocks his readers in the comforting descriptions of God's grace or energetically takes them to rhetorical heights in his impassioned descriptions of the glory and power of God's sovereign rule. Calvin also devotes many sections of the *Institutes* to teaching his students the content of divine wisdom. When his purposes are pedagogical, he deploys the classical rhetorical form of deliberative speech. The pace of discourse slows down and, by making extensive use of examples and simple images, he presents his position in language appropriately accommodated to a classroom setting.

In this manner, Calvin uses his rhetorical skills to construct doctrines that produce in his readers a certain play of mind, a play of mind that has as its final goal the inculcating of a faithful disposition. When I begin to develop a rhetorical reading of the *Institutes* in chapter 3 of this study, discerning the various strategies he uses to manipulate these plays of mind will prove of central importance to my analysis. At times, discerning his strategy will be easy: his presentation will lend itself to a straightforward analysis of his tactics. However, as I will show, there are also times when his rhetorical manipulations become quite complex and subtle, and it will not be as clear how his doctrinal constructions are contributing to the formation of specific dispositions. Calvin is also not beyond tricking his audiences: He may appear to be engaged in teasing out a play of mind when he suddenly subverts, turns on its head, or collapses it. Or he may initiate a particular play of mind that he soon fractures into multiple mind plays, some of which are positive, others of which he forthrightly condemns. When these sorts of moves occur, it becomes clear that Calvin's tactics, strategies, and rhetorical goals often resist the reader's attempts to categorize them simply.

One may ask at this point why it is important to attend to these dimensions of Calvin's theology. One possible answer is to signal the fact, as already noted, that Calvin himself attached great significance to this dimension of theological discourse, to its capacity to move and dispositionally orient his audience. A fuller answer to this question will also develop as the fruits of this kind of reading appear more clearly in later chapters.

What will become apparent is that a rhetorical reading may alter or expand the interpretations Calvin's doctrines have traditionally received. For now, a brief example will serve to make this point. I shall look at the flow of Calvin's treatment of the doctrine of creation.

Calvin begins his discussion of "knowledge of God the creator" (chapters 3 through 5 of Book 1) with a lengthy description of the various forms of natural knowledge that, if Adam had not fallen, would testify clearly to the reality of God's presence in and sovereignty over the created order. Having put forth this description of natural sources of knowledge, Calvin then firmly and emphatically announces to the reader that all this evidence is for naught because "all degenerate from the true knowledge of him," and "scarcely one man in a hundred is met with who fosters it."[65] Following these chapters in which Calvin has first built and then deconstructed a "natural theology," he turns in chapters 6 through 8 to an extensive description of the role played by the Bible and the Holy Spirit in ascertaining true knowledge of God the creator. Having in turn laid this foundation, he then addresses the topic of creation for a second time: in chapters 13 through 15, he argues that once illumined by faith, creation quite rightly witnesses to the glory of the creator through both its splendor and its order.

If theologians approach these chapters on the knowledge of creation—both the initial deconstructive chapters and the later, more constructive ones—with the goal of simply ascertaining the propositional content of the doctrine of creation, they might be content with the conclusion that the purpose of this discussion is to assert and support the claim that apart from faith, there is no natural source for knowledge of God. However, Calvin makes it clear that his aims are much broader. Not only does he argue against the claims of natural theology, he also intends for the first chapters on creation to inculcate in the readers an inescapable sense of their own guilt and hence the correlative attitudes of humility and gratitude toward the God whose testimony in creation has shone upon their closed and blinded eyes. He makes this point most sharply when he concludes at the end of chapter 5, "Therefore, we are justly denied every excuse when we stray off as wanderers and vagrants even though everything points out the right way."[66]

The fact that Calvin ends his entire description of natural theology with this statement suggests that the affective, dispositional function of the discussion may be as significant as its more obvious propositional content. Could it be that Calvin has situated this particular argument at the beginning of the *Institutes* in order to break down any arrogant pretensions to self-knowledge his audience might have, and thereby to clear the way for them to understand truly the real source and power of divine wisdom? This type of consideration has rarely been addressed in the long history of theological interpretations of this section, and hence, significant interpretive possibilities have been overlooked in the search for the "logic" of Calvin's position on natural knowledge of God. When read rhetorically, the dialectical play between the critical and constructive moments in his doctrine of creation appears not as a problem for the reader to solve logically but as a discursive play of mind for the reader to embrace affectively.

As this example demonstrates, Calvin was exceptionally skilled at taking traditional doctrines and rhetorically reworking them so that they became the occasion not only for setting forth "the principles of faith" but also, more importantly, for the shaping of Christian character. Calvin's predilection for attending to the affective dimensions of doctrine is particularly clear in passages where he discusses theological topics for which he has no use apart from their character-forming potential for Christians. When he turns to the topic of angels, he admits at the outset that he has no interest in the treatment of angels proffered by the Scholastics, especially when these theologians engage in lengthy arguments about the number and hierarchies of angels. Such arguments, he states, are unnecessary because they "indulge in curiosity or in the investigation of unprofitable things."[67] However, he does not entirely exclude a discussion of angels from his text. Rather, he argues that scripture speaks of angels for a very practical purpose:

> Scripture strongly insists upon teaching us what could most effectively make for our consolation (*consolatio*) and the strengthening (*confirmatio*) of our faith: namely, that angels are dispensers and administrators of God's beneficence toward us. . . . Thus, to fulfill that task of protecting us the angels fight against the devil and all our enemies, and carry out God's vengeance against those who harm us.[68]

This discussion of angels exemplifies a fascinating dynamic that appears frequently in the *Institutes*. Calvin was a serious student of both scripture and patristic theology and, as a sign of his respect for their divine authority, he was reluctant to dismiss traditional doctrines even though he clearly considered some doctrinal formulations highly suspect. Caught between his respect for tradition and his commitment to teach only things that are "sure and profitable," Calvin deploys an interesting strategy. He reclaims what he believes would otherwise be confusing doctrines—such as the doctrine of the Trinity,[69] the belief in the devil and angels, and the complicated incarnational language used in traditional Christologies[70]— by asking the question: what aspect of this doctrine might serve either to strengthen the faith of believers or to judge the impiety of the reprobate? Having answered this question, he then foregoes an extended philosophical discussion of these doctrines and directly launches into a rhetoric fashioned to evoke the desired disposition. In this manner, he sheds new light on what should be considered the meaning of these doctrines. As these examples suggest, Calvin assessed meaning not only in terms of propositional content but in terms of social function as well. And again, his rhetorical sensibilities shine through.

Throughout the *Institutes*, Calvin continues to struggle with a tradition of Christian doctrines that he respects and yet often feels compelled to re-work. In pursuing this struggle, Calvin follows yet another piece of advice offered by Cicero. As Cicero suggests in *Orator*, truly persuasive discourse will draw upon the vast storehouse of rhetorical resources left behind by past generations of writers and thinkers. The activity of mining these re-sources is referred to by Cicero as the art of *copia*, as noted earlier. It should not take the reader of the *Institutes* long to realize that the copiousness of Calvin's own discourse would have been pleasing to Cicero. In fact, Calvin's skills in the art of *copia* are immediately manifest in the opening paragraph of the text. Here, in his discussion of the sources of divine wis-dom, he deploys images and arguments drawn from Aristotelian logic, Neoplatonic metaphysics, the tradition of Christian mysticism, and the pragmatic rationalism of the humanists.[71] Similarly, a few pages later, Calvin exhibits his knowledge of classical Latin and Greek literature by making explicit reference to such figures as Gaius Caligula (a Roman em-peror), Diagoras (an atheist cited by Cicero), Plato the philosopher, and Gryllius (a commentator on Cicero). Who other than a theologian trained in classical rhetoric, and hence one determined to prove the copiousness of his work, would find it necessary or valuable to include such references, particularly in the first pages of a book on the "Christian Religion"?

When Calvin sought material for his own work, classical literature was not the only storehouse from which he drew. As stated earlier, the revela-tion of God in scripture was his norm and guide and as such, provided the richest storehouse of resources for his writing. In addition, he drew heav-ily upon the wisdom of a variety of patristic writings, gleaning therefrom many of the insights and metaphors that adorn his work. Quite surpris-ingly, Calvin also turned to Scholastic theology to collect arguments, themes, and images to strengthen his own argument and presentation. Despite his repeated denunciations of Scholastic dialectics, he was not be-yond employing dialectical argumentation when it helped to build his case and persuade his audience. This is particularly clear in his "Prefatory Address to King Francis I of France." In this short piece, he frequently takes the arguments of his Scholastic opponents and skillfully reworks them. With dialectical precision, he then turns the arguments given by the Scholastics against the Scholastics themselves. In doing so, he exhibits his own facility for logical analysis and metaphysical philosophy. However, as this example of his copiousness suggests, when Calvin used "voices from the past" to buttress his own position, he did not feel constrained to use them as they had previously been used. Rather, keeping his own discursive agenda ever before him, he assessed them in terms of their pragmatic usefulness and employed them only insofar as they served to promote what he considered to be sound teaching.

Calvin's attitude toward medieval dialectics typifies Calvin's approach to other Christian and philosophical sources as well. He uses them as he sees fit, or better, as he is able to accommodate them to serve his overarching project. For instance, Calvin often displays profound respect for his favored theologian, Augustine. But this does not mean that Augustine is beyond critique or that Calvin will only use Augustine's arguments in the way Augustine himself used them. It is precisely this tendency in Calvin, his copious use of bits and pieces of linguistic images and arguments borrowed from past generations, that has made it difficult for Calvin scholars to tie his work to one school of theology or one philosophical tradition. He exploits many sources, and he does so quite freely. For this reason, it helps to view Calvin's use of the traditions, of both theology and philosophy, as extremely ad hoc. On the one hand, he is clearly dependent on prior authors. This is beyond dispute, and a copious writer like Calvin would have celebrated this dependence. On the other hand, he exercises considerable creativity and freedom in his use of prior materials, and the only standard that guides and constrains this creativity is Calvin's attempt to be faithful to the witness of scripture and, thereby, to construct doctrines that are as accommodative and persuasive as God's own revelation. When Calvin's theology is viewed from this perspective, his methodological affinities with the twentieth-century theologian Karl Barth become quite apparent.

Calvin's creative use of sources suggests that he also follows Cicero's advice on the rhetorical companion of *copia*, the art of *imitatio*. As Cicero explains it, truly copious discourse requires that one thoroughly digest borrowed material by studying the life and context of the original author. One then makes this material a part of oneself by rearticulating it in a language suited to one's present context, thereby re-presenting a position that has become, by the end of the process, the product of two authorial natures. When one turns to the *Institutes*, it is obvious that Calvin digested this advice. For example, when he deploys bits and pieces of insight and images borrowed from the tradition, he seldom identifies his source directly and, when he does, he usually paraphrases the original text.[72] This is particularly evident in his use of scripture. When referring to a particular part of the "Holy Wisdom" found in the Bible, he freely translates a given passage into a language accommodated to his own context. In fact, his use of scripture is occasionally so free that it is difficult to locate the actual passage he is using. The same holds true for his references to the "church fathers" and to other theologians. While this proclivity to paraphrase and to leave sources unnamed makes tracing Calvin's references quite complicated, it does reveal that unlike modern theologians, he was not as concerned with the accuracy of his references as he was with capturing their general sense and accommodating that sense to fit his own discursive agenda. The looseness of his paraphrases may suggest as well that Calvin, as an orator trained in the art of memorizing lengthy materials, was working with many of these sources from memory.[73]

Calvin's frequent use of the first person further demonstrates his penchant for the paraphrastic and hence his skill at *imitatio*. Even when he is using scripture or repeating an Augustinian position, Calvin marks the theological discourse he produces as his own by putting these words in his own style. For a well-trained rhetorician in early modern Europe, this skillful maneuver would not have been considered deceptive. Rather, it would have been viewed as an indication of his eloquence in so far as he was able to pull it off with rhetorical finesse. Indeed, Calvin's ability to inscribe his own identity upon the text would have been considered a sign of the text's strength rather than its weakness. It would have signaled the truly eloquent blending of two natures, his own and the authorial nature of his sources. Furthermore, marking the text as a distinct product of his own authorial voice did not preclude the possibility that the doctrines he articulates are "more God's than his own."[74] According to the practice of *imitatio*, the more the voice of another author became his own voice, the more his writings would be able to reproduce the intentions of the original author, be that author a biblical scribe, a patristic theologian, or a classical "pagan" like Cicero.

As these reflections on the role rhetoric plays in the *Institutes* suggest, Calvin's early training in humanism continued to influence his writing, even as late as 1559. And this influence is manifest at a variety of levels. It shapes his understanding of the task of theology, a task that he conceives as an inherently persuasive enterprise. Following Renaissance patterns of discourse, Calvin also maintains that shaping the disposition of his audience is of primary importance, and he accommodates his language to this end. As he seeks to move his audience, he also displays his facility for blending the forensic, deliberative, and demonstrative forms of appeal. Likewise, his rhetoric is fully adorned with the stylistic ornaments described by the classical rhetoricians: he attends to rhythm, rhyme, metaphorical imaging, and a broad spectrum of tropological gestures. And in the process of employing these rhetorical tools, Calvin exhibits his skill at the arts of *copia* and *imitatio* by weaving a discursive tapestry rich in both tradition and his own creative style.

When Calvin's theology is read with an eye toward these dimensions of his text, new interpretive avenues appear. They are avenues that do not necessarily bypass or cut off previous readings of Calvin. Rather, they are capable of expanding and nuancing the subjects upon which discussions of his theology move. One of the perennial questions that has marked these subjects concerns the overarching principle or structure that ties the *Institutes* together as a coherent whole. As I have argued, it is difficult to find one conceptual framework, philosophical system, or systematizing principle through which Calvin organizes his thought. Consequently, I join a number of Calvin scholars in suggesting that it is a mistake to characterize the *Institutes* as a systematic work in so far as "systematic" implies a tightly knit logical coherence among and within the various doctrines he treats. While it is possible to point to places where Calvin, for argumentative purposes, seeks to justify his position on the basis of such a standard, systematic rigor does not appear to have been his major concern, and for this reason, the standards he uses frequently vary. In fact, given Calvin's obsession with discursive clarity and with practically shaping the disposition of his readers, it is questionable whether he could have been rigorously systematic and still have accomplished his desired ends.

However, as my discussion of Calvin's understanding of the theological enterprise suggests, there remain two "principles" that unify his thought: first, his struggle to follow faithfully the scriptural witness to God's revelation in history, and second, his very practical concern to edify, uplift, and defend the particular community of faith to whom he speaks (and to whom, he believed, the scriptures speak as well). In his concern to accomplish these ends, Calvin took great liberties, often reshaping and reforming the tradition so that it might more concretely respond to his community's needs and capacities and bear witness to the often unsystematic testimony of the biblical text. It thus appears that what counts for "coherence" in Calvin's *Institutes* may be best determined scripturally, rhetorically, and socially rather than systematically, logically, or philosophically. If this is the case, then it is necessary not only to attend to Calvin's use of scripture but also to situate Calvin's doctrines in their original social context in order to interpret their rhetorical / social goals. To this task, I now turn.

NOTES

1. Robert M. Kingdon, *Geneva and the Coming Wars of Religion in France: 1555–1563* (Geneva: Librairie E. Droz, 1956), 14–15.

2. Francis Higman, "Calvin the Writer" (manuscript, 1989).

3. For a general overview of the relation between Christian theology and Roman rhetoric, see George A. Kennedy, *The Art of Rhetoric in the Roman World: 300 B.C.–A.D. 300* (Princeton, N.J.: Princeton University Press, 1972), and *Classical*

Rhetoric and Its Christian and Secular Traditions from Ancient to Modern Times (Chapel Hill: University of North Carolina Press, 1980).

4. For an excellent study on the place of rhetoric in the medieval academy, see James J. Murphy, *Rhetoric in the Middle Ages: A History of Rhetorical Theory from Saint Augustine to the Renaissance* (Berkeley: University of California Press, 1974). Also see Maria Colish, *The Mirror of Language: A Study in the Medieval Theory of Knowledge* (Lincoln: University of Nebraska Press, 1983).

5. On the variety of topics covered by these rhetorical works, see Paul O. Kristeller, "Rhetoric in Medieval and Renaissance Culture," in *Renaissance Eloquence: Studies in the Theory and Practice of Renaissance Rhetoric*, ed. James Murphy (Berkeley: University of California Press, 1983), 1–19.

6. On the thought of Petrarch, Salutati, and Valla, see Charles Trinkaus, *"In Our Image and Likeness": Humanity and Dignity in Italian Humanist Thought*, vol. 1 (Chicago: University of Chicago Press, 1970). For more on Salutati's life, see Berthold L. Ullmann, *The Humanism of Coluccio Salutati* (Padua: Editrice Antenore, 1963); on Bruni's career, also see Lauro Martines, *The Social World of the Florentine Humanists: 1390–1460* (Princeton, N.J.: Princeton University Press, 1960). I have also found Kristeller's work on the Italian humanists helpful. See Paul O. Kristeller, *Studies in Renaissance Thought and Letters* (Rome: Edizioni di storia e letteratura, 1956–1985).

7. On the social function of lawyers in early modern Europe, see William Bouwsma, "Lawyers in Early Modern Culture," *American Historical Review* 78 (1973): 303–37; Donald Kelley, "Civil Science in the Renaissance: Jurisprudence in the French Manner," in *Foundations of Modern Historical Scholarship: Language, Law, and History in the French Renaissance* (New York: Columbia University Press, 1970); and Myron Piper Gilmore, *Humanists and Jurists: Six Studies in the Renaissance* (Cambridge, Mass.: Belknap Press of Harvard University, 1963), 61–86.

8. Bouwsma, "Lawyers," 311, 314. "Their role, in short, was to man the frontiers between the safe and the familiar on the one hand, the dangerous and the new on the other; between the tolerable and the intolerable, the conventional world and the chaos beyond it. They constituted a kind of civil militia whose difficulties were compounded by the fact that the precise location of the frontiers to which they were assigned was rarely clear, and these frontiers were constantly changing."

9. Bouwsma makes this argument in his article on lawyers in early modern Europe, "Lawyers," 318. It merits quoting at length.

> Litigation in secular courts had been forbidden by the early Church; Augustine, who knew the courts well, had pointed to lawsuits to illustrate the persistent sinfulness of earthly society The notion of a relative natural law appropriate to man's fallen state had resolved the practical problems of life in a society that, although professedly Christian, remained imperfect. But the acceptance of conflict was, in this view, also relative; it could never be tolerated as normal and inevitable. Justice was itself finally an absolute; and this meant that a legal decision was ideally concerned not so much to resolve conflict as to transcend and abolish it by resort to ultimate principles. In this light coercion by legal authority was an effort to bend the refractory wills of men into conformity with a final vision of justice. But increasingly the lawyers of early modern Europe, whatever the formulas to which they sometimes still appealed, disregarded such conceptions. Their task was practical and limited; they aimed not to transcend conflict but to manage it. In their world the essential tensions were not between sin and ultimate justice but between antithetical human interests that generally seemed morally ambiguous on both sides. Their activity was directed to the effective

resolution of conflict, not to the realization of a lofty vision; their rise signified and accelerated the breakdown of a traditional view in which social values were defined in accordance with final ends.

10. Bouwsma, "Lawyers," 319.

11. Gilmore, *Humanists and Jurists*, 67. For this reason, many prominent figures in early modern Europe had studied law but failed to put it to professional use in their later careers, such as Servetus, Samuel Butler, Voltaire, Diderot, and David Hume. See Bouwsma, "Lawyers," 307.

12. For a short overview of the various ways contemporary scholars have typified the humanist movement, see William Bouwsma, *The Interpretation of Renaissance Humanism* (Washington, D.C.: Service Center for Teachers of History, 1959, 1966). For additional summary treatments of Renaissance humanism, I have found the following books helpful: Ernst Cassirer, *The Individual and the Cosmos in Renaissance Philosophy*, trans. Mario Domandi (Philadelphia: University of Pennsylvania Press, 1963); Hannah Gray, "Renaissance Humanism: The Pursuit of Eloquence," *Journal of History of Ideas* 24 (1963): 497–514; Werner L. Grundersheimer, ed., *French Humanism, 1470–1600* (London: Macmillan, 1969); P. O. Kristeller, *Renaissance Thought: The Classic, Scholastic, and Humanist Strains* (New York: Harper Torch Books, 1961); and Charles Trinkaus, *The Scope of Renaissance Humanism* (Ann Arbor: University of Michigan Press, 1983).

13. On Erasmus's life and his relation to the Reformation, see P. S. Allen, *The Age of Erasmus* (Oxford: Clarendon Press, 1914); Johan Huizinga, *Erasmus and the Age of Reformation*, trans. F. Hopman (New York: Harper, 1957); and Louis Bouyer, *Autour d'Erasme: Études sur le christianisme des humanistes catholiques* (Paris: Editions du Cerf, 1955). On Budé's life and work, see David McNeil, *Guillaume Budé and Humanism in the Reign of Francis I* (Geneva: Librairie Droz, 1975). Also see Marie-Madeline de La Garanderie, "Guillaume Budé: A Philosopher of Culture," *The Sixteenth Century Journal* 19:3 (1988): 379–87.

14. My reconstruction of Calvin's early education in France represents no new historical research on my part. I have drawn upon the research found in a series of excellent biographies on Calvin, all of which cover these years in much more detail than my analysis will provide. The biographies I have depended on most heavily are the following: Williston Walker, *John Calvin, The Organizer of Reformed Protestantism, 1509–1564*, trans. N. Weiss (New York: Schocken Books, 1969); Quirinus Breen, *John Calvin: A Study in French Humanism* (Grand Rapids: Wm. B. Eerdmans Publishing Co., 1931); Alexandre Ganoczy, *The Young Calvin*, trans. David Foxgrover and Wade Provo (Philadelphia: Westminster Press, 1987); François Wendel, *Calvin: The Origins and Development of his Religious Thought*, trans. Philip Mairet (New York: Harper & Row, 1963); and Bouwsma, *John Calvin*. I have also drawn upon the more detailed description of Calvin's life found in Emile Doumergue's monumental seven-volume biography, *Jean Calvin: Les hommes et les choses de son temps* (Lausanne: Georg Bridel, 1899–1927).

15. For a more in-depth analysis of Alciati's life and work, see P. E. Viard, *André Alciat, 1492–1550* (Paris: Société anonyme du Recueil Sivey, 1926). Although Calvin developed a growing passion for humanist scholarship at this point in his studies, his response to Alciati, personally, was often less than enthusiastic; he did not like Alciati's repeated, sarcastic attacks on his venerable teacher at Orleans, Pierre de l'Estoile. For a discussion of Calvin's mixed reaction to Alciati, see Ganoczy, *The Young Calvin*, 69–70.

16. Bouwsma, *John Calvin*, 14.

17. *Calvin's Commentary on Seneca's "De clementia,"* ed. and trans. Ford Lewis Battles and André Malan Hugo, introduction by Battles (Leiden: E. J. Brill, 1969). For discussion of this period of Calvin's life, see Ganoczy, *The Young Calvin*, 71–76. Also see Battles, "Introduction," *Calvin's Commentary on Seneca's "De clementia,"* 32–36.

18. Battles's introduction to *Calvin's Commentary on Seneca's "De clementia,"* 19.

19. For a more developed discussion of this controversy, see Ganoczy, *The Young Calvin*, 80–83.

20. For the English text of Nicolas Cop's famous address delivered on assuming the rectorship of the University of Paris, see Ford Lewis Battles's translation and annotation of the 1536 edition of the *Institutes*, titled *Institutes of the Christian Religion, Embracing almost the whole sum of piety, & whatever is necessary to know concerning the doctrine of salvation: A work most worthy to be read by all persons zealous for piety, and recently published* (Grand Rapids: Wm. B. Eerdmans Publishing Co., 1989), 363–72.

21. Battles's *Institutes* (1536) also has the text from "The Placards of 1534," 339–42.

22. Ganoczy, *The Young Calvin*, 91–93. There has been much debate in the history of Calvin scholarship as to whether or not Calvin wrote the address for Cop.

23. For the most recent English edition of this work, see the second edition of Ford Lewis Battles's translation and annotation of the 1536 edition cited above.

24. For the purpose of my analysis, I have used the Latin and English versions of these texts found in the Loeb Classical Library. (Reference noted when used.)

25. Cicero, *De inventione*, 1.5.7, pp. 14–17; 1.9.12, pp. 24–27, trans. H. M. Hubbell, Loeb Classical Library (Cambridge: Harvard University Press, 1976).

26. In writing of the students of rhetoric, I will be referring to both men and women. This decision is not purely the product of authorial preference, however. During the fifteenth and sixteenth centuries, there were women of substantial power and prestige who were well known for the eloquence of their public orations. These women were, for the most part, taught in the Royal courts by humanist teachers and were highly accomplished in the rhetorical arts I will be describing. Although they were recognized as orators and humanists, these women were not allowed to obtain legal degrees or to practice official juridical arbitrations. Evidence suggests, however, that they often functioned as informal arbitrators. For a recent treatment and full bibliography of women rhetoricians, see Margaret King, *Women of the Renaissance* (Chicago: University of Chicago Press, 1991). For a discussion of their role as informal arbitrators, see Katherine Gill, "Open Monasteries for Women in Late Medieval and Early Modern Italy: Two Roman Examples," in *The Crannied Wall: Women, Religion, and the Arts in Early Modern Europe*, ed. Craig A. Monson (Ann Arbor: University of Michigan Press, 1992).

27. This notion thus reflects the deep appreciation the Romans and Greeks had for the intertextual character of all discursive practices.

28. Quintilian's "imitation theory" is discussed in *Institutio Oratoria, Bk X*, vol. 4, trans. H. E. Butler, Loeb Classical Library (Cambridge, Mass.: Harvard University Press, 1966). See Terence Cave, *The Cornucopian Text: Problems of Writing in the French Renaissance* (Oxford: Clarendon Press, 1979), 36–39.

29. In his introductory discussion of Renaissance rhetoric, Terence Cave outlines the effects of this proliferation. See Cave, *The Cornucopian Text*, ix.

30. See Victoria Kahn, *Rhetoric, Prudence, and Skepticism in the Renaissance* (Ithaca, N.Y.: Cornell University Press, 1985), 38; Richard J. Shoeck, "Lawyers and Rhetoric in Sixteenth Century England," in *Renaissance Eloquence: Studies in the Theory and Practice of Renaissance Rhetoric*, ed. James Murphy (Berkeley: University of California Press, 1983), 275–76.

31. It is because of this fundamental insight that modern critics frequently trace the origins of a functionalist notion of language to the writings of Cicero.

32. Cicero, *Orator* 21.69, p. 357; "ut probet, ut delectet, ut flectat" (*Orator* 21.69, p. 356). This reference and those that follow are taken from *Orator*, trans. H. M. Hubbell, The Loeb Classical Library (Cambridge: Harvard University Press, 1971).

33. Cicero, *Orator* 8.24, p. 323; "Semper oratorum eloquentiae moderatrix fuit auditorum prudentia. Omnes enim qui probari volunt voluntatem eorum qui audiunt intuentur ad eamque et ad eorum arbitrium et nutum totos se fingunt et accommodant" (*Orator* 8.24, p. 322).

34. Bringing the three together would have been encouraged by sixteenth-century rhetoricians but not by Cicero.

35. Cicerio, *Orator* 3.12, p. 313; "fateor me oratorem, si modo sim aut etiam quicumque sim, non ex rhetorum officinis, sed ex Academiae spatiis exstitisse" (*Orator* 3.12, p. 312).

36. Cicero, *De oratore* 2.1.5, p. 201, trans. E. W. Sutton, Loeb Classical Library (Cambridge, Mass.: Harvard University Press, 1967); "neminem eloquentia, non modo sine dicendi doctrina, sed ne sine omni quidem sapientia, florere unquam et praestare potuisse" (*De oratore* 2.1.5, p. 200).

37. Cicero, *De inventione* 1.1.1, p. 3, trans. H. M. Hubbell, Loeb Classical Library; "ratio ipsa in hanc potissimum sententiam ducit, ut existimem sapientiam sine eloquentia parum prodesse civitatibus, eloquentiam vero sine sapientia nimium obesse plerumque, prodesse nunquam" (*De inventione* 1.1.1, p. 2).

38. Petrarch, *"De vita solitaria,"* ed. G. Martellotti, in *Prose: Francesco Petrarcha*, ed. G. Marellotti, P. G. Ricci, E. Carrara, E. Bianchi (Milan, Naples: R. Riccardi, 1955), 540. Translation taken from Jerrold E. Seigel, *Rhetoric and Philosophy in Renaissance Humanism: The Union of Eloquence and Wisdom* (Princeton, N.J.: Princeton University Press, 1968), 46–47; "circa notitiam sui reflectendumque ad se animum et circa contemptum inanis glorie" (47). Jerrold Seigel has an excellent discussion of the combination of Stoic, Peripatetic, Skeptical, and Platonic sentiments that, together with the thought of Augustine, provided the philosophical underpinnings of Petrarch's and his students' view of rhetoric. See "The Ideals of Eloquence and the Silence of Petrarch," in *Rhetoric and Philosophy*, 31–62.

39. The full statement reads: "The object of the will, as it pleases the wise, is the good; that of the intellect truth. It is better to will the good than to know the truth." See Petrarch, "On His Own Ignorance," in *Renaissance Philosophy of Man*, ed. Ernst Cassirer, Paul Oskar Kristeller, and John Herman Randall, Jr. (Chicago: University of Chicago Press, 1969), 105. In Latin, Petrarch's statement reads, "Satius est autem bonum velle quam verum nosse" (*Opera Latini di Francesco Petrarcha a cura di Antonietta Bufano* [Torinese: Unione, 1975], vol. 2, 1110).

40. On Valla's skepticism, see *The Skeptical Tradition*, ed. Myles Burnyeat (Berkeley: University of California Press, 1983). On Valla's pragmatism, see Victoria Kahn's extended discussion in *Rhetoric, Prudence, and Skepticism in the Renaissance*. Nancy Struever touches upon similar trends in Valla's writing: "Lorenzo Valla: Humanist Rhetoric and the Critique of the Classical Languages of Moral-

ity," *Renaissance Eloquence*, 191–206; *The Language of History in the Renaissance* (Princeton, N.J.: Princeton University Press, 1970); and *Rhetoric and the Pursuit of Truth: Language Change in the Seventeenth and Eighteenth Centuries*, papers read at Clark Library Seminar, 8 March 1980, by Brian Vickers and Nancy Struever (Los Angeles: University of California Press, 1985).

Valla's distrust of philosophy eventually led him to proclaim that it was rhetoric and not the science of dialectics that should occupy the position of "the queen of disciplines." See Valla's work "On the True Good," in *Scritti Filosofici e Religiosi*, ed. Giorgio Radetti (Florence, 1953), 30–31. Cf. Seigel, *Rhetoric and Philosophy in Renaissance Humanism*, 142. Valla even appealed to the examples of biblical figures and the writings of patristic theologians in order to support his claim for the primacy of oratory and the ineptitudes of philosophy. He argues that Saint Paul himself "seems to be distinguished for no other thing than for eloquence." See *Elegantiae linguae latinae*, IV, *Opera*, Vol. I, of *Monumenta Politica et Philosophica Rariora* (Turin, 1962), 117–120. Cf. Seigel, *Rhetoric and Philosophy in Renaissance Humanism*, 154–155.

41. The work of Victoria Kahn, *Rhetoric, Prudence, and Skepticism in the Renaissance*, has been my principal source on the importance of educating the reader's "disposition" in Renaissance literature.

42. See Petrarch, *De sui ipsius et multorum ignorantia*, in *Prose: Francesco Petrarcha*, 748; English translation by Hans Nachod, "On His Own Ignorance," in *Renaissance Philosophy of Man*, 105. Cf. Seigel, *Rhetoric and Philosophy in Renaissance Humanism*, 35; "Hi sunt ergo . . . virtutum utiles magistri, quorum prima et ultima intentio est bonum facere auditorem ac lectorem, quique non solum docent quid est virtus aut vitium preclarumque illud hoc fuscum nomen auribus instrepunt, sed rei optime amorem studiumque pessimeque rei odium fugamque pectoribus inserunt," vol. 2, 1108, 1110.

43. For instance, Victoria Kahn has traced the intentionality with which authors as diverse as Erasmus, Montaigne, and Hobbes constructed their writings in a manner that encouraged the development of the reader's deliberative skills. Nancy Struever has pursued a similar line of criticism in her interpretation of Lorenzo Valla. With regard to Valla's famous attack on Scholasticism, Struever argues that one of his primary concerns is to nurture a kind of Stoic skepticism in his readers in order to train them to be suspicious of any form of absolute truth claim. He accomplishes this training in skepticism through a series of very clever rhetorical strategies. In his study of the rhetorical structures of Tudor dramas, Joel Altman also takes a similar tack. He convincingly demonstrates that the dramatic structures of many sixteenth-century plays were designed to induce particular "plays of thought" in the minds of their audiences. Inducing a "play of mind" involved teaching the audience a certain mode of inquiry that might assist them in sorting a myriad of questions related to human intention, desire, and moral action. Altman further illustrates that Tudor dramatists utilized more than just the story line of their plays in order to encourage rhetorically their audience to pursue this mode of inquiry.

See Kahn, *Rhetoric, Prudence, and Skepticism*; Struever, "Lorenzo Valla," in *Renaissance Eloquence*, 191–206; Joel B. Altman, *The Tudor Play of Mind: Rhetorical Inquiry and the Development of Elizabethan Drama* (Berkeley: University of California Press, 1978). Two other texts in which I found useful discussions of the literary practices of Renaissance writers are Richard A. Lanham, *The Motives of Eloquence:*

Literary Rhetoric in the Renaissance (New Haven, Conn.: Yale University Press, 1976), and Ronald Lavao, *Renaissance Minds and Their Fictions: Cusanus, Sidney, and Shakespeare* (Berkeley: University of California Press, 1985). On the Renaissance understanding of "making" the self, see Stephen Greenblatt, *Renaissance Self-Fashioning: From More to Shakespeare* (Chicago: University of Chicago Press, 1980).

44. Higman, "Calvin the Writer," 5.

45. Ibid., 6.

46. For a rhetorical analysis of his early writings in Strasbourg, see Benoit Girardin, *Rhétorique et théologique: Calvin, Le Commentaire de L'Epitre aux Romains* (Paris: Editions Beauchesne, 1979). For a thorough analysis of the '36 *Institutes*, see Ford Lewis Battles's annotated edition of this text. Francis Higman was the first to embark upon such an analysis of Calvin in his rhetorical study *The Style of John Calvin in His French Polemical Treatises* (Cambridge: Oxford University Press, 1967).

47. Bouwsma's *John Calvin* represents the most thorough and recent study of the role played by rhetoric in the *Institutes*. The first contemporary scholar to actually engage in an exploration of the discipline of rhetoric in Calvin's writing was Quirinus Breen in his article "John Calvin and the Rhetorical Tradition," *Church History* 26 (1957): 3–21. For more recent discussions, see Ford Lewis Battles, "God Was Accommodating Himself to Human Capacity," *Interpretation* 31 (1977): 19–38; and David Willis, "Rhetoric and Responsibility in Calvin's Theology," *The Context of Contemporary Theology*, ed. Alexander J. McKelway and E. David Willis (Atlanta: John Knox Press, 1974), 43–63. Also see Brian Armstrong's argument that rhetorical coherence may be the best approach to discerning the structure of the *Institutes*; Armstrong, "The Nature and Structure of Calvin's Thoughts according to the *Institutes*: Another Look," in *John Calvin's Institutes: His Opus Magnum* (Proceedings of the Second South African Congress for Calvin Research, July–August 1984, Potchefstroom University for Christian Higher Education Press, 1986), 55–81. Although each of these texts discusses rhetoric, only Willis approaches the task as a systematic/historical theologian, but his approach is markedly different from the approach I take in my analysis of the *Institutes*.

48. *Inst.* 1.14.4, p. 164; "Theologo autem non garriendo aures oblectare, sed vera, certa, utilia docendo, conscientias confirmare propositum est" (OS, 3:157. 11–13).

49. *Inst.* 1.10.2, p. 97; "eius agnitio vivo magis sensu, quam vacua et meteorica speculatione constet" (OS 3:86. 18–19).

50. *Inst.* 1.5.9, pp. 61–62; "invitari nos ad Dei notitiam, non quae inani speculatione contenta in cerebro tantum volitet, sed quae solida futura sit et fructuosa si rite percipiatur a nobis, radicemque agat in corde" (OS 3:53. 11–14).

51. *Inst.* 1.14.4, p. 164; "in lectione Scripturae, iis continenter quaerendis ac meditandis immoremur quae ad aedificationem pertinent" (OS 3:156. 21–23).

52. *Inst.* 1.7.4, p. 79; "testimonium Spiritus omni ratione praestantius esse . . . non ante fidem reperiet sermo in hominum cordibus quam interiore Spiritus testimonio obsignetur. Idem ergo Spiritus qui per os Prophetarum loquutus est, in corda nostra penetret necesse est, ut persuadeat fideliter protulisse quod divinitus erat mandatum" (OS 3:70. 1–8).

53. *Inst.* 1.7.4, p. 78; "nobis indubie persuasum sit, authorem eius esse Deum" (OS 3:36. 29–30).

54. *Commentary on First Corinthians*, 1:17. From William Bouwsma, *Calvinism as Theologia Rhetorica*, Protocol of the Fifty-fourth Colloquy, 28 September, 1986; Cen-

ter for the Hermeneutical Studies of Hellenistic and Modern Culture (Berkeley: General Theological Union and University of California Press, 1987), 3; "pareclara esse Dei dona, quibus homines tamquam organis ad bonas usus adiuvantur . . . a spiritu sancto sint profectae" (OC vol. 49, col. 321).

55. In his article "Rhetoric and Responsibility in Calvin's Theology, " 43–63, Willis offers a detailed discussion of Calvin's understanding of faith itself as a form of "affective persuasion."

56. From Calvin's *Commentary on Jeremiah*, 18:11. English translation taken from Bouwsma, *John Calvin*, 115; OC vol. 38, col. 300.

57. *Inst.* 1.2.1, p. 40; ". . . persuasi simus fontem omnium bonorum esse: nequid alibi quam in ipso quaeramus. . . . quem ab omnibus oporteat coli et adorari" (OS 3:34. 29–30 and 28–29).

58. For a fuller discussion of Calvin's use of "accommodation," see Battles, "God Was Accommodating Himself to Human Capacity." Also see Edward A. Dowey's examination of the theological import of Calvin's conception of accommodation. Edward A. Dowey, *The Knowledge of God in Calvin's Theology* (New York: Columbia University Press, 1952), 3ff.

59. *Inst.* 1.5.9 p. 62; "se propinquum nobis familiaremque reddit, ac quodammodo communicat" (OS 3:53. 22–23).

60. *Inst.* 1.14.3, p. 162; "Moses vulgi ruditati se accommodans, non alia Dei opera commemorat in historia creationis nisi quae oculis nostris occurrunt" (OS 3:154. 28–30).

61. *Inst.* 1.5.10, p. 62; "non modo ad Dei cultum excitare nos debet, sed ad spem quoque futurae vitae expergefacere, et erigere" (OS 3:54. 1–2).

62. *Inst.* 1.14.1, p. 160; "quae apprime utilis est cognitio . . . cognito mundi exordio, clarius eluceat Dei aeternitas, nosque in sui admirationem magis rapiat" (OS 3:152. 17–20).

63. *Inst.* 1.14.22, p. 181; "animadvert[ere] in bonum ac salutem nostram Deum omnia destinasse, simul in nobis ipsis, et tantis quae in nos contulit bonis, sentimus ipsius potentiam et gratiam: inde nos ad ipsius fiduciam, invocationem, laudem, amorem excitemus" (OS 3:172. 23–27).

64. *Inst.* 1.5.8, pp. 60–61; "propositis eiusmodi exemplis colligit, qui censentur esse fortuiti casus, totidem esse providentiae caelestis testimonia, praesertim vero paternae clementiae: atque hinc piis dari materiam laetitiae, impiis vero et reprobis ora obstrui" (OS 3:52. 23–26).

65. *Inst.* 1.4.1, p. 47; "omnes tamen degenerant a vera eius notitia. . . . vix centesimus quisque reperitur qui conceptum in suo corde foveat" (OS 3:41. 4–5 and 40. 32–41.1).

66. *Inst.* 1.5.15, p. 69; "Quare omni prorsus excusatione merito excludimur, quod vagi et palantes aberramus: quum omnia rectam viam demonstrent" (OS 3:59. 34–36).

67. *Inst.* 1.14.4, p. 164; "non curiositati aut rerum inutilium studio indulge[nt]" (OS 3:156. 23–24).

68. *Inst.* 1.14.6, pp. 166–67; "Quod autem ad consolationem nostram fideique confirmationem facere maxime poterat, in eo docendo plurimum insistit Scriptura: nempe Angelos divinae erga nos beneficentiae dispensatores esse et administros. . . . Itaque quo istud protectionis nostrae munus impleant, contra Diabolum omnesque hostes nostros depugnant, et vindictam Dei adversus eos qui nobis infesti sunt exequuntur" (OS 3:158. 22–25 and 159. 11–14).

69. One of the most interesting examples of this dynamic is found in Calvin's treatment of the doctrine of the Trinity in Book 1. In order to accommodate "the sum of what God meant to teach us in his word" to the capacity of "simple folk," Calvin believed the doctrine of the Trinity, like all other doctrines, should be presented as perspicuously and concisely as possible. He also recognized this was particularly difficult in the case of the Trinity, given its convoluted history and the highly speculative character of its traditional renderings. Thus, when he begins to treat the doctrine, he only briefly ventures into the terminological debates over the use of "person," "substance," and "essence." He then withdraws from the conversation altogether, confessing that he himself finds the whole thing overly complicated and confusing. He thus urges theologians engaged in terminological debates to step back from the conversation and "weigh the necessity that compels us to speak thus, that gradually they may at length become accustomed to a useful manner of speaking" (*Inst.* 1.13.5, p. 127). In the name of finding a "useful manner of speaking," Calvin searches for a simple Trinitarian formula that he believes will "render the truth plain and clear" (1.13.3, p. 124). Therefore, at least in the first stages of his treatment of the Trinity, it is obvious that practical/rhetorical considerations influence the shape of the formula he eventually adopts.

As his discussion of the Trinity progresses, one finds Calvin struggling to find a meaningful, clear, and accessible way of presenting his position. Finally, in the midst of what appears to be growing frustration on his part, he opts for a metaphor that he finds conceptually problematic but nonetheless "useful" because it is "easy to understand." Before submitting wholeheartedly to the metaphor he has chosen to depict the distinctions that inhere in the Godhead, he openly admits his dislike for it: "I really do not know whether it is expedient to borrow comparisons from human affairs to express the force of this distinction" (1.13.18, pp. 142–43). And yet he continues,

> Nevertheless, it is not fitting to suppress the distinction that we observe to be expressed in scripture. It is this: to the Father is attributed the beginning of activity, and the fountain and well-spring of all things; to the Son, wisdom, counsel, and the ordered disposition of all things, but to the Spirit is assigned the power and efficacy of that activity. (Ibid.)

Then, he goes on to adopt and unpack this particular formulation on the grounds that it accommodates itself to the natural capacity of the human mind: "For the mind of each human being is naturally inclined to contemplate God first, then the wisdom coming forth from him, and lastly the power whereby he executes the degrees of his plan" (ibid.)

What this whole discussion reveals is the extent to which the audience's conceptual capacities influenced the shape of the metaphor Calvin finally judged to be appropriate, even if such a metaphor is found insufficient on strictly theological or philosophical grounds. This discussion, however, also demonstrates that Calvin felt constrained enough by the biblical witness that he used a "way of speaking" found in scripture, even though it was not particularly "expedient." Thus, eloquence once again finds itself determined by wisdom even as that same eloquence gives shape and depth to the very wisdom that constrains and directs it.

70. For a fuller discussion of Calvin's Christology, a topic that has long baffled Calvin scholars, see David Willis, *Calvin's Catholic Christology*, Studies in Medieval and Reformation Thought, vol. 2 (Leiden: E. J. Brill, 1966).

71. This particular example of Calvin's copiousness and its rhetorical function will be explored extensively in chapter 3.

72. His interpretive activity more closely resembles that of Erasmus than it does the strict linear translations promoted by a school of Renaissance humanists known as the Ciceronians. For a discussion of Erasmus's view of interpretation/translation and its relation to the work of Quintilian, see Cave, *The Cornucopian Text*.

73. On this particular point, Brian Armstrong's comments refreshed my own memory concerning the significance of Calvin's skills at working from memory.

74. See his prefatory letter, "Subject Matter of the Present Work" (*Inst.* p. 8); "estre de Dieu, plus que mien" (OS 3:8.15).

2

CALVIN'S CONTEXT:
PREFACING AND PLACING

'Tis those whose cause my former booklet pled
Whose zeal to learn has wrought this tome instead.

Quos animus fuerat tenui excusare libello,
Discendi studio magnum fecere volumen.
Calvin, 1559 *Institutes*

As a hush fell over the crowd gathered in the Great Hall of downtown Geneva in 1561 and Calvin stepped forward to speak, the collective energy in that room must have been immense. People from many vastly different walks of life had come to hear the reformer lecture, and most likely, the only expectation shared by all was the certainty that, in the course of his lecture, Calvin would say something that spoke directly to each of them, to their individual concerns and to their particular life circumstances. If they knew Calvin's style of lecturing well, then they also knew that he would speak kindly to some and harshly to others; he would speak words of comfort to some and words of judgment to others. And this alone would have been enough to make the crowd restless, maybe a bit uncomfortable, and most assuredly full of anticipation, ready for a mental and emotional workout and braced to hear both the heartening and terrifying words that would come from the lips of this well-known Christian orator.

Over the centuries, readers from many lands and many walks of life have experienced the same restlessness and exhilaration as they have worked through Calvin's *Institutes* because, in the pages of this text, he manages to capture the energy and tension that typified his public lectures. One can hardly read a single paragraph in the *Institutes* without feeling drawn to its author and personally addressed by his message. When the text speaks to its audience as "you"—"you know God to be your Creator"—it is difficult not to feel that it is directly speaking to you, even if you live in the late twentieth century. And when Calvin owns his words and states, "I say that God is the author of your life," it almost seems as if he is standing before you as he did in that Great Hall four centuries ago. The power of Calvin's public addresses is also captured in the *Institutes* insofar as one gets the sense that many different readers are being pulled into the text at the same time. At points, it is clear that the text is gently nurturing the faith of the newly converted while at other points, it launches a bitter attack against readers whose faith and politics Calvin obviously despises. It is precisely these tensions and conflicts that make it virtually impossible to read the *Institutes* without having a strong reaction to it.

These reactions are particularly evident to me when I teach a course on Calvin's *Institutes*. Every week, students arrive either inspired and compelled by the assigned readings, or indignant and enraged by Calvin's often caustic arrogance. But if they have attended to the rhetorical and theological subtleties of the text, both reactions are tempered by an overwhelming respect for the beauty and honesty of Calvin's reflections on scripture and his commitment to making it come alive for his readers— whatever form that "coming alive" might take. The force of these students' reactions has made it clear to me that one could very easily do an analysis of the rhetorical movement of the *Institutes* as it is read by and affects the lives of contemporary readers. To do such an analysis, one need not understand Cicero's thoughts on rhetoric or the history of Calvin's training as a lawyer and humanist. The rhetorical pull of the text is so powerful that one need not know even the text's original audiences in order to recognize that its discursive maneuvers are complex and that its intended readers are expected to be diverse. All one needs to do is to sit in a modern-day class on Calvin and witness the text's ability to recreate the immense energy and tensions of the Genevan Great Hall, and recognize that when this occurs, the field of opportunities for rhetorical textual analysis is wide open.

I have also found, however, that students' appreciation for the text's rhetorical play is increased when they become aware of Calvin's background in rhetoric and when they learn about the audiences the text was originally designed to address. When this information is provided, it does not prevent students from responding to the text with the immediate passions and concerns of twentieth-century readers (nor should it), but it does deepen their respect for the theological, cultural, and political aspirations of the text as it functioned in a different era and attempted to reach out to people whose lives were very different from their own. It also allows students to gain critical leverage on a text by exposing what biases they bring to the activity of reading and by raising questions about their respect for the historical limits of the text. Once one realizes that Calvin was speaking to an early modern audience of students, pastors, merchants, princes, spies, and other perceived "friends and enemies," the theological import of his doctrines may feel and sound quite different than it does if these doctrines are simply applied to present-day Calvinists and their critics. If this interpretive reorientation to Calvin's theology can be accomplished by providing historical background, it may also help students to better understand the historical thickness of their own lives and theology as well.

Anchoring the text in a historical context is not an easy task, however, particularly if one is doing it in the interest of informing a rhetorical reading. On the one hand, like any other piece of historical investigations, it requires that one digest some basic historical facts. For this part of the project, historians of early modern Europe are necessary conversation partners, especially when their area of study is France and Geneva in the sixteenth century. The second section of this chapter engages directly in this conversation. On the other hand, if one wants to discern the character of the audiences Calvin sought to address and if one intends to get a sense of the "play of mind" he hoped his rhetorical gestures might engender in these audiences, then digesting historical facts is not sufficient. It is not enough to know the names and background of all those people who sat waiting for him to speak in the Great Hall because this information will not necessarily tell one how Calvin perceived these people and how he imagined his rhetoric might engage and shape their habits of thinking, their attitudes, beliefs, and dispositions. These latter insights are important to grasp when analyzing the rhetoric of the *Institutes* because one needs to imagine the rhetorical goals that drove Calvin to write to these people. One must try to enter the rhetorical mind-set of the author in order to determine what rhetorical "plan of action" guided his pen as he wrote. In doing so, one is required to step gently into a fragile and ambiguous area of analysis: the imaginative world of Calvin's intentions, or, as I refer to it in the third section of this chapter, "the world according to Calvin."

This world is fragile and ambiguous because it is finally impossible for anyone to know with certainty what Calvin actually thought about his audiences and his rhetorical goals. Historical distance makes it impossible as does the reality that a person's intentions are not transparent; they continually shift, and they remain endlessly open to interpretation, even to the interpretive processes of the very person who is "intending." It is thus critical that a historical reconstruction of Calvin's "rhetorical plan of action" be tempered by an acknowledgment that the reconstruction requires the readers to make imaginative leaps that are neither historically neutral nor analytically precise. This does not mean, however, that such a reconstruction must always be considered a product of "pure" imagination on the part of the modern reader. As mentioned above, the work of historians helps to set limits that make such a reconstruction historically "respectful" and plausible. And even more importantly, as one attempts to reconstruct Calvin's intentions, there are clues that the text offers as guides, clues that Calvin himself has left behind, allowing the reader to enter the world of his articulated intentions, the world of his own imagined audiences and goals.

These clues come in the form of three prefaces, each of which served to introduce the original readers to various editions of the *Institutes*. In this chapter, I will be using these prefaces to reconstruct imaginatively the "rhetorical plans of action" that may have guided Calvin over the many years he devoted to writing this text. In each of these prefaces, the reader is given a glimpse of Calvin's perceptions of his social context. Calvin offers the reader a series of mini portraits that depict the aims and aspirations, as he imagined them, of his varied audiences. Through the prefaces, one is also offered brief narratives of sixteenth-century history, albeit history according to Calvin, and in these narratives it is possible to discern a list of the reasons why Calvin found it important to speak to particular communities. He tells his reader what he wants the text "to do," what dispositions he hopes it evokes, and what kinds of rhetoric he intends to deploy as he shifts from audience to audience.

Again, the information offered in the prefaces is not historically neutral; it is colored and shaped by Calvin's own life experiences, and one can be certain that those persons identified as his enemies would paint a radically different portrait of the same era if they were to write their own prefaces to the text. It is also important to remember that in Calvin's world, claims about historical neutrality and objectivity did not hold the same mythic power that they do in our own day. As Cicero tells his students, the work of a truly eloquent orator is never disinterested; rather it is always shaped by a vision of what the orator believes to be "the good," and therefore it is structured by political aims and rhetorical gestures designed to inculcate a sense of that "good" in the audience. For Calvin, the vision of the "good" was a vision of a creation that knows and loves the God who created and redeemed the world. And as Christian orator, Calvin causes his discourse to follow a course marked for it by both scripture and his own accommodative perceptions of the political and cultural world in which the newly emerging evangelical church might better struggle to know and worship the divine. These are the conceptual and practical parameters that may not be empirically or historically measurable, but they are parameters that nonetheless structure Calvin's worldview. And if one is to read his text in a historically, theologically, and rhetorically informed manner, then this is the world that the reader also must enter with the tools of scripture, Calvin's prefacing remarks, a sense of Calvin's social context, and one's own imagination as guides.

WHY WRITE A PREFACE?

I have just discussed several theoretical reasons that Calvin's prefaces play a central role in reconstructing a rhetorical map of the *Institutes'* intended audiences and goals. There is, however, one additional reason that it is useful to begin the process of reconstructing Calvin's "rhetorical plan of action" by starting with the prefaces. It is quite simply the fact that Calvin wrote the prefaces so that his audiences would read through them before launching into the main body of the *Institutes*. And given Calvin's meticulous attentiveness to the language and structure of his discourse, it is safe to assume that he did not haphazardly throw together a series of opening remarks to introduce the reader to his work. To the contrary, Cicero would have taught him that beginnings play a critical role in determining whether one's rhetoric will soar to eloquent heights or crash aimlessly upon deafened ears. In light of this advice, it would seem that these prefaces play a significant role in orienting his audiences to the rest of the *Institutes*. Thus, as a way of entering the text's rhetorical world at the very place where Calvin would have one enter, let me begin by exploring the general role that the prefaces might have played in this regard.

Development of Calvin's Three Prefaces

Calvin commenced the 1559 edition of the *Institutes* with two prefaces. The best known of these prefaces, titled "The Prefatory Address to King Francis I of France" (*Praefatio ad Regem Gall*), was not written originally to introduce the 1559 edition but was penned in 1535 during Calvin's stay in Basel. In its first publication, it served as the introduction to his 1536 edition of the *Institutes*.[1] However, Calvin used it in its original, unaltered form to introduce each successive edition of the *Institutes* as well.[2] Given the early date of the letter's initial composition, it may seem surprising that Calvin would use the letter, in an unrevised form, as the introduction to a work as late as the 1559 edition, a text written more than twenty years after the letter's initial penning.[3] During these years, many dramatic changes had occurred in the French situation described in the preface, changes such as the death of the letter's addressee, King Francis I, and Calvin's own transformation from a recently exiled and marginal French intellectual to a powerful and internationally famous religious leader.[4] These shifts in context prompt us to ask why Calvin used an outdated preface to introduce a new, updated edition of the *Institutes*.

It is difficult to know the mind of Calvin on this matter, for his writings during this period do not record his views on the function this preface served in the 1559 edition of the text. However, the very fact that Calvin decided to keep the unaltered letter as an introduction to the 1559 *Institutes*—a text he had never hesitated to alter, expand, or reorganize when necessary—suggests that it continued to serve well the task of introducing the reader to his work. The letter might have served this role because the situation it describes still found strong resonances in the lives of his readers in France and Geneva, despite the historical distance of twenty years. This possibility finds support in the fact that although the historically particular characters in Calvin's prefatory story of the conflicts surrounding the evangelical community in France had obviously changed over the years, the tensions it narrates had not disappeared. During these years, intervals of increased toleration had occurred, but constantly shifting relations of power between the Roman Catholic Church and the French crown kept the threat of persecution a living and often terrifying reality for the evangelical community Calvin defends in the letter. In this context, it could be that Calvin used this preface to introduce each successive edition of the *Institutes* because he wanted his readers to recall the events of the 1530s as the context for his present reflections, situating the text in a prior time of tumult and crisis, and hence, using the past as a key to illumining the present. It could be, as well, that Calvin chose to retain the preface for scholarly reasons, wanting to preserve the textual integrity of at least part of the original *Institutes*. This possibility, however, seems less likely given that in his other writings, Calvin is seldom interested in marking those places where he has preserved or revised original texts, be they his own or another's.

Whatever Calvin's reasons may have been, it is certain that the letter's introductory role, in its 1536 form, was rhetorically important to the 1559 *Institutes*. It is thus critical that when the preface is interpreted, its original social context be taken into account, for Calvin's own dating of the text points the 1559 reader to the year 1536. But in addition to the 1536 context, it is also crucial that the letter be interpreted with reference to what it would have meant to the 1559 reader in his or her own context, for it is clearly this reader, not the reader of 1536, to whom the preface speaks in this final Latin edition of the *Institutes*. Within this context, then, one needs to consider the recent events in France and imagine how the letter may have appealed to the 1559 readers who—with their current contextual interests and expectations—would have read the letter, in its final position, as narratively part of the same literary structure of the updated text it prefaces.

Similar interpretive challenges attend the second prefatory letter to the 1559 *Institutes* titled "John Calvin to the Reader" (*Iohannes Calvinus Lectori*).[5] In its initial form, this letter commenced Calvin's 1539 *Institutes*, a text penned while he was in Strasbourg, teaching in Johann Sturm's newly founded academy and tending to a French parish.[6] In the 1543 *Institutes*, Calvin expanded the letter very slightly, adding a concluding reference to Augustine. However, with the 1559 edition, Calvin not only reworked several of the letter's original sentences, he expanded and updated the text as whole, adding comments that refer explicitly to events that occurred in 1558.[7] These changes, blended directly into the original text of the letter, make it appear as if this preface were written specifically for the 1559 edition.

This blending of editorial additions into the original represents a literary strategy quite different from the one found in the 1536 preface. When Calvin placed the 1536 preface in the 1559 text, he left it untouched, keeping even the original date and place at the end of the letter. However, with this second preface, the original text is altered, new references are added, and perhaps most important from a rhetorical point of view, the date and place at the end of the letter reflect the new audience to whom the updated text is designed to speak. With the new ending reading "Geneva, 1st August 1559," it most likely would have appeared to the 1559 reader of the text that the preface was designed especially to introduce this particular Latin edition.

Given the nature of these changes, it seems that Calvin did not wish to invoke this letter's original 1539 context with the same directness he invokes the original context of the 1536 letter. This changes the dynamics of how one interprets the letter's function in relation to the larger text, suggesting that while historical information about the 1539 audience might be interesting, it is not information toward which the letter itself points. Instead, all references to 1539 have been revised in the letter's new form, thus changing the very character of the contextual notes it offers its reader. For instance, in light of the changes Calvin makes to the letter, the reference to "instructing candidates in sacred theology" in the 1539 text—a reference that referred to French students in the school of Strum in Strasbourg—would have become, by the time he wrote the 1559 edition, a reference to the "candidates in sacred theology" whom he taught in "Geneva, August 1st, 1559."[8] In this manner, the older sections of the text take on new rhetorical meaning as they are blended into what appears to be a seamless narrative directed toward a contemporary audience of readers. Thus, if one is to read this letter as it would have been read by its new audience, it is important to focus most particularly on its 1559 context.

The third preface I examine presents many of the same interpretive challenges raised by the previous two. Titled "The Subject Matter of the Present Work" (*Argument du present livre*), it was composed in 1539 and expanded two years later to introduce the 1541 French edition of the *Institutes*.[9] Calvin then revised it only slightly to introduce the French edition of 1560, and this final version is the one used in the present study. In addition to these comments about its dates and editions, it is also important to note that, unlike the previous two letters, it did not appear in the 1559 Latin text. In this regard it is anomalous, for it was not a calculated part of Calvin's 1559 rhetorical plan of action and should not be read as if it functioned in this context. Despite this difference, I have chosen to include it in this study because it tells the contemporary reader of the *Institutes* a good deal about Calvin's view of his French audience, both in 1541 and around the time he was writing the 1559 Latin text. It thus provides useful contextualizing information with respect to questions of readership and rhetorical strategy.[10]

In addition to establishing the different dates and historical contexts of each of these three prefatory letters, one must note as well that the main text of Calvin's *Institutes* is also composed of different editorial layers.[11] Like Calvin's "Preface to the Reader," these editorial layers make it difficult to identify a single audience and historically stable context for the text as a whole. As the above discussion of Calvin's letters suggests, he worked on the *Institutes* for many years, during which time he moved geographically, the conflicts he engaged in shifted, and his audiences changed and grew accordingly. And these changes affected the shape of the main text. For example, the three opening chapters of the *Institutes*, which I examine in chapters 3, 4, and 5 of this study, were drafted for the 1539 edition while Calvin was teaching in Strasbourg. In 1543, shortly after Calvin's return to Geneva, the text of these chapters was only slightly revised for a new Latin edition of the book as a whole. Then again, in preparation for the 1559 edition, Calvin expanded these chapters in the 1550s, adding material and occasionally revising prior statements. Accordingly, each of these textual layers had an "original" audience and an "initial" rhetorical function specific to its 1539 writing, and a later audience and function accommodated to its 1559 context.

As one reads these chapters rhetorically, it is important to recognize the presence of these layers and the different historical contexts each evokes, just as it is crucial that each preface be appropriately historicized. As with the prefaces, however, one can also make some general observations about the audiences and contexts of the *Institutes* over the years. Using the prefaces as a guide, one can construct loose historical "types" of audiences/readerships that appear to stay with the *Institutes* throughout its editorial revisions. Likewise, the prefaces and the main text allow one to identify broadly structured "types" of rhetoric, which Calvin uses to address these audiences each time he reformulates the text. While conceiving such broad types alone overlooks the wealth of rhetorical insight one might gain from a more detailed analysis of the context and audience of each edition, it has the advantage of giving one enough historical information to situate the text while remaining general enough to allow one to trace the integrated rhetorical flow of the final 1559 edition as a whole.

What are these types? In the following pages, I use Calvin's prefaces to identify the following four audiences and textual functions: (1) the students whom Calvin sought to instruct; (2) the friends and followers in French parishes whose faith Calvin sought to strengthen and console; (3) the community of humanistically minded scholars and aristocrats whom he sought to convert to the cause of reform; and (4) a diverse collection of "enemies" whom he sought to attack polemically and marginalize. Although this particular list of audiences is clearly not exhaustive, it helps to get a rhetorical reading of Calvin off to a firm start. I have jumped ahead of the text, however, by introducing these figures before the prefaces have had a chance to tell their own story. So, let me return to text and continue to explore how Calvin uses these prefaces to introduce his readers to the project at hand.

Rhetorical Function of the Three Prefaces

There are many ways one can begin the process of analyzing the rhetorical function served by these prefaces. One interesting angle of approach is to begin with a general question concerning the overarching literary function of this group of prefaces as a "genre" before turning to more historical questions concerning the nature of each preface and its audiences, contexts, and rhetorical character. To raise this general question is, in short, to ask: Why write a preface? Why engage in the literary activity of prefacing? And why do it in the form that Calvin has?

Although the dates of the two prefaces that begin the 1559 *Institutes* are different, they have several similarities that offer clues to their shared function as a literary genre. First, it is clear from the beginning of each that they are both occasioned by Calvin's concern that his writings have been misinterpreted by his readers. In the preface "John Calvin to the Reader," he describes his fear of false readings: "Since I undertook the office of teacher in the church, I have had no other purpose than to benefit the church by maintaining the pure doctrine of godliness. Yet I think that there is no one who is assailed, bitten, and wounded more by false accusations than I."[12] He then recounts events that occurred at the 1558 Diet of Augsburg, where rumors of his defection to the papacy had spread. In response to these rumors, Calvin announces that in this edition of the *Institutes*, he intends to offer his "godly readers" (*piis lectoribus*) "new proof" (*novum documentum*) of his continued loyalty to the cause of reform and his opposition to the papacy.[13]

In his "Prefatory Address to King Francis I of France," Calvin expresses this same concern but in a different context. Calvin explains here that he intended the letter to serve as the opening remarks of an extended defense of the evangelical church against the charges of heresy and sedition. He makes this point at the beginning of the letter when he asserts his intention to tell the king of France the truth about this faithful community and thereby to counter the "many lying slanders" (*mendaces calumniae*) his opponents have incorrectly attributed to them. Appealing to the king's sense of justice, Calvin claims he has written the *Institutes* so that "from this you [King Francis] may learn the nature of the doctrine against which those madmen burn with rage who today disturb your realm with fire and sword."[14] Thus, in contrast to the lying slanders of the opposition, Calvin intends to present the king with a true account of his community's faith, an account that performs the critical task of correcting false reports.

In his third preface to the French reader, Calvin again reiterates his concern that his text may be misunderstood. However, he refers here to the reception it may receive, not in the hands of his detractors, but in the hands of the truly faithful who share his theological perspective. He states his hope that he has not "misused words" (*abuser de parolles*) and thereby made it difficult for the French community to grasp the text's meaning.[15] He further urges his readers not to despair if they cannot understand all the contents of his book but to press onward, "hoping that one passage will give [them] a more familiar explanation of another."[16] These references to "misused words" and "the lack of understanding" reveal Calvin's continued fear that his text may be misinterpreted, even in communities sympathetic to his cause.

Thus, whether the *Institutes* was to be read in the court of the king, in large ecclesial meetings, or in the hands of a pious French reader, correcting previous readings and protecting the text from potential abuses appear to have been major motivations behind Calvin's writing of each preface. This zealous desire to thwart the text's misappropriation suggests that Calvin recognized the possibility that his book could generate a multiplicity of interpretations by readers who stood in a variety of contexts. According to Calvin, these misreadings might be intentionally occasioned by the political interests of opponents, such as described in the "Address" to the king, or false interpretation might spring from rumors and lies, as conveyed in his preface to the reader in the 1559 edition. He also suggests that misreadings might be the product of limited knowledge and inexperience, the problem addressed by Calvin's preface to the 1560 French edition.

Whatever the reason behind false readings, the activity of prefacing indicates that Calvin appreciated the degree to which textual meaning "travels" as the text travels, shifting from place to place, from audience to audience, from function to function.[17] Or to use Calvin's words in his *Commentary on Seneca's De clementia*, meaning is a function of use.[18] Calvin was not unique in his belief that meaning travels as a text's context and function change. Such a notion was common parlance among many of his contemporaries in the humanist movement. However, Calvin did not hold, as did some of his colleagues, that this functional understanding of meaning required one to forfeit all claims to a true or correct reading.[19] The prefaces demonstrate quite the opposite. The fact that Calvin refers to these misreadings as "abuses" presupposes the possibility of a correct or respectful reading and the corresponding possibility that his readers are capable of grasping it.[20]

How does Calvin intend to ensure his text is read correctly and not falsely interpreted or distorted? Once again, the prefaces provide the reader with the answer, pointing to a second similarity in the functional genre of these letters. A respectful or "proper" reading will follow, Calvin suggests, if the text is set in its appropriate social context and read in light of its intended social function, and Calvin lists these contexts and functions. He writes in the preface to the 1559 edition, "It has been my purpose in this labor to prepare and instruct candidates in sacred theology for the reading of the divine Word, in order that they may be able to both have easy access to it and to advance in it without stumbling."[21] Similarly, he positions his text in its intended context in the opening paragraph of the letter to the king; he explains, "My purpose was solely to transmit certain rudiments by which those who are touched with any zeal for religion might be shaped to true godliness. And I undertook this labor especially for our French countrymen."[22] Likewise, the 1560 preface offers similar contextualizing information. Calvin's purpose is "to help simple folk . . . and as it were to lend them a hand, in order to guide them and help them to find the sum of what God meant to teach us in his Word."[23]

In light of these assertions, it is possible to expand the answer to the question concerning the rhetorical function of the prefaces. Based on Calvin's comments, one may conclude that these letters represent an attempt to defend the text against possible misreadings by locating it in its proper communal context. In this sense, the prefaces serve a distinctly limiting function in relation to the larger text. They limit the sphere of possible readings by anchoring the text in specific situations. The implicit assumption is that when properly located and used as intended, the text's meaning will be clear. Thus, Calvin's recognition that meaning is a function of usage is complemented by a set of contextual parameters that delineate for the reader usage rules guaranteeing a correct reading. When the prefaces are read with this rhetorical function in mind, it is clear why Calvin found the activity of prefacing to be essential to the theological project undertaken in the remainder of the text: without the introductory letters, the readers might wander from the path of truly accommodative divine wisdom and become lost in the endless chaos of multiple meanings.

Theological Significance of the Prefaces

Despite Calvin's explicit concern to set boundaries around the interpretive act of reading, many of his more recent theological interpreters have chosen not to follow the advice of the prefaces and to read the text without reference to the communal parameters that bind it. One example of such a reading is Wilhelm Niesel's well-known interpretation of Calvin's thought, *The Theology of John Calvin*.[24] In his opening comments, Niesel acknowledges that Calvin's purpose in writing the *Institutes* was to teach students the elements of the faith and to edify the community of believers. Niesel thereby makes an initial gesture toward locating the work in its original context. However, when he begins to interpret the meaning of Calvin's doctrinal formulations, these historical gestures become fewer and fewer as his central thesis grows increasingly focused. Arguing that Calvin's theology is fundamentally Christocentric in orientation, Niesel sets Calvin in a Barthian framework and constructs a picture of the *Institutes* reflecting the all-encompassing centrality of the revelation of God in Jesus Christ. Niesel's position on this matter is well argued, his evidence quite convincing, and he succeeds in setting a new course for contemporary readings of Calvin's overarching agenda. On this score, Niesel's project deserves hardy applause.

But what about history? What about Calvin's opening comments on the purpose of the *Institutes?* Niesel occasionally ventures into the realm of history, most frequently to make note of those places where Calvin parts ways with Luther, or where his Augustinian sympathies appear with greatest clarity. However, the majority of Niesel's comments on Calvin are made without historical reference.[25] This lack of contextualizing gestures suggests that Niesel envisions a text that speaks to an ahistorical audience of Christian readers. Similarly, there is an implicit assumption that the message the text speaks can be extracted from its rhetorical clothing and restated with a propositional clarity that captures the text's true meaning, its rhetorically unencumbered doctrinal truth. As a result, Niesel offers a reading of Calvin divorced from the type of dispositional knowledge of truth—truth that is rhetorically evoked—that Calvin intended his texts to elicit. Thus, while Niesel's reading may not be "wrong," it is limited in its understanding of textual meaning. Given Calvin's oratorical training, rhetoric would not have been dismissed as the mere "clothing" of his doctrines because it is precisely through the power of his rhetoric that he communicates dispositional truths to his audience. Furthermore, Calvin understood that rhetorical ornamentation rarely has universal applicability. It must always be carefully accommodated to the conventions of a particular audience. In this sense, history is linked to rhetoric and together they form the contextual terrain within which meaning occurs.

It may well be that Niesel's evaluation of Calvin's Christocentrism is correct. But if one intends to make such a determination from a rhetorical perspective, the arguments given in support of Niesel's position would look very different from the arguments he offers. A rhetorical reading designed to argue in favor of Niesel's thesis might focus on the discursive gestures Calvin deploys in order to rivet the attention of his audience upon the person and work of Jesus Christ. And a good deal might also be made of Calvin's rhetorical transposition of his audiences' identity with the biblical rendering of the narrative identity of the disciples. Indeed, there is ample rhetorical space for arguing that Calvin's theology is quite Christocentric. However, it may also be the case that a rhetorical exploration of Calvin's christological claims might critically challenge or reshape Niesel's description of what makes Calvin's text Christocentric and how that Christocentrism shapes the affective disposition of the reader. Again, the interpretive possibilities engendered by rhetorical conversations with Calvinist theologians such as Niesel are endless.

But testing Niesel's thesis and carrying on this particular conversation are beyond the scope of this chapter. So let me now return to the task of discerning Calvin's own "rhetorical plan of action" and, following his advice, attend to the historical character of the audiences and goals he identifies in the prefaces.

A HISTORICAL MAP OF THE
TERRAIN OF THE *INSTITUTES*

The Terrain of Early Modern France

In the deep valleys that cut through the Alps of Dauphiné, peasants still tell stories of the pastors from Geneva, who four hundred years ago stole their way from house to house, impelled by religious conviction and a sense of mission, to win converts to Calvinism. People raised in the Protestant tradition can still point out the hidden paths these men pursued between the sheer rock faces that flank the valleys. They can also point out substantial stone farmhouse[s] set at one day's march from each other that still contain secret hiding-places behind chimneys or in cellars, where a hunted man could find shelter. But only an especially persistent and interested stranger will ever see any part of this underground network that unites Dauphiné. It has served many causes in the past, most recently the Resistance in the Second World War.[26]

With this description of the precarious paths taken by Calvin's students as they slipped into France on the eve of a civil war that would rock that country for the next forty years, Robert Kingdon begins his account of the "Genevan Company of Pastors," an organization instituted under Calvin's direction to send missionaries into this conflicted area. It is likely that some had with them, among the few books they could carry, copies of Calvin's writings: perhaps a letter from Calvin to one of his many contacts in France; perhaps one of his short polemical tracts; perhaps a biblical commentary for use in their preaching; perhaps even a copy of the *Institutes*, which had long been available to them in both French and Latin.[27] The paths they followed, writings in hand, were fraught with political tensions and intrigue, with secrecy and subversion, and they were paths frequently soaked with the blood of both Calvin's followers and their enemies.

If a contemporary reader chooses to follow the "path" of reading set by Calvin in his introduction to the *Institutes*, then he or she must begin by imaginatively traveling along these and other paths in order to understand, if only partially, the world of audiences and actions that constituted the terrain upon which this text was formed and disseminated. Like the paths of the pastors, these interpretive paths are precarious, for historical distance makes it impossible to calculate the many turns the text will take into unknown political battles, secret negotiations, and eclipsed theological controversies. However, to "the especially persistent and interested stranger," the now aged markings of these paths are still visible. Following the simple directions that Calvin provides in the prefaces, they are paths that even in their sketchiness promise to bring new insights into the meaning of Calvin's doctrines and the "divine Word" to which they witness.

The broadest parameters of this map can be provided by a brief overview of the cultural terrain of Europe in the mid–sixteenth century. In short, it was a terrain marked by many deep and destabilizing fractures in the social structure of its territories.[28] As I have already noted, early modern Europe saw the beginnings of the rise of national bodies and identities that challenged and subsequently began to change the boundaries that defined and separated not only geographical regions but human subjects as well. The rise of nation- and city-states disrupted age-old alliances between sovereign rulers and the ecclesial institutions of Rome. At the same time, these emergent political bodies created new tensions between the various aristocratic power blocks that sought to renegotiate their relations to both king and church. It was thus a period of fluid political boundaries and intense warfare aimed at more tightly securing territorial borders. It was also a period marked by tremendous economic change. Beginning in fourteenth-century Italy, the traditional feudal economic configurations that had ordered much of Europe for centuries were slowly eroding, giving way to a new form of economic arrangement, the still nascent form of capitalism. And with this transition came a period of economic instability. New trade paths emerged as the avenues of economic exchange increased. Peasants flooded into cities across Europe, guilds of artisans formed, and a merchant class of entrepreneurs, the bourgeoisie, began to emerge.

With this growth in the cities came increased social unrest. In France, crippling taxes were laid upon the middle sectors as well as on the already impoverished peasantry in order to fund the king's wars with the Holy Roman Empire. As a result, plagues, hunger, and local rioting threatened daily.[29] Fueling this social unrest was the previously unprecedented production of written materials in vernacular languages that poured off the newly invented printing press.[30] As a result, Europe began for the first time to witness the rise of a literate class of entrepreneurs and artisans.

Social unrest reverberated in the intellectual world of the academies as well. In France and Italy it took the form of the challenges that humanism brought to bear upon the medieval Scholastic tradition. Breakthroughs in science, as well as the violently wrought "discoveries" of different peoples and cultures in the "new world," added to the force of these challenges. Thus, like Europe's geographical boundaries, intellectual and cultural boundaries were fluid, and the battles waged to stabilize them were fierce. Along with these challenges, out of Germany came voices that shook the northern territories, the voices of Luther, Melanchthon, Zwingli, Bucer, and other reformers who struggled to articulate a new religious identity for Christian Europe. Thus, even the ideological mainstay of medieval society, Christian culture, was being challenged and in many cases, slowly dismantled.

As this map of the forces fracturing sixteenth-century Europe suggests, the cultural world of Calvin and his followers was marked by uncertainty and change. The old order was eroding and the possibilities held by the future as yet remained unclear. It was an era marked by anxiety, an anxiety wrought by the tensions of a world caught between the traditions of the Middle Ages and the seemingly endless possibilities of the beckoning modern era.[31] In short, the geographical, political, and cultural map of Europe—which provides the broadest parameters for the context in which I shall place Calvin's text—was a map with boundaries as fluid as its possibilities. And this map designates a time in which the articulation and marking of those boundaries had become, by necessity, an obsession, and one which the powerful and politically astute writer of the *Institutes* shared.

It is in Calvin's three prefaces that one encounters the most explicit account of his struggle to articulate these new boundaries. As I have previously argued, he accomplishes this by first marking the cultural boundaries of his own discourse, and as I shall show, these particular boundaries were as complex as the world he sought to engage. In order for the modern reader to sort through their complexity, it is necessary to take these prefaces apart and to distinguish, one by one, the audiences and functions that mark the terrain upon which Calvin intended his *Institutes* to stand. The way to begin the process of distinguishing audiences is to look at the largest and most prominent group of persons to whom Calvin appealed, his students.

The Main Audience: Calvin's Students

As I have previously remarked, in his preface "John Calvin to the Reader," Calvin states that he intends his book to be used as a teaching tool.[32] "It has been my purpose in this labor to prepare and instruct candidates in sacred theology for the reading of the divine Word, in order that they may be able both to have easy access to it and to advance in it without stumbling."[33] He further stresses the text's teaching function when he writes,

> For I believe I have so embraced the sum of religion in all its parts, and have arranged it in such an order, that if anyone rightly grasps it, it will not be difficult for him to determine what he ought especially to seek in Scripture, and to what end he ought to relate its contents.[34]

On the basis of these comments, it is fair to say that Calvin's principal agenda in the *Institutes* is pedagogical insofar as his principal audience appears to consist of persons he seeks to instruct. Given that he forthrightly admits his concern to arrange and structure the book so that students will be able to grasp its contents, it is also clear that Calvin gave careful consideration to the rhetorical requirements best suited to teaching. In his *Commentary on First Corinthians,* Calvin reflects further on the rhetoric of teaching as he explains the decorum of good pedagogy: "A wise teacher accommodates himself to the understanding of those who must be taught. He begins with first principles in teaching the weak and ignorant and should not rise any higher than they can follow. In short, he instills his teaching drop by drop, lest it overflow."[35] As one scholar has noted, Calvin takes his own advice quite literally, carefully crafting a text that, divided into small sections, can be slowly absorbed by the reader.[36] In addition to attending to the text's arrangement, Calvin adopts—in the body of the *Institutes*—a rhetoric that aims at simplicity and clarity of presentation. His writing is terse and to the point, as he avoids excessive ornamentation in his choice of words and images. Similarly, while he is in his teaching mode, Calvin presents his arguments in a clean and straightforward manner so that the reader will easily follow the movement of the text.

In another reflection on the task of teaching, Calvin states that accommodating one's discourse to an audience of students involves much more than adopting a suitable arrangement, style, and vocabulary. The very content of the teaching itself must be shaped to speak to the social context of the students. "It would be a cold way of teaching," he explains, "if the teacher does not carefully consider the needs of the times and what is appropriate to the people for in this matter nothing is more unbalanced than absolute balance."[37] Here one finds Calvin expanding the notion of accommodation to include the "needs of the time" (*quid exigat tempus*), needs that would have been political and social as well as religious.

On the basis of this last comment, it is evident that if one is to appreciate the way in which Calvin accommodates his rhetoric to speak to his students, then one must have some sense of their needs and expectations.

What was their background? What was Calvin training them to do? What were the particular "needs of the time" that the *Institutes* was designed to meet? To answer these questions, it is necessary to turn, once again, to historians of early modern Europe.

The Genevan Academy

Although Calvin had been lecturing and training students in Strasbourg and Geneva since the late 1530s, it was not until 1559 that the city's municipal council formally established Calvin's famous Genevan Academy.[38] Given the late date of its founding, this academy is not the place one would have found the actual students Calvin spoke of when he penned the text. More than likely, those students were his students at Sturm's school in Strasbourg and his earlier students in Genevan schools. However, a brief look at the Genevan Academy provides a glimpse of the ideal educational context Calvin may have had in mind when imagining his student audience, for the school represents in its design and curriculum the epitome of the classical/religious education Calvin applauded throughout his career.[39] Designed to nurture students from childhood through advanced studies, the Genevan Academy sought to provide its pupils with a classical education comparable to that of Europe's finest universities. It was divided into two sections: the *schola privata*, where elementary Latin, Greek, and French were taught, and the *schola publica*, where advanced training in theology and biblical exegesis was provided.

In each of these schools, the educational environment created under the direction of Calvin clearly reflected his continued respect for the educational reforms and interests of humanism.[40] If one may judge from the list of books in its library, the academy's students were expected not only to be well grounded in the works of Cicero and Quintilian (and consequently, the rhetorical tradition) but also to learn Greek, to study the philosophy of Aristotle and Plato, and to read in the fields of Greek and Roman history. This suggests that the frequent references in the *Institutes* to the works of these classical figures would not have gone unnoticed by students aspiring to the copiousness requisite for elegant and informed scholarship. Students were also expected to give extensive attention to the French language, an expectation revealing Calvin's approval of the humanist movement's belief that the wisdom of the vernacular was equal to that of academic Latin. In addition to this material, students in the *schola publica*, the more advanced theological section of the school, were expected to master not only the contents of sacred scripture but also the major texts of both patristic and contemporary theologians.[41] Given this type of training, it is not surprising that in the *Institutes* Calvin refers to scriptural passages and cites theological texts in a familiar manner that suggests his confidence in a reader who would be able to follow his references with ease, perhaps even from memory. What kind of student body would one find studying at such an academy in the mid–sixteenth century? By 1561, two years after the publication of the 1559 *Institutes*, the Genevan Academy had officially registered 162 students. This number is deceptive, however, because there were many students who never formally enrolled but regularly attended lectures. Based on the impression of one of Calvin's contemporaries, it appears that at the peak of the school's popularity, Calvin's public lectures attracted more than one thousand auditors, including a number of already famous international figures.[42] If this were the case, then Calvin must have shaped his teachings to appeal to students representing a considerable breadth and diversity of backgrounds.

Records of the school show that the largest percentage of these students were from France, and many of them were enlisted in the work of the Genevan Company of Pastors founded in 1555 for the purpose of dispatching missionary preachers to the French provinces. The background of these pastors was diverse. Many of them came from the French aristocracy, although the largest group appears to have been drawn from the upper ranks of the French bourgeoisie. They were frequently lawyers, wealthy merchants, university students, and persons previously employed as royal officials. A smaller, though by no means negligible number of candidates also came from the higher levels of the artisan class, while the largest mass of the population, the peasantry, seems to have made only a marginal appearance, if any.[43] These percentages reflect, to a large degree, the makeup of the Calvinist parishes in France that sent their student-pastors to Geneva.

The Evangelical Churches in France

The Protestant communities in most French towns revolved around churches whose adherents were predominantly skilled craftspersons, while the leadership consisted primarily of notables and a few aristocrats who provided the church with financial and military support.[44] This constituency also reflects the class composition of the majority of French refugees who had been immigrating to Geneva since the mid-1550s.[45] In fact, by 1557, the number of French immigrants in the city was greater than its indigenous population.[46] Although many of these refugees were never granted the full rights of Genevan citizenship, they nonetheless provided Calvin with a large and outspoken block of support.

In terms of assessing the audience and function of the *Institutes*, it is thus safe to assume that although Calvin's student audience was international in its range, the primary focus of his teaching lay in training persons to respond to the immediate needs of the struggling church in the homeland from which he had been exiled. In this context, as a teacher, Calvin would not only have been concerned with presenting the content of sacred doctrine in a clear manner in order that it would be easily understood and disseminated; he would also have attempted to structure the rhetoric of his teachings to speak to the present situation of that struggling church and thereby begin to nurture in it a disposition appropriate to its situation. For a scholar trained in rhetoric, as I have illustrated, teaching was not only a matter of explicating a certain body of propositional truths; it was also a moral enterprise and its concern was that of inculcating an appropriate Christian character and eliciting desired social actions. In the context of the struggling French church, these needs were multiple and in response to them, the *Institutes* served a variety of social functions that supplemented its overarching pedagogical agenda. Thus, adding these contours both refines and complicates the construction of the rhetorical map upon which the *Institutes* was situated.

As I stated earlier, the France into which these pastors were sent was a country on the verge of civil war. Although the persecution of the reforming, evangelical community dates back even farther than the events that precipitated Calvin's exile, France had signed a treaty with Spain in 1559 that once again increased the incidences of violence against followers of the Reformation.[47] An example of this increase was the rise in the number of French pastors sent from Geneva who were executed upon returning to their home parishes. Of the eighty-eight who were sent into France between 1555 and 1562, ten of them are known to have been killed. In most cases, they were not burned for heresy but hanged on charges of sedition.[48] This suggests that in spite of Calvin's avowed support of the king, Calvin's students were generally perceived as posing a specifically political threat not only to the Roman church but to the royal crown as well.

In addition to this mounting persecution, economic troubles in the major cities of France created a siege mentality among the middle- and upper-class persons who constituted the majority of Calvin's followers. On the one hand, they were burdened with crippling taxes imposed by a king who did not extract the same economic toll from clerical establishments in the provinces. On the other hand, the growing number of the poor, predominantly Catholic, and anti-Protestant peasantry flooding into the cities threatened the middle- and upper-sector Calvinists' sense of social stability and order. These combined factors created an environment in France that was anything but welcoming to the small but growing Protestant movement of artisans, merchants, and aristocrats who awaited the theological and political assistance that Calvin and his students had to offer. As to the precise form of this assistance, let me return again to the prefaces and begin to reconstruct "the world according to Calvin."

THE WORLD ACCORDING TO CALVIN

As the ideological backbone of this movement, Calvin's writings and teachings served a critical social function: construction of a narrative framework within which this still-young community of believers could locate themselves and make sense of the chaos surrounding them. For Calvin, this task would have been particularly difficult given the fluidity of the cultural boundaries that marked this period in French history. In the midst of the community's struggles he was to assist them by creating a language that could bind them together. In this sense, he was called upon to help them construct their identity, to form a name for themselves, in short, to articulate the language of their shifting and emerging subjectivity. If one is to appreciate fully the degree to which Calvin's writings participated in the shaping of this communal identity, then one must recognize that the audience to which he spoke was an audience not only marked by the material and social conditions I have outlined; they were also an audience who stood in the middle of a process of becoming a people. They were an audience Calvin's rhetoric not only responded to but in fact helped to create, and, as noted earlier, the identity that Calvin narrates for this community is not historically neutral but woven out of the narrative fabric of his own discursive sensibilities and beliefs.

That Calvin sought to speak to this fragile French community throughout his lifetime is evidenced in all three of his prefaces. In his letter to the reader of the 1559 *Institutes*, he makes explicit reference to those "whose cause he pleaded"—referring to the church he had been defending since his exile in 1534.[49] Similarly, in his preface to his 1560 French edition, he explains that he has translated the text into French because of his desire "to communicate what could bear fruit for our French nation."[50] However, to get a sense of the narrative framework within which Calvin sought to situate this community, it is necessary to look at the 1536 "Prefatory Address to King Francis I of France." Here one finds the most graphic description of Calvin's view of that community's emerging self-understanding. It is graphic in the sense that it is full of images and metaphors depicting the key players in the drama surrounding the reforming movement in France. And these same images and metaphors frequently reappear in the body of the *Institutes*. Furthermore, the fact that Calvin insisted on commencing every edition of the text with this preface suggests, as I have argued earlier, that it continued to play a critical role in contextually framing the drama of the *Institutes*, even as late as 1559, when the economic situation of French evangelicals had improved significantly but the persecution—described so vividly in the 1536 letter—had continued nonetheless.

If one looks at this preface as a narrative frame, what kind of characters does one meet, and what plotline does one discover? The first characters encountered are the faithful members of the French community of reformers. Calvin begins his description of this community by detailing the abuses inflicted upon them. They are portrayed as a people who have been "unjustly charged" with sedition and sentenced "without a hearing." The doctrine they espouse is described as being "punished by prison, exile, proscription and fire, . . . exterminated on land and sea."[51] They are pictured as helpless victims of cruel scourgings, maimings, rackings, and burnings.[52] And the graphic details continue as Calvin explains, "Some of us are shackled with irons, some beaten with rods, some led about as laughingstocks, some proscribed, some most savagely tortured, some forced to flee. All of us are oppressed by poverty, cursed with dire execrations, wounded by slanders and treated in most shameful ways."[53]

On the basis of these statements, it is clear that Calvin perceived this community as the powerless and innocent victims of a brutal and unjust oppressor. He narrates this identity, again, in rather explicit terms:

> The poor little church has either been wasted with cruel slaughter or banished into exile, or so overwhelmed by threats and fears that it dare not even open its mouth. And yet, with their usual rage and madness, the ungodly continue to batter a wall already toppling and to complete the ruin toward which they have been striving.[54]

Calvin describes their situation as one of social marginality, severe and violent oppression, and limited political power. In sum, Calvin identifies them as a community under siege, struggling for their very survival.

As Calvin narrates the contours of this communal identity, he stresses its moral righteousness. In addition to living a life of "quiet and simplicity," its members abide in communities known for their "chastity, generosity, mercy, continence, patience, modesty and all other virtues."[55] He further confesses that this community is humble; it is not filled with pride or self-adulation but rather recognizes itself as "mean and lowly" before God.[56] As Calvin proceeds through the letter, these depictions of faithfulness, humility, and virtue, when woven together with depictions of the violence meted out against them, form a narrative weave that makes the struggle of the French evangelical church almost indistinguishable from the life of faithful struggle carried on by the prophets and apostles in biblical times. In fact, at one point, the letter directly compares the plight of the evangelical church to the situation of the apostles: "[T]he apostles in their day experienced the same things that are now happening to us."[57] Furthermore, the letter uses christological images to describe the church's plight. Calvin portrays church members as "sheep destined for the slaughter"[58] and as victims of the "tyranny of certain Pharisees."[59] Quoting from 1 Timothy 4:10, Calvin pleads with the king to understand that "we toil and suffer reproach because we have our hope set on the living God."[60] Thus, in addition to their social marginality, this community is identified as a community of the truly faithful who are being unjustly persecuted for righteousness' sake.

Just as Calvin introduces the reader to the French community of Reformers, so too he offers the reader a character profile of its persecutors and oppressors. In contrast to his portrayal of the truly faithful as powerless, Calvin depicts their opponents as men of power, men who have gained the confidence of the king. In the opening section of the letter, he observes, "I perceived that the fury of certain wicked persons has prevailed so far in your realm that there is no place in it for sound doctrine."[61] Furthermore, Calvin limits his description of the oppressors to men institutionally aligned with the Roman church. In typifying the moral character of the clerical oppressor, Calvin uses imagery that stands in direct contrast to the moral virtue of the faithful. He writes:

> Now look at our adversaries (I speak of the order of priests, at whose nod and will the others are hostile toward us), and consider with me for a moment what zeal motivates them. . . . for them "their God is their belly" [Phil. 3:19]; their kitchen their religion! If these are taken away, they believe that they will not be Christians, not even men! . . . Consequently, the one most concerned about his belly proves the sharpest contender for his faith. In fine, all men strive to one goal: to keep either their rule intact or their belly full.[62]

As in his description of the faithful, he also uses biblical images to represent these powerful persecutors: they are "the ungodly," "the Pharisees," and they are compared even to "Satan" himself.[63]

In addition to introducing the major actors in the drama the *Institutes* will engage, the letter to the king provides the reader with a story line, a narrative plot with many interesting twists and turns. As the preceding comments suggest, these two groups, the good parishioners and their evil Roman Catholic persecutors, are embroiled in a fierce struggle. In terms of sheer brute force and political power, the clerical establishment is portrayed as the stronger party. They control the land. However, the weaker party, the "poor little church," is not without its strength, a strength that flows from the power of God who stands with them on the side of goodness and truth. God, in short, is their fortress and their shield.

Calvin also describes the struggle between these two groups in terms of boundaries and spatial territories that are being transgressed or over-stepped. In terms of their political actions and concrete social power, the evil oppressors are described as "false apostles intruding into the true church," "to batter a wall already toppling," conquering the land and forc-ing the faithful into exile or imprisonment.[64] Calvin thus discursively po-sitions the faithful as the other, the outsider, the marginal. The territorial space of their identity and faith is the space the ungodly transgress.

However, Calvin adds an interesting twist to the plot when he rhetori-cally inverts this order. He states that in terms of their theology, the evil ones "transgress the limits set by our fathers," "they remove the bound-aries" set by the true church,[65] and "they stray very far from the truth when they do not recognize the church unless they see it with their very eyes, and try to keep it within limits to which it cannot at all be con-fined."[66] In contrast to these transgressions, the community of evangelical Christians is depicted as the people appropriately respecting the limits on doctrine and behavior set by the ancient church. As such, they are de-scribed as rightfully laying claim to the territory of the true faith. There-fore, when viewed from the perspective of divine truth, the weak and op-pressed but faithful French evangelical community actually appears as the more powerful party. Consequently, in this scenario, their oppressors stand on the outside as the exiled, the other, and the marginal with respect to God's providence and power.

Into this narrative of contestation and conquest, Calvin introduces a third party represented by the king, whose support is one of the prizes for which the battle between these polar opposites is being waged. As such, the king is never rhetorically imaged as standing solely on the side of the reforming church or on the side of the Roman Catholic clerics. Rather, Calvin discursively situates him in a position not unlike that of a judge be-fore whom both the accused and the accusers must argue their case. In fact, Calvin reinforces this image of the king as judge throughout the let-ter by the forensic language he uses to describe both the role of the sover-eign arbitrator who adjudicates justice and the role of the adversarial par-ties who must plead their cause before him. However, it is not clear which group occupies the positions of either defendant or prosecutor. At one level, the persecuted Christians are identified as the accused. Referring to the accusations of sedition lodged against the evangelical church by their opponents, Calvin tells the king, "Indeed, I know with what horrible re-ports they have filled your ears and mind, to render our cause as hateful as possible to you. But, as it fits your clemency, you ought to weigh the fact that if it is sufficient merely to make accusation, then no innocence will remain either in words or in deeds."[67] Following this remark, Calvin pre-sents a "just defense" of those whom he believes have been wrongly ac-cused. And he argues their case in the hope that his testimony might convince the king of the righteousness of their faith and their loyalty as the king's subjects. Thus, at this level of the letter's narrative, Calvin positions the struggling French church in an essentially apologetic position vis-à-vis the French state. As Calvin explains to the king, "This preface has already grown almost to the size of a full-scale apology."

However, in arguing his case, Calvin frequently adopts a strategy that inverts these courtroom roles and puts his opponents on the defensive. Instead of simply refuting his opponents' accusations against the supposedly seditious evangelical reformers, he puts the theology as well as the moral character of the clerics on trial. He accomplishes this by means of a clever argumentative strategy that takes the accusations lodged by his opponents and attempts to demonstrate how the content of the accusations reveals not only the seditious effects of clerical abuses but also the heretical status of their religious convictions. They are consequently placed in the position of the accused with regard to their loyalty both to the king and to the true faith. On the basis of this inversion, the narrative framework of the letter suggests that a strong polemic against the oppressor constitutes part of Calvin's apologetic stance toward the king.

Thus, through the images and argumentative strategies contained in Calvin's letter to the king of France, the reader is introduced to the principal character descriptions and the central story line through which Calvin narrates the shape of the situation his text addresses, a narration that played a normative role in shaping the self-understanding and worldview of the French parishioners and their pastors. The main plot and characters are simple, but the weave of their interactions is more complex. At the center of the story stands the persecuted, powerless, and yet faithful community of evangelical Reformers in France. Opposite them stands the morally bankrupt and faithless but powerful oppressor, the French clerics. And the two are engaged in a violent struggle, where the force of divine truth arms the weak while military strength and popular opinion aid the cause of the stronger. In addition, the king appears as a third party, standing on the sidelines in the position of judge or referee, and although he is depicted as neutral, he is recognized as having thrown his support behind the clerics in the past. Before this judge, the struggling evangelical community is forced to come and plead its case, to witness to the righteousness of their faith, and to expose the malevolence of their opponents.

A RHETORICAL MAP OF THE
TERRAIN OF THE *INSTITUTES*

The purpose of this analysis of the narrative framework put forth in the letter to the king of France is to offer the modern reader a glimpse of the world and the characters Calvin sought to address in the *Institutes*. It is particularly useful because it introduces a vocabulary of images and depictions that Calvin will employ often in the body of his text. It is also helpful because it gives one a sense of the complicated power relations Calvin's discourse had to negotiate. However, the point of this study is not simply to read the prefaces; rather, the purpose is to interpret rhetorically the doctrines found in the text that this letter only introduces. Therefore, in order to apply these insights to Calvin's doctrinal discussion, one must step back from this framework and sort through the list of audiences, agendas, and forms of rhetoric it offers. In doing so, one can further expand the map of Calvin's creatively wrought "rhetorical plan of action."

A Pedagogical Rhetoric

As I have previously stated, the most obvious audience of the *Institutes* was Calvin's students. With regard to this sector of the population, it is clear that Calvin would have used a pedagogically accessible rhetoric to address them.[68] But it is also evident that Calvin intended to speak to the struggling reforming churches in France. In terms of this audience, Calvin's rhetorical strategies would have been devised to address their needs and concerns and subsequently to upbuild this community of faith. Looking at the narrative framework of the "Prefatory Address to King Francis I of France" gives further insight into the types of rhetorical gestures best suited to this upbuilding. Once these gestures are identified, it will be easier to discern both to whom Calvin is speaking in specific portions of the *Institutes* and why he adopts a particular style of writing when he does.

A Consolatory Rhetoric

One of the most evident needs in this context was the need to hear a word of hope and encouragement to persevere in the midst of adversity. In addressing this need, Calvin constructed doctrines designed to console and comfort the faithful as they faced the violence of their oppressors. Referring to the rhetoric of consolation in a sermon on Job, Calvin describes this task: Consolation, he suggests, requires "a singular prudence," for "afflictions are like sicknesses; if a doctor used the same remedy for every sick person, how would that be? It is necessary in the first place to consider what people are like, and then, how to deal with them."[69] If Calvin has followed his own advice in the writing of the *Institutes*, he will have articulated the content of divine wisdom in a way that would serve as a remedy to the specific afflictions of the French reforming churches, the afflictions of political persecution and social marginality. Thus, when modern readers approach Calvin's doctrines, it is important to interpret them in light of this consoling function and the specific social "sicknesses" they seek to remedy.

In the body of the *Institutes*, it is possible to identify certain rhetorical strategies that Calvin typically deploys when he wants to emphasize this consoling function. When Calvin is speaking to the community of the faithful, he frequently draws upon images taken from the scriptures, just as he used biblical imagery to identify their plight in his address to King Francis. The stress upon the lay study of scriptures in the French reforming communities most likely would have guaranteed their understanding and appreciation of such images. Similarly, when appealing to these communities, Calvin often speaks in an exhortative voice, which gives the reader the sense that Calvin is preaching to them rather than simply lecturing. These passages of exhortation also display a high proportion of words with devotional connotations. By adopting a homiletic voice and style, Calvin thus exploits a range of rhetorical strategies suited to the need for consolation.

An Apologetic Rhetoric

Consolation, however, was not the only form of appeal that served the cause of the Reformers in France. Calvin's text was also called upon to provide its students with the skills required to convert others and convince them to join in their religious struggle. Historical evidence suggests that one of the main strategies used by the French missionaries sent by the Genevan Company of Pastors was to target and convert the nobility to the Calvinist cause in order not only to win the sympathy of the Royal Court but also to acquire the financial and military support needed by the movement.[70] Throughout his career, Calvin personally followed a similar strategy in dealing with the French nobility. His frequent and long-standing correspondence with Louis XII's daughter, Renée de France, Duchess of Ferrara, procured the establishment of an oasis for French Reformers in her court at Montargis, and his successful appeal to Louis I de Bourbon, Prince of Condé, produced a convert who later became a military and political leader of the Huguenot party.[71]

In addition to the French nobility, there were several other political blocks whose sympathies the movement repeatedly tried to win. One of these groups consisted of pioneers of French evangelicalism like Gérard Roussel, the bishop of Oléron, who, although he was known to support the cause of the Reformation, nonetheless continued to enjoy episcopal dignities by maintaining his ties to Roman Catholicism.[72] In his early polemical tracts, Calvin refers to people like the bishop as "Nicodemites" who pretend inwardly to champion the evangelical faith while outwardly refusing to break their ties with the Roman church.[73] Such figures as

Calvin's humanist mentors Budé, Erasmus, and Lefèvre would also have been included in this group.

The Calvinist movement continued to court the sympathies of a younger generation of humanists as well. They were often up-and-coming young scholars whose already critical posture toward the conservatism of the mainline religious establishment made them easy targets for conversion.[74] This group was the stratum of French intellectuals who comprised the majority of Calvin's students and who subsequently provided the core leadership around which the reforming churches in the Provinces revolved. Thus, rhetorically structuring doctrines that would appeal to this sector of the population, while simultaneously persuading the aristocracy, formed an essential part of a theology designed to address "the needs of the time" and strengthen the reforming community.

Consequently, along with the text's pedagogical and consoling agendas, one can also discern in the *Institutes* the presence of a rhetoric designed to render an apology for Calvin's cause in the hopes that he might convert the sympathies of persons in these various political groups. Just as the prefatory letter to the king reveals Calvin's use of a distinctly forensic vocabulary when he is arguing his case before the royal judge, so too in the body of the *Institutes,* one finds Calvin often using figurative images drawn from a courtroom setting to make his point. Similarly, there are places in the text where the voice of the author pleads with the reader as if she or he were in a position to judge and perhaps be converted by the persuasiveness of the testimony he offers. Part of this testimony frequently involves the construction of tightly woven arguments whose conclusion leads to one of two results: to the complete dismantling of the opposition by means of an emphatic statement of their conviction before the court, or to an exhortative proclamation of the righteousness of the truly faithful.[75]

In addition to these overt apologetic strategies, the text also makes more subtle appeals aimed at converting those who may be sympathetic to but not yet completely convinced by Calvin's cause. These appeals are usually hidden and work by virtue of subtle manipulations that occur between the authorial voice and the pronouns used to identify the reader's relation to the text. Noting the way in which Calvin plays with "we," "you," and "them" helps to locate places where his apology moves beneath the surface of the text's narrative. In the next chapter, where I begin to work through several of Calvin's doctrinal formulations, the force of this type of apologetic strategy will become more apparent.

A Polemical Rhetoric

Closely related to this apologetic agenda is another social function that Calvin's teachings would have been required to perform in the process of preparing his students for the struggling church in France. Not only did the church need an apologetic strategy designed to convert possible allies, it also needed a strategy for fending off the accusations and attacks of its opponents. As the narrative of the prefatory letter suggests, part of Calvin's defensive strategy in this regard is to invert the social order of power relations by putting the opposition on trial. He accomplishes this rhetorically by launching into full-blown polemics against the opposition's moral virtue as well as their theological and political positions.[76] Apart from the prefatory letter, Calvin develops this tactic most clearly in his many polemical tracts, which were put into pamphlet form and smuggled into France. However, even though the *Institutes* is not, strictly speaking, a piece of polemical propaganda, its doctrinal formulations nonetheless bear the marks of this strategy. In fact, Calvin devotes large segments of the text to refuting the position of a variety of opponents. Furthermore, even in segments where a polemical agenda does not appear to be the primary one, Calvin is rarely able to resist the opportunity to assail someone or some group.

These assaults come in a variety of shapes and forms, all of which reveal the author's skill as a political rhetorician. Sometimes he argues against his adversaries by illustrating how their position contradicts the writings of the church fathers. At other times he carefully dissects the faulty logic of their theology. Most frequently, however, he attacks his opponents by simply caricaturing them with a wealth of unpleasant images drawn from proverbial and colloquial sources. When I turn to an analysis of his doctrine, the force of his polemical language will make identifying the presence of this agenda an easy task.

Summary: Four Social Functions of the *Institutes*

Thus far, I have attempted to draw a rough map of the rhetorical and historical terrain upon which Calvin constructed the *Institutes* in order to identify the types of theological "meanings" his text intended to present to its readership. Based on the evidence afforded in the prefaces along with supplementary historical information, it appears that Calvin designed the text to serve a variety of social functions. I have described at least four of these functions and the rhetoric appropriate to each: the pedagogical agenda, which brings with it a clear and concise style of presentation; the consolatory agenda, which offers solace and encouragement to a marginalized community in the face of persecution and does so by using rhetoric laden with biblical imagery and terms with devotional connotations; the apologetic agenda, which frequently resorts to a forensic rhetoric in addition to more subtle manipulations of the reader; and the polemical agenda with its harsh attacks and figurative caricatures.

One shortcoming of this outline, however, is that by isolating each social function and identifying the type of rhetoric particular to it, one may
get the impression that the text can be neatly divided into segments according to function and style. Thus, it may appear that as one reads
Calvin's doctrines, it is possible to point to a sentence or paragraph and,
on the basis of its rhetoric, clearly delineate the nature of the specific community it engages and the discrete agenda it attempts to address. While it
is true there are parts of the text that can easily be divided in this fashion—
for instance, some of Calvin's polemical sections are clearly marked as
such—the majority of the doctrines are developed in a manner that defies
such facile distinctions. In the case of the doctrines I will examine in the
next three chapters, all of these agendas, audiences, and social functions
are simultaneously negotiated, often in the same paragraph or sentence
and sometimes even in the same turn of phrase or figurative image. For
instance, a word of consolation for the oppressed church may at times take
the form of a polemical attack on its persecutors. Similarly, some of
Calvin's strongest apologetic gestures may depend on the persuasiveness
of his polemic against an opponent or on the attractiveness of the encouragement he offers to the faithful. Given the synchronic nature of these textual negotiations, one must therefore consider each doctrine in light of the
effect it might have produced as it interacted with the entire map of the
audiences and social agendas in the *Institutes*.

Another limitation of the map I have outlined is that it focuses on only
four particular aspects of Calvin's context. I have highlighted, most specifically, the various "present needs" that would have been felt by the students who were instructed by Calvin's work and by the churches in
France that sought his theological guidance in a time of crisis. In addition
to these audiences, by 1559 Calvin's texts had long been distributed
throughout Europe and thus to many audiences. Consequently, in each of
the various contexts in which the *Institutes* was disseminated, it would
have addressed a different readership and a different set of "present
needs," some of which the reformer would have recognized in the process
of writing the text and others which he could not have anticipated. Even
in the Genevan context, Calvin's text was designed rhetorically to address
and intervene in a number of conflictive situations that are missed when
the focus rests solely on Calvin's French students. Both the Genevan
church and the city's governing councils were fraught with internal contradictions and conflicts. As a politically astute rhetorician, Calvin undoubtedly structured his rhetoric to promote the policy decisions he
found most acceptable. Indeed, until the mid-1550s, he was involved in an
intense and occasionally violent battle with the Perrin party in Geneva, a
group often referred to as "the Libertines," and this struggle most assuredly left its marks upon the text.[77] Similarly, although the Anabaptist

conflict had long been resolved by 1559, early editions of the text that were incorporated into the final edition continue to bear the marks of this struggle as well.[78] And the list of particular events to which the *Institutes* responded goes on.[79]

THE UNIVERSAL READER

In the preceding section, I outlined the historical contours of Calvin's context in order to provide a sense of the kinds of audiences to which his text was designed to speak and the various types of social functions his text served. If Calvin had followed the lead of several of his early modern literary counterparts and had held the view that human beings are fundamentally social constructs, it would have been sufficient for my purposes here simply to present an outline of these historical audiences and functions. However, Calvin did not hold this view. In fact, in several sections of the *Institutes* he reflects at length on the universal nature of the human person created by God. In light of these considerations pertaining to "general humanity," it is necessary to explore the contours of Calvin's universal anthropology, highlighting a series of additional considerations that influenced his analysis of the *decorum* appropriate to his doctrines.[80]

Calvin's remarks on the essential and universal nature of human persons are divided into two parts: his discussion of the human being before the Fall, and his discussion of the fallen and sinful creature. In Book 1, beginning in chapter 15, he presents the first part, which consists of a rather ad hoc compilation of reflections on the nature of human persons before they turned away from God. In this section, he explains that the human person represents the union of a body and a soul. By the soul, Calvin means "an immortal yet created essence, which is [our] nobler part."[81] It is the soul that separates human beings from other brute animals by allowing humans to have knowledge of both the world and God. The soul is "set in the body, it dwells there as in a house; not only that it may animate all its parts and render its organs fit and useful for their actions, but also that it may hold the first place in ruling man's life."[82]

Following the classical model, he further explains that the soul consists of two principal parts, the intellect and the will. He describes the power of the intellect in two basic ways. First, the intellect is the faculty that allows the person to grasp and analyze the world as it actually is.[83] Thus, Calvin embraced a traditional, medieval epistemology in which the mind is perceived as mirroring the world it encounters. Second, and even more important, Calvin highlights the power of the intellect "to distinguish between objects, as each seems worthy of approval or disapproval."[84] By emphasizing the power of the intellect to distinguish what is good from what is bad, Calvin stresses the distinctly moral character of the intellect's task. In this, he demonstrates his affinities for the anthropological perspective of the early modern humanists and their preoccupation with those aspects of the intellect that influence one's social action and shape one's disposition. In addition to these two aspects, the intellect is further distinguished by Calvin as that faculty which in the original created order was capable of truly knowing God and therefore of attaining the highest form of truth and happiness.

As the second faculty of the soul, the will represents the faculty of choice and, as Calvin explains, it can choose either to follow or reject what the intellect has deemed good or bad. It is consequently this faculty that allows one to characterize human beings as essentially free; and as such, it is the faculty that allowed for the possibility of the Fall. The will can also be influenced by the emotions or the appetitive faculties. Furthermore, when Calvin turns to his discussion of faith, the will takes priority over the intellect as the faculty that must be turned toward God. Although Calvin never offers a full account of the anthropology of faith, which would allow one to explore it more fully, this prioritizing of the will follows the oft-repeated Petrarchan motto (as cited earlier) that "it is better to will the good than to know the truth." While this description of the will may seem a bit obscure and underdeveloped, it is difficult to be much more precise in delineating its contents because Calvin does not appear to have been particularly concerned about its conceptual precision. After all, he continually reminds the reader, he is not a speculative philosopher.

In Book 2, Calvin introduces a series of equally ad hoc and philosophically underdeveloped reflections on the basic nature of the human person after the Fall. Stated in philosophical terms, this level of analysis concerns the structure of the creature's faculties as they are given under the limitations of existence, as opposed to the essential structure that inhered in the original creation. In Adam's fall, Calvin explains, the will did not choose to follow God but in disobedience turned toward the self in an act of unfaithfulness. "Unfaithfulness, then, was the root of the Fall. But thereafter ambition and pride, together with ungratefulness, arose" and brought forth "works of the flesh," works whose primary sin lies in seeking equality with God.[85] Because of this sinful turning, the human creature is now suffused through and through with a blind self-love that not only prohibits any innate knowledge of God but also marks humans as inescapably prideful creatures. The will, as the faculty whose turning precipitated the Fall, is now marked by a narcissistic desire to draw the world into itself. Similarly, the intellect is affected by the Fall in its inability to grasp intuitively the divine object of knowledge. However, even though the mind can no longer grasp the divine, Calvin makes it clear that the Fall does not obliterate the basic structure of the human faculties. The human person continues to be a creature governed by the intellect and thus capable of perceiving the real structure of the world and making responsible decisions even though the will has been irrevocably bent by pride.

In the light of this description of the creature's capacities before and after the Fall, it is possible to discern several ways in which the rhetoric of the *Institutes* has been accommodated to address the human person living under these conditions. At the broadest and perhaps most obvious level, one can account for the distinctively noetic cast of the entire text on the basis of the importance Calvin places on the intellectual faculty and reason. Given that human persons are partially ruled by the intellect and its capacity to reason, it makes sense for Calvin to construct arguments aimed at acquiring the intellectual assent of his audience. Calvin uses primarily ocular and auditory terms to describe this mental activity of intellective knowing. He describes the creature as seeing the world as well as hearing the word of revelation.[86] Consequently, in order to appeal to the reason of his audience, Calvin frequently deploys a language designed to portray or visually depict his position for the reader. Similarly, he frequently writes in a style that attempts to capture the aesthetic power of the spoken word, hence appealing to his readers' auditory faculties.

Calvin's anthropology also highlights the importance of the will in determining human actions and the role the emotions play in affecting the will. It thus makes sense that he designed his doctrines to appeal broadly to a variety of emotions that may play an even more crucial role than the intellect in turning the creature toward the divine. Further, given that the will distorted by pride precipitates the act of sinful turning from God, it follows that affecting and transforming the will would be the most direct path to regeneration. Finally, given his conviction that unbelief, pride, and self-interest are the most powerful impulses at work in the fallen creature, it makes sense that Calvin describes the content of God's revelation in terms of the "benefits of faith" it provides for the creature. Thus, in a rhetorically clever move, he fashions the appeal of revelation to meet the self-interested, unfaithful needs of human creatures in their fallen, prideful state.

In the next three chapters, I will expand this list of places in the text where one finds Calvin accommodating his doctrine to meet the essential as well as existential needs and capacities of the human person conceived in universal terms. The few that I have mentioned simply serve as suggestive examples of the various ways in which his theological anthropology informs the rhetoric of his doctrines. Before concluding this section, however, I want to make one final observation about the shape of Calvin's general anthropology.

Since his theological anthropology is one of the many "doctrinal formulations" to which I have been referring, it seems that the more immediate historical needs of Calvin's audience would have been as instrumental in the shaping of this doctrine as those needs would have been in the shaping of others. Without going into a detailed analysis of this doctrine in order to ferret out all the ways in which it was structured to speak to the needs of Calvin's context, I would like to focus on one place in his discussion where it is possible to identify clearly the normative role played by his historical audience's "particular" capacities in shaping the substance of this supposedly "universal" doctrine. In his discussion of the soul's faculties, Calvin states that although he finds certain aspects of Plato's anthropology "enlightening," given the task at hand, "for the upbuilding of godliness, a simple definition will be enough for us. . . . Although these things [written by Plato] are true, or at least are probable, yet since I fear they may involve us in their own obscurity rather than help us, I think they ought to be passed over."[87] Here it appears Calvin is ready to jettison a major segment of the widely accepted Platonic anthropology because he believes it is too complicated for his audience to follow. Thus, even though he feels Plato's analysis is most likely true, he discards it in favor of an anthropology that could be more readily understood by his students. This suggests that even his most general comments on the shape of the human person are predicated upon rhetorical decisions that take seriously the practical limits of his immediate audiences. Calvin's anthropology thus appears to be universal in scope but pragmatic and hence functional in origin, a curious and rather challenging combination indeed!

With this doctrine as an example of the kinds of surprises one encounters when Calvin's text is placed upon a map of its rhetorical terrain, it is now possible to turn to the first pages of the *Institutes* and begin exploring the many interpretive avenues opened up by following the map's directions. Like the paths followed by Calvin's students on their clandestine journeys into French territories, these paths remain rather treacherous and are often hard to find, but if one is an "especially interested and persistent stranger," the journey promises to be a productive one.

NOTES

1. *Inst.* (1559), pp. 9–31; OS 3:9. 1–30.19.
2. During this period, Calvin also penned a preface for the French Bible of his cousin, Olivétan. It offers depictions of the situation in France that closely parallel the description presented in this letter to Francis I. For a fuller discussion of the additional preface, see Ganoczy, *The Young Calvin*, 94–98. For an English translation of the biblical preface, see the second edition of Battles's translation of the 1536 *Institutes*, 373–77; OC vol. 9, cols. 787–90.
3. The same preface is also used, in its original form, to introduce every successive edition of the *Institutes* after 1536.

4. In addition to the death of Francis I, it is quite clear that by 1559, the French Protestant community described by Calvin is no longer as "small" and "weak" as the 1536 letter suggests. Rather, it had become strong enough to be the source of even more heightened political concern to the French crown. Similarly, at the time of the letter's initial composition, Calvin had been quite concerned about the Anabaptist situation at Münster (1534–35), but by the time he wrote the 1559 edition, this conflict had subsided and its international significance had lessened, a fact that further complicates the meaning of Calvin's decision to use an outdated letter to commence a new edition.

5. *Inst.*, pp. 3–5; OS 3:5.1–7.9.

6. For an overview of Calvin's circumstances in Strasbourg, see Alister E. McGrath, *A Life of John Calvin: A Study in the Shaping of Western Culture* (Oxford: Basil Blackwell Publisher, 1990), 100–102.

7. Two such references are first, a comment regarding his struggle with "quartan fever" (malaria) in the fall of 1558 and the spring of 1559; and second, remarks concerning the Diet held at Augsburg during the spring of 1558. *Inst.*, pp. 3, 4; OS 3:5.19 and 6.5ff.

8. For further discussion of this section of the letter, see pages 60–63 of this chapter.

9. *Inst.*, pp. 6–8; OS 3:7.14–8.26. For a fuller discussion of Calvin's 1541 French edition of the *Institutes*, see Jacques Pannier's introduction to his edition of the 1541 French text, *Institution de la Religion Chrestienne*, ed. Jacques Pannier (Paris: Société d'Edition "Les Belles Lettres," 1961), vii–xxxi. For the French text of the 1541 Preface, see pages 3–5 of that work.

For a more detailed discussion of Calvin's 1560 French edition of the *Institutes*, see the editor's comments in McNeill's 1559 *Inst.*, "Introduction," xxxviii–xxxix.

10. For excellent discussions of Calvin's French *Institutes*, see Francis Higman, "The Reformation and the French Language," *L'Esprit créateur* 16 (1976): 20–36; "Theology in French: Religious Pamphlets from the Counter-Reformation," *Renaissance and Modern Studies* 23 (1979): 128–46; and "De Calvin à Descartes: La création de la langue classique," *Revue d'Humanisme et Renaissance* 15 (1986): 5–18. For a comparative analysis of the Latin and French editions of the *Institutes*, see J. W. Marmelstein, *Etude comparative des textes latins et français de l'Institution de la Religion chrestienne par Jean Calvin* (Paris, Groningen, The Hague, 1921).

11. Many of the questions I have raised regarding the various editions and uses of the prefaces could also be applied to the three chapters of the 1559 *Institutes* that I work with in the next three chapters of this study. Each of these chapters, like his prefatory letters to the reader, Calvin produced through a process of continued editing and additions. As such, the texts comprise several layers of writings, each of which no doubt had its own original audience and context. Given the presence of these different layers, it would be possible, and most likely quite revealing, to do a rhetorical reading of each edited layer, engaging in a type of redaction criticism that would correlate sections of the text with their original audiences and then would trace their shifting functions as the text moves through its many revisions.

12. *Inst.*, "John Calvin to the Reader," 4; "nihil ex quo officium doctoris in Ecclesia suscepti, mihi fuisse propositum quam Ecclesiae prodesse, sinceram pietatis doctrinam asserendo: neminem tamen esse puto qui pluribus impetatur, mordeatur et laceretur calumniis" (OS 3:6. 1–5).

13. *Inst.*, "John Calvin to the Reader," p. 4; OS 3:6. 1–5.

14. *Inst.*, p. 9; "unde discas qualis sit doctrina in quam tanta rabie exardescunt furiosi illi, qui ferro et ignibus regnum tuum hodie turbant" (OS 3:9. 18–20).

15. *Inst.*, p. 8; OS 3:8. 22.

16. *Inst.*, p. 8; "esperant qu'un passage luy donnera plus familierement exposition de l'autre" (OS 3:8. 24–25). Calvin's French lacks some of the accent marks one expects today.

17. Edward Said, "Traveling Theory," in *The World, the Text, and the Critic* (Cambridge, Mass.: Harvard University Press, 1983), 226–47.

18. In a rare instance in which Calvin actually reflects on the nature of language, he explicitly states that meaning is a function of usage. "What difference is there between a tyrant and a King? Whatever difference there is, usage rather than etymology or original meaning determines it"; "Quid interest inter tyrannum & regem. Quicquid est differentiae, vsus potius quàm verbi etymon aut proprietas constituit." Both English and Latin references taken from Battles and Hugo, eds., *Calvin's Commentary on Seneca's "De clementia,"* 1.81, 200–201.

19. In contemporary literary theory, Harold Bloom uses the term "misreading" to suggest that all readings, because they are influenced by culture and convention, amount to misreadings. See Bloom, "The Necessity of Misreadings," in *Kabbalah and Criticism* (New York: Seabury Press, 1974). For a discussion of early modern writers who celebrate the triumph of convention as the final and only arbiter of meaning, see Lawrence Manley, *Convention: 1500–1750* (Cambridge, Mass.: Harvard University Press, 1980).

20. The prefaces repeatedly claim that, in contrast to distorted reports, the contents of the *Institutes* represent "sound doctrine" that is in truth "more God's" than Calvin's (*Inst.*, pp. 7–8). And the perspicuity of the text in this regard is never questioned. Calvin never claims that the *Institutes* represents a summary of only his temporary and therefore limited interpretation of scripture. Rather, the truth that it articulates is as singular as the truth to which it witnesses, the truth of God's revelation to the human creature.

21. *Inst.*, p. 4; "Porro hoc mihi in isto labore propositum fuit, sacrae Theologiae candidatos ad divini verbi lectionem ita praeparare et instruere, ut et facilem ad eam aditum habere, et inoffenso in ea gradu pergere queant" (OS 3:6. 18–21).

22. *Inst.*, p. 9; "Tantum erat animus rudimenta quaedam tradere, quibus formarentur ad veram pietatem qui aliquo religionis studio tanguntur. Atque hunc laborem Gallis nostris potissiumum desudabam" (OS 3:9. 6–9).

23. *Inst.*, p. 6; "de subvenir aux simples . . . et quasi leur prester la main, pour les conduire et les ayder a trouver la somme de ce que Dieu nous a voulu enseigner en sa parolle" (OS 3:7. 27–29).

24. Wilhelm Niesel, *The Theology of Calvin,* trans. Harold Knight (Philadelphia: Westminster Press, 1956).

25. When it comes to Calvin's treatment of the Trinity, however, Niesel gives an account of Calvin's position on the basis of distinctively historical considerations, viewing it as a response to the accusations of Arianism brought against him in the wake of the 1536 edition of the *Institutes* and Calvin's later confrontation with Servetus. While these comments on the part of Niesel do help to clarify the discussion of the Trinity, one wonders why the same practice of contextualization is not applied to all the text. The fact that this does not occur represents a fallacious

assumption on Niesel's part, namely, that in sections of the text where there is no ambiguity, there is no need for this type of contextualization.

26. Kingdon, *Geneva and the Coming Wars of Religion*, 5.

27. In *Censorship and the Sorbonne: A Bibliographical Study of Books in French Censored by the Faculty of Theology, 1520–1551* (Geneva: Librairie E. Droz, 1979), Francis Higman traces the records of censorship in France and thus provides an account of Calvin's texts that were most likely being circulated in France during this period.

28. There is a wealth of informative historical work on this period, which I have drawn upon to construct the brief overview that follows. Of these many texts, a few of the more recent ones that I have found particularly helpful in describing the world of sixteenth-century France, Geneva, and Germany are Natalie Zemon Davis, *Society and Culture in Early Modern France* (Stanford, Calif.: Stanford University Press, 1975); Donald Kelley, *The Beginning of Ideology: Consciousness and Society in the French Reformation* (Cambridge: Cambridge University Press, 1981); J.H.M. Salmon, *Society in Crisis: France in the Sixteenth Century* (New York: St. Martin's Press, 1975), and *Renaissance and Revolt: Essays in the Intellectual and Social History of Early Modern France* (London: Cambridge University Press, 1987); Lucien Febvre, *Life in Renaissance France*, ed. and trans. Marion Rothstein (Cambridge, Mass.: Harvard University Press, 1977); Thomas A. Brady, Jr., *Ruling Class, Regime, and Reformation in Strasbourg, 1520–1555* (Leiden: E. J. Brill, 1978); Miriam Usher Chrisman, *Strasbourg and Reform: A Study in the Process of Change, 1520–1555* (New Haven, Conn.: Yale University Press, 1967); and James Tracy, *The Politics of Erasmus: A Pacifist Intellectual and His Political Milieu* (Toronto: University of Toronto Press, 1978.) On the Reformation, I have also drawn upon the previously cited works of Ozment, Kristeller, and Oberman.

29. See Henry Heller, *The Conquest of Poverty: The Calvinist Revolt in Sixteenth-Century France* (Leiden: E. J. Brill, 1986), for an account of the economic conditions of France in the mid–sixteenth century, with principal reference to its effects on urban populations.

30. See Miriam Usher Chrisman, *Lay Culture, Learned Culture: Books and Social Change in Strasbourg, 1480–1599* (New Haven, Conn.: Yale University Press, 1982); and Natalie Zemon Davis, "Printing and the People," in *Society and Culture*, 189–226, 326–36.

31. William Bouwsma, *John Calvin*, and "Anxiety and the Formation of Early Modern Culture," in *After the Reformation: Essays in Honor of J. H. Hexter*, ed. Barbara C. Malament (Philadelphia: University of Pennsylvania Press, 1980), 215–46.

32. For a fuller discussion of the relation of the *Institutes* to the teaching function of the commentaries, see Girardin, *Rhétorique et théologique*.

33. *Inst.*, p. 4; OS 3:6. 18–21. See note 21 for Latin text.

34. *Inst.*, p. 4; "siquidem religionis summam omnibus partibus sic mihi complexus esse videor, et eo quoque ordine digessisse, ut siquis eam recte tenuerit, ei non sit difficile statuere et quid potissimum quaerere in Scriptura, et quem in scopum quicquid in ea continetur referre debeat" (OS 3:6. 21–25).

Both of Calvin's sentences quoted here, referring to the teaching function of the *Institutes*, are part of the original letter to the reader, written while Calvin was instructing students at Sturm's school in Strasbourg. Thus, in the original version, the students referred to here were most likely students in this academy as well as the many "self-taught" students that Calvin's book tutored in the field. By the time the text had been revised and traveled the distance of twenty years to Geneva, the students referred to in the letter were most likely located in a growing network of academies where Calvin's evangelical theology was taught, in Geneva as well as internationally. It is also quite likely that Calvin continued to be read, in 1559, by "students" who were pastors and laypersons engaged in self-teaching at home or in their local parishes.

35. Calvin, *Commentary on First Corinthians*, 3:2. English translation taken from William Bouwsma's introductory article "Calvinism as Theologia Rhetorica," in *Calvinism as Theologia Rhetorica*, 2; "Prudentis ergo doctoris est, eorum, quos docendos suscipit, captui se attemperare: ut apud infirmos et rudes ab elementis incipiat, nec altius conscendat quam sequi possint: ut denique paulatim instillat doctrinam" (OC vol. 49, col. 347).

36. Higman, *The Style of John Calvin*, 47–82.

37. John Calvin, *Commentary on Matthew*, 3:7. English translation taken from Bouwsma, *Calvinism as Theologia Rhetorica*, 2. "Et sane frigida erit docendi ratio, nisi prudenter expendant doctores, quid exigat tempus, et quid personis conveniat: nec quidquam in hac parte magis inaequale est, quam perpetua aequalitas" (OC vol. 45, col. 116).

38. Calvin first mentions his desire to establish this institution in the ordinances he helped to formulate for the city in 1541. For an exhaustive account of the history of the Academy established in 1559, see Charles Borgeaud, *Histoire de l'Université de Genève* (Geneva, 1900–1934). Volume 1 deals with "L'académie de Calvin" from 1559 to 1789, pp. 21–83. Cf. Breen, *John Calvin*, 156.

39. Using the Genevan Academy as a model context for examining Calvin's students is not without its limits, particularly given the fact that the Academy was not formally instituted until May of 1559, and the final Latin edition of the *Institutes* was written in the winter of 1558 and the spring of 1559. In addition to this limitation, the Genevan Academy would have had within its ranks of students only a small slice of the many readers who would have studied the *Institutes* in their own homes or in parishes and schools both within and outside Geneva. Despite these limitations, however, the advantage of focusing on the Genevan Academy lies in the amount of historical material available for studying this student population. Furthermore, in light of the influential role Calvin played in instituting the Academy, it is not unlikely that the student it strove to produce was, in Calvin's mind, the model or ideal student in the Geneva of the 1550s.

40. Breen notes the influence of Mathurin Cordier, the educational reformer and Calvin's former teacher, *John Calvin*, 157. Also see A. Ganoczy, *La bibliothèque de l'Académie de Calvin* (Geneva: Droz, 1969), for a discussion of the library Calvin developed for the Academy.

41. During their training in this part of the Academy, students were required to master the classical corpus of the primary school, but they also received additional training designed to prepare them for the tasks of Christian ministry. Following the contours of Calvin's own educational background, the curriculum for this section of the academy included theological and biblical works from a variety of fields. According to one pastor's booklist, cited by Kingdon, this material ranged from the textual commentaries of Erasmus to the logic of Ramus and the controversial theology of Luther. Kingdon, *Geneva and the Coming Wars of Religion*, 16.

42. Ibid., 15. Because this is only an "impression," it may well be a laudable but exaggerated view of the size of Calvin's audience.

43. Ibid., 6–8.

44. Heller, *The Conquest of Poverty*, 143. I use the term "Protestant" here very tentatively because it could be taken mistakenly to imply the existence of a firmly established "French Protestant Church" in France at this time. However, at this early stage in the reforming community's development, there is no one, consolidated, Protestant identity or institution in France. Thus, it is more accurate to refer to these communities as being part of "a reforming movement" or to describe them as being "evangelical" or "reforming churches." In order to note their connection to Calvin's Company of Pastors in Geneva, it is also appropriate to refer to these communities, very loosely, as "Calvinist," although this term, again, is not meant to suggest that an institutional identity called "Calvinism" existed in France during this period.

45. For a more fully developed analysis of the class background of the French Calvinists and the reasons they were attracted to Calvin's teaching, see Davis, *Society and Culture*, and Heller, *The Conquest of Poverty*.

46. William E. Monter, *Calvin's Geneva* (New York: John Wiley & Sons, 1967), 165.

47. Ibid., 81–97.

48. Kingdon, *Geneva and the Coming Wars of Religion*, 51.

49. *Inst.*, p. 5; OS 3:7.5–6.

50. This particular text first appeared with the 1541 French edition of *Institutes*. *Inst.*, p. 7; "de communiquer ce qui en pouoit venir de fruit a nostre Nation Françoise" (OS 3:7.42–3:8.1).

51. *Inst.*, p. 9; "carcere, exilio, proscriptione, incendio mulctandam, quam terra marique exterminandam" (OS 3:9.21–23).

52. *Inst.*, p. 31.

53. *Inst.*, p. 14; "alii nostrum vinculis constringuntur, alii virgis caeduntur, alii in ludibrium circumducuntur, alii proscribuntur, alii saevissime torquentur, alii fuga elabuntur: omnes rerum angustia premimur, diris execrationibus devovemur, maledictis laceramur, indignissimis modis tractamur" (OS 3:13.29–14.1).

54. *Inst.*, p. 11; "paupercula vero Ecclesia aut crudelibus caedibus absumpta sit, aut exiliis abacta, aut minis ac terroribus perculsa ne hiscere quidem audeat. Et instant etiamnum qua solent insania et ferocitate, fortiter in parietem iam inclinatum, et ruinam quam fecerunt incumbentes" (OS 3:11.10–15).

55. *Inst.*, p. 30; "vita nostra, castitatis, benignitatis, misericordiae, continentiae, patientiae, modestiae, et virtutis cuiusvis exemplum esse possit" (OS 3:29.19–21).

56. *Inst.*, p. 12.

57. *Inst.*, p. 29; "eadem expertos esse suo seculo Apostolos quae nunc usu nobis veniunt" (OS 3:27.37–38).

58. *Inst.*, p. 31; "oves mactationi destinatae" (OS 3:30.11).

59. *Inst.*, p. 11; "Pharisaeorum id quidem quorundam tyrannide" (OS 3:11.6–7).

60. *Inst.*, pp. 13–14; "in hoc nos laborare, et probris affici quia spem reponimus in Deo vivo" (OS 3:13.25–26).

61. *Inst.*, p. 9; "quum perspicerem usque eo quorundam improborum furorem invaluisse in regno tuo, ut nullus sanae doctrinae sit istic locus" (OS 3:9.13–15).

62. *Inst.*, p. 14; "Intuere iam in adversarios nostros (de ordine sacrificorum loquor, quorum nutu et arbitrio alii nobiscum inimicitias exercent) et mecum

paulisper reputa quo studio ferantur. . . . illis Deus venter est, culina religio: quibus sublatis, non modo non Christianos, sed ne homines quidem futuros se credunt? . . . Ideo ut quisque eorum pro ventre est maxime solicitus, ita pro sua fide deprehenditur bellator acerrimus. Denique huc ad unum omnes incumbunt, vel ut regnum incolume, vel ut ventrem confertum retineant" (OS 3:14.1–4, 17–19, 22–25).

63. *Inst.*, pp. 27–28.

64. *Inst.*, p. 11; OS 3:11.10–15.

65. *Inst.*, pp. 19–21.

66. *Inst.*, p. 24; "non parum a vero ipsi aberrant, dum Ecclesiam non agnoscunt nisi quam praesenti oculo cernant, et eam iis finibus circumscribere conantur quibus minime inclusa est" (OS 3:23.34–36).

67. *Inst.*, pp. 9–10; "Equidem scio quam atrocibus delationibus aures animumque tuum impleverint, ut causam nostram tibi quam odiosissimam redderent: sed id tibi pro tua clementia perpendendum est, nullam neque in dictis, neque in factis innocentiam fore, si accusasse sufficiat" (OS 3:9.23–10.1).

68. For a more detailed account of Calvin's pedagogical strategies, see pp. 60–63.

69. Translation from Bouwsma, *John Calvin*, p. 116; "car il y a une prudence singuliere requise en cest endroit [i.e., consolation], ainsi que nous avons vue par ci devant. Car les afflictions sont comme maladies: et si un medecin use d'un mesme remede envers tous malades, et que sera-ce? . . . il faut en premier lieu regarder quelles sont les personnes, et puis comme nous les voyons disposees" (OC vol. 34, col. 206); the original has no accents, and no indication of quotations.

70. Kingdon, *Calvin and the Coming Wars of Religion*, 58–59.

71. Ibid., 59. Also see F. Whitfield Barton, *Calvin and the Duchess* (Louisville, Ky.: John Knox Press, 1989), and Charmarie Blaisdell, "Calvin's Letters to Women: The Courting of Ladies in High Places," *The Sixteenth Century Journal* 12, no. 3 (1982): 67–84; "Renée de France between Reform and Counter-Reform," *Archiv für Reformationsgeschichte* 63 (1972): 196–226.

72. Heller, *Conquest of Poverty*, 115ff.

73. See John Calvin, "Excuses des messieurs les Nicodemites" (1544), in *Three French Treatises*, ed. Francis M. Higman (London: Athlone Press, 1970), 131–53; 166–68.

74. Heller, *Conquest of Poverty*, 122.

75. Higman, *The Style of John Calvin*, 108.

76. The purpose of his polemics is not to convert his opponents but merely to attack them. It should thus be distinguished from apologetics as a strategy that serves apologetics. "It has been my particular intention to lead by the hand those who are teachable but not to strive hand to hand with the inflexible and contentious" (*Inst.* 1.8.21, pp. 145–46).

77. For a short summary of Calvin's interactions with the "Libertines" of Geneva, see Ross William Collins, *Calvin and the Libertines of Geneva* (Toronto: Clarke, Irwin & Co., 1968).

78. Willen Balke offers an excellent overview of the Anabaptists in Switzerland and Calvin's relation to them in *Calvin and the Anabaptist Radicals*, trans. William Heynen (Grand Rapids: Wm. B. Eerdmans Publishing Co., 1981). For a more general discussion of the history of Anabaptism during the Reformation, see Peter

Claus, *Anabaptism: A Social History, 1525–1618: Switzerland, Austria, Moravia, South and Central Germany* (Ithaca, N.Y.: Cornell University Press, 1972).

79. The text most certainly would have served functions that were not as overtly political or internationally significant as the ones I have just mentioned. One such function may have been, for Calvin, a quite personal one. In his letter "John Calvin to the Reader," Calvin explains to his audience that in this textbook he hopes to "furnish a very clear testimony of [his] great zeal and effort to carry out this task for God's church" (*Inst.*, p. 3); "quanto studio ad operam hanc Ecclesiae Dei praestandam incubuerim, luculentum testimonium proferre" (OS 3:5.16–18).

When this letter was reworked for the 1559 edition, it appears that Calvin had just come through a serious illness and was facing the reality that his years were numbered. In light of this illness, could it be that Calvin took up the task of rewriting the *Institutes* not only for the continued purpose of building up faithful communities, but also for the purpose of once again offering personal testimony to his readers and to his God of his unending faithfulness as a servant of his savior Jesus Christ? When the text is approached from the rhetorical perspective of "personal testimony," a whole host of interpretive possibilities opens up which, unfortunately, this study will not explore.

80. For a more elaborate account of his anthropology, see T. F. Torrance, *Calvin's Doctrine of Man* (London: Lutterworth Press, 1952). I have also found Mary Potter Engel's book, *John Calvin's Perspectival Anthropology* (Atlanta: Scholars Press, 1988), extremely interesting since it approaches the question of Calvin's anthropology from a perspective that is open to the insights a rhetorical reading generates.

81. *Inst.*, 1.15.2, p. 184; "essentiam immortalem, creatam tamen . . . quae nobilior eius pars est" (OS 3:174.27–28).

82. *Inst.*, 1.15.6, p. 192; "corpori tamen inditam illic quasi in domicilio habitare: non tantum ut omnes eius partes animet, et organa reddat apta et utilia suis actionibus, sed etiam ut primatum in regenda hominis vita teneat" (OS 3:182.25–29).

83. This part of Calvin's anthropology is not developed in 1.15, but it is implied throughout the text. See Bouwsma, *John Calvin*, 98ff.

84. *Inst.*, 1.15.7, p. 194; "inter obiecta discernere, prout unumquodque probandum aut improbandum visum fuerit" (OS 3:185.3–4).

85. *Inst.*, 2.1.4, p. 245; "Proinde infidelitas radix defectionis fuit. Hinc autem emersit ambitio, et superbia, quibus annexa fuit ingratitudo" (OS 3:232.6–7).

86. Bouwsma correctly points out that Calvin preferred to use metaphors of hearing rather than seeing to describe how the creature receives (hears) the word of God. This emphasis on hearing partially explains Calvin's belief that public preaching and oral teaching were critically important parts of Christian communication. "The living voice has a greater effect in exciting our attention, or at least teaches us more surely and with greater profit, than simply seeing things without oral instruction." Translation from Bouwsma, *John Calvin*, 158 (*Commentary on the Psalms*, Ps. 19:1). However, Calvin's attention to the ocular also bears mentioning. In the *Institutes*, ocular metaphors begin to appear very early in the text, as in the instance of Calvin's use of the metaphors of blindness and sight to describe the beginnings of our knowledge of God (*Inst.* 1.1.2, p. 38). Similarly, in his discussion of creation, Calvin often uses the image of the "showing" or "displaying" of God in

the created order (*Inst.* 1.5.1, p. 52; 1.14.1, pp. 160–61; 1.14.2, p. 162.) Again, playing off the ocular metaphor, Calvin describes the function of scripture as "the spectacles" of faith (*Inst.* 1.14.1, pp. 160–61).

87. *Inst.* 1.15.6, p. 193; "nobis ad aedificandam pietatem simplex defnitio sufficiet. . . . Haec ut vera sint, aut saltem probabilia: quoniam tamen vereor ne magis nos sua obscuritate involvant quam iuvent, omittenda censeo" (OS 3:183.19–20 and 184.2–4).

3
AN APOLOGY FOR DIVINE WISDOM

A Reading of Chapter 1 of Book 1 of the *Institutes:*
"The Knowledge of God and That of Ourselves
Are Connected. How They Are Interrelated"

One's opening remarks, though they should always be carefully
framed and pointed and epigrammatic and suitably expressed, must
at the same time be appropriate to the case at hand; for the opening
passage contains the first impression and the introduction of the
speech, and this ought to charm and attract the hearer straight away.

Principia autem dicendi semper cum accurata et acuta et instructa senten-
tiis, apta verbis, tum vero causarum propria esse debent; prima est enim quasi
cognitio et commendatio orationis in principio, quaeque continuo eum qui
audit permulcere atque allicere debet.

Cicero, *De oratore*

In the opening chapter of the 1559 *Institutes,* Calvin begins his discussion
of the basic doctrines of the Christian faith by presenting his readers with
a puzzle. Having asserted that "nearly all of the wisdom we possess . . .
consists of two parts: the knowledge of God and of ourselves," Calvin tells
the reader that it is "not easy to discern" how one should approach the
task of determining the nature of this wisdom. Should one begin with an
inward glance aimed at understanding the nature of the self and from
there proceed to knowledge of God? Or should one begin the quest for
true wisdom by looking solely to the divine and on the basis of this knowledge alone proceed to analyze the nature of the self? This is the puzzle that
Calvin poses and, having set it forth as a problem to be solved, Calvin devotes the remainder of the chapter to this very task. However, the solution
with which the reader is left at the end of the chapter is strangely ambiguous. Does he finally opt for self-knowledge or divine knowledge as
the starting point for the theological endeavor? The ambiguity of his answer does not seem to have troubled Calvin.

The same cannot be said for many twentieth-century theologians who
have pondered and endlessly debated this puzzle. In the famous Barth-
Brunner debate on natural theology, each of these theologians offers a different interpretation of Calvin's position on this matter, and they both describe in great detail the enormous theological import of their differing
interpretations.[1] For Brunner, Calvin's text allows for the possibility that
the quest for divine wisdom begins with an inward glance, and that
through this inward glance one gains insights into the wisdom of God.
Brunner therefore holds that "self-knowledge" can function as a starting

point or "point of contact" in the search for divine wisdom. In stark contrast to this interpretation, Barth argues that this inward glance is theologically vacuous, that one discovers nothing significant about God simply by looking at one's self, and that the only source of divine wisdom is the knowledge of God that God alone reveals to the creature. Barth thus asserts the singular priority of divine wisdom in the human quest for knowledge of the divine. In addition to this debate, there is another contemporary theologian who tries to bring clarity to Calvin's ambiguity on this issue. In the first volume of his *Systematic Theology*, Paul Tillich argues that divine wisdom is essentially correlative in character.[2] Using this opening chapter of Calvin as a proof text, Tillich describes the way in which human experience presents human beings with questions that divine wisdom in the form of revelation is able to answer. Tillich thus reads Calvin as holding these two types of knowledge in tension.

I mention these three interpretations of Calvin's "puzzle" not because I intend to explore their positions further. To do so would require moving beyond the scope of my present enterprise. I mention them solely because these three readings of Calvin currently provide the major parameters of the debate about how one should interpret Calvin's intentions in his opening statement.[3] In this chapter, I intend to broaden those parameters by giving a rhetorical reading that challenges each of these interpretations and in doing so suggests a fourth option. It is an option that attempts to honor the text's rhetorical movement by exploring the possible reasons why Calvin would have found this seeming ambiguity on the relation between self-knowledge and divine knowledge to be theologically productive. It involves placing the text in its historical context and exploring the practical functions this puzzle may have served. In this manner, the fourth option is predicated upon a reading of Calvin's puzzle that sees the puzzle as more than an abstract discussion of theological methodology. As to the content of this "more" . . . I shall turn to the text.

RHETORICAL READING OF BOOK 1, CHAPTER 1

In my rhetorical reading of the first chapter, I have followed Calvin's own paragraph divisions and have structured his argument in the following manner:

A. The opening sentences: The two parts of wisdom
B. The first thesis: "Without knowledge of self there is no knowledge of God."
C. The second thesis: "Without knowledge of God there is no knowledge of self."

D. The third thesis: The human person must stand in awe before God's majesty.
E. A pedagogical postscript: The order of right teaching

The Opening Sentences: The Two Parts of Wisdom

As my own opening comments suggest, no two sentences in the corpus of Calvin's writings have received as much scholarly attention as the beginning lines to Book 1, chapter 1. Here, Calvin introduces his readers to the *Institutes* with the simple and straightforward claim that "nearly all the wisdom we possess, that is to say, true and sound wisdom, consists of two parts: the knowledge of God and of ourselves (*Dei cognitio et nostri*). But while joined by many bonds, which one precedes and brings forth the other is not easy to discern" (*Inst.* 1.1.1, p. 35; OS 3:31.6–10). Often heralded as the hallmark of his theology, this statement marks the distinctively noetic cast of the project at hand. First, rather than taking up the traditional question of the nature of God's being, the author alerts the reader that this text, the *Institutes*, will consider the nature of God's wisdom or knowledge. Second, he directs the reader's attention to the objects of the wisdom considered, namely, God and ourselves. Thus, with regard to the content of Calvin's project, this opening statement functions to situate his text's epistemological scope and its dual object.

In addition to situating the textual scope and object, this inaugural statement accomplishes a series of other "situatings" that are equally important in defining the nature of the project at hand. As rhetorical gestures, these two short sentences assume and thereby textually construct a myriad of relationships between author, text, and audience, relationships that play a crucial role in determining the "meaning" of the entire chapter.

One of the primary tasks this opening statement accomplishes is establishing a relationship of identity between the author and his audience by using the terms "we" and "ourselves." By invoking a common field of experience, "the wisdom we possess" (*sapientia nostra*), this sentence embraces the audience by assuming that Calvin and his readers stand together in the textual space marked by "we."[4] This assumed unity functions to characterize the text's relation to the audience in several ways. At one level, the use of "we" creates an air of collegiality. The audience is not made the distant object of Calvin's discourse by the use of "you" or "one," both of which are forms of address employed at other times in the *Institutes*. Here, Calvin approaches his audience on friendly terms. The sense of intimacy is further enhanced by the conversational tone and straightforward, nonornamental style of his language. This unity of sentiment between text and reader is also implied by the oblique reference to a space outside the text, and hence outside the community of readers, where a wisdom resides that is other than "true and sound" (*vera ac solida*). It is a place, in other words, where "we" are not.

At another level, the invocation of this common space inscribes a particular set of power relations between the text and its audience. By drawing the reader into the text by means of a general statement about "our wisdom," the text takes upon itself the task of definition. It assumes its own ability to speak for the "we" and to adjudicate the distinction between "true and sound wisdom" and its opposite. In this manner, Calvin reminds the reader of the pedagogical impetus behind the construction of the *Institutes*. The reader is told that he or she stands as student before teacher. The narrative of the text has assumed the position of legislating the constitutive narrative of its pupil, the reader. Therefore, in addition to courting the audience, the text has firmly established a relation of power between itself and the readership, namely, that of master and student.

At a third level, this statement initiates the construction of a relation between text and author. The use of the first person plural firmly ties the voice of the text of the *Institutes* to the voice of its author. As the origin of this text's speech, Calvin remains ever before the reader. He is present directly in the surprising "I" comments scattered here and there as reminders of the particular human mind from which the text emerged. In light of this highly personalized form of address, it is rather surprising that the *Institutes* is so often viewed as a cold and impersonal work. While it may differ markedly from Luther in the paucity of its autobiographical references and its much more dispassionate and authoritarian rhetoric, it nonetheless remains equally marked by the voice of its author. The text of the *Institutes* is clearly Calvin's, and for this reason, the terms "the author" and the "text" of the *Institutes* become interchangeable references for that discursive body which engages the reader. Following this practice, my reading will use "Calvin" and "the text" interchangeably.[5]

This identity created between the work and its author immediately distinguishes the rhetoric of this text from the more disinterested textual presentation of "the philosophers" and the dreaded "Scholastics" whom Calvin opposes. In sharp contrast to medieval Scholastic literary conventions, this personalizing of the act of writing reflects the Renaissance humanists' conviction that the true meaning of a classical text resides in a blending of the author's mind and the ancient source. On the basis of this conviction, the author is beckoned to enter the text boldly. Furthermore, as the rhetorical handbook of Cicero teaches, the use of the audience's positive assessment of the speaker's moral character is one of the most effective forms of persuasion.[6] If Calvin had completely effaced his authorial presence in the text by writing in the third person, he would have sacrificed the persuasive power of his reputation, a sacrifice that a skilled rhetorician would most assuredly have avoided.[7] In addition to introducing the text's subject matter and instituting a series of relations between text, author, and audience, these opening sentences also serve to locate the text within the intellectual and political world of Calvin's day. By the simple act of an assertion, namely, that this text is to be concerned with the twofold character of "wisdom" (sapientia), Calvin has already contested as well as embraced certain popular assumptions about the proper scope and object of theology. In order to obtain a fuller sense of the rhetorical play of this statement, it is useful to note some of the text's implied intertextual references.

To begin with, the position of several classical schools is echoed in this statement. At one level, it echoes the ancient Platonic sentiment that people know themselves only by self-contemplation of Nous in the knowledge of God.[8] That Calvin was quite familiar with Plato is suggested by the number of explicit references he makes to Plato throughout the Institutes.[9] At another level, this opening statement would have struck familiar chords in those acquainted with the ancient Stoic tradition. For the Stoics, exploring the relation between self-knowledge and divine knowledge was a principal project, and this is particularly evident in the writings of Cicero and Seneca.[10] As has been previously illustrated, Calvin was quite familiar with the philosophy of both of these figures.[11] In the light of these two classical allusions, the Platonic and the Stoic, it seems that Calvin's formulation of the opening sentences would have signaled to his readers that the author stood firmly within a long tradition of classical philosophers who had put forth their projects in a similar manner.

This act of anchoring the text in the context of the classical tradition would have been particularly appealing to Calvin's humanist audiences because they shared Calvin's appreciation for the ancient philosophers. Furthermore, Calvin's humanist colleagues were extremely interested in self-knowledge and its relation to knowledge of the divine, and his reference to this twofold nature of wisdom at the outset of the text would have signaled to them that his project included within its scope interests that they shared.[12] It is also significant that Calvin's statement echoes the sentiments of two divergent philosophical schools, the Platonic and the Stoic, because it was between these two schools that the Renaissance humanists had divided their loyalties. Therefore, by embracing both positions in his opening statement, Calvin would have captured the attention of a broad range of humanists. Finally, the most persuasive evidence of Calvin's intention to spark the interests of the community of humanist scholars is found in the fact that Calvin's opening line resembles the words of Budé in his famous De transitu.[13] As the "father of French humanism" and as

Calvin's former teacher, Budé's influence on this opening statement would have been apparent to those who knew the work of Budé and particularly to those who knew the history of Calvin's relation to this highly respected scholar.

However, the community of French humanists was not the only one that would have found familiar echoes in these opening lines. Anyone well versed in patristic theology would have noted the similarities between Calvin's opening formulation and the theological position of at least two of Calvin's favored classical Christian mentors. For persons attuned to these echoes, the formulation of the twofold character of wisdom would have recalled the claim of Clement of Alexandria that "if one knows oneself, one will know God."[14] Similarly, Augustine's famous assertion, "I desire to know God and the soul," most likely would have reverberated through the minds of readers familiar with Augustine's writings.[15] For these reasons, the opening statement of Calvin's text would have sparked the interest of those sixteenth-century students of theology who recognized and respected the works of both Augustine and Clement.

As far as this theologically inclined audience is concerned, these opening lines provide further evidence that Calvin intended his text to appeal to the community of Reformers in the Swiss and German lands, as well as to the Reformers in his own homeland, France. For example, when one compares Calvin's work to a treatise by the Swiss reformer Zwingli, *Commentary on True and False Religion*, the similarities between their opening comments are quite remarkable.[16] Similarly, in his *Enarrationes*, Martin Bucer, the Strasbourgian reformer, remarks that "if we know God and ourselves, we will ascribe to God glory in all things, but to ourselves confusion."[17] As both these intertextual references suggest, Calvin would have immediately kindled the interest of the community of Reformation theologians by casting his opening sentence in the manner that he does.

Nevertheless, within the community of Reformers, Zwingli and Bucer differed widely on the question of whether one should begin with self-knowledge or knowledge of God. Zwingli's theology grants the possibility of gaining insights into the nature of the divine by beginning with self-knowledge. In contrast, one finds Bucer much more resistant to the claim that an inward glance unaccompanied by divine knowledge can generate theologically substantive content. As his statement cited above implies, Bucer held that this inward glance will provide one with nothing but "confusion," and that one should properly begin by "ascribing to God glory in all things." I mention these differences because they point to the fact that Calvin has formulated his opening sentence in a manner that would have avoided alienating the students of either theologian. Thus, as with his sweeping embrace of two divergent humanist schools, Calvin structures his opening address in a language that would have appealed to two divergent groups within the community of Reformation theologians. In the light of the intertextual traffic that this opening sentence would have stimulated, it becomes clear that Calvin has accomplished a rather monumental task in his initial statement of the scope and object of his text. He has situated the text in the middle of highly contested terrain within both the humanist and reforming camps, and he has structured his statement in such a way that none of the various schools of thought whose position he echoes would have felt themselves excluded from the scope of his theological endeavor. As I continue to analyze the rhetoric of the remainder of the chapter, it will become increasingly clear why this initial gesture is so crucial for the project Calvin has set for himself.

But before moving on to the second stage of Calvin's argument, let me review what sort of rhetorical and social determinations Calvin has established in these opening lines. First, in terms of the content of the *Institutes,* Calvin has set forth the epistemological scope and dual object of his project and conceded the nature of the problem that will drive the remainder of the chapter, namely, the order of procession for knowledge of God and self. Second, in terms of his work's location within the intellectual milieu of his day, Calvin has situated it in the middle of a highly contested area, but he has done so by appealing to a broad and diverse audience. By beginning with a widely acceptable premise, the text has cleverly drawn those with refined humanist proclivities into its project. Similarly, Calvin has made broad appeal to several camps within the community of reforming theologians. Third, the text rhetorically reenacts this initial gesture of invitation and embrace by assuming a bond of community between reader and author, both through the use of the inclusive first person plural and by means of an appeal to common experience and common authorities. Thus, even those readers who were unfamiliar with the subtleties of the text's intertextual allusions would have felt embraced by this initial gesture. And finally, Calvin has filled the text itself with his own voice and thereby his authority. As far as readers are concerned, why should such an authority be contested when it affirms their own sentiments? In sum, by virtue of this opening statement, Calvin has managed to bring many "friends" on board the project of the *Institutes,* while keeping the rudder firmly in hand. The skilled rhetorician now begins carefully to maneuver a course toward his own position.

The First Thesis: "Without Knowledge of Self There Is No Knowledge of God"

Having put forth the subject matter of the text and having posed a puzzle for the reader in his opening sentences, Calvin turns quickly to the task of exploring the nature of the problem he has presented. In each of the three sections or paragraphs that constitute chapter 1, Calvin approaches the problem from a different angle. In the first paragraph, he explores the possibility that self-knowledge can lead to knowledge of the divine. In the second paragraph, he discusses the limits of self-knowledge, and in the third, he defends the position that one should properly begin with knowledge of the divine and not with knowledge of the self. What is distinctive about Calvin's argument in each of these three paragraphs is his development of each position by deploying a series of highly suggestive images, each designed to present the reader with a different configuration or picture of the God / self-knowledge relation. As such, the "argument" of this chapter is predicated upon a stringing together of metaphors and images rather than the development of a tightly constructed defense that seeks conceptual clarity through the use of syllogistic reason.

As a rhetorical strategy, this form of argumentation has caused Calvin's interpreters endless frustration and worry precisely because it lacks the kind of conceptual and logical rigor required for clean renderings of Calvin's "meaning." Instead of carefully laying out his position in a style that invites a close philosophical or theological analysis, Calvin uses a language and an argumentative form that resist textual closure. It is partially because of this resistance that contemporary interpreters of Calvin have come up with such a wealth of differing readings of the chapter. In most cases, these contemporary readings attempt to get at Calvin's meaning by penetrating his figurative images in search of the propositional truth that lies buried beneath them. This type of approach is evidenced clearly in the readings given by Brunner, Barth, and Tillich. In their quest for Calvin's "cleaner" meaning, each of these theologians wants to dig beneath the text's rhetoric and uncover the truth it hides.

In contrast to this more analytical approach to deciphering the logic of these three paragraphs, I want to suggest that the "meaning" of the text resides in the play of these images and the effect they have on the reader. Through a rhetorical analysis of these three stages of Calvin's argument, I will illustrate that these paragraphs were designed to situate Calvin's reader in a particular position. Therefore, their logic is more dispositional than syllogistic. In other words, the function of these three paragraphs lies in the kind of orientation they effect in the reader and not in the conceptual clarity they are able to bring to the puzzle Calvin has posed. Through his images and metaphors, Calvin takes his readers through an interesting "play of mind" in which the text leads its audience through the activity of glancing inward by performing the inward glance for them. Having begun with self-knowledge, Calvin then turns the readers' glance upward and presents to them the possibilities opened up by a theological perspective that begins with knowledge of the divine. I believe it is only after one has come to appreciate these dimensions of Calvin's enterprise that one can truly understand the theological content of his position in this opening chapter. So I shall now turn to the text and see what kinds of theological insight this rhetorical reading can generate.

In the first stage of Calvin's "argument," he explores the contention that one might productively begin the quest for divine wisdom by starting with self-knowledge. He states this quite succinctly in the third sentence of the first paragraph. He begins, "In the first place (*nam primo*), no one can look upon (*aspicere*) himself without immediately turning his thoughts to the contemplation (*intuitus*) of God, in whom he 'lives and moves' [Acts 17: 28]" (*Inst.* 1.1.1, p. 35; OS 3:31.10–12).[18] As this statement suggests, Calvin is not going to argue that one can simply be content with self-knowledge and never turn one's attention to the divine. Quite to the contrary, Calvin argues that true self-knowledge always requires that one immediately turn one's attention to God. But he nonetheless suggests, at least at this stage of the argument, that one can discover something in that inward glance that drives one to the divine. In this sense, self-knowledge can be said to "precede and bring forth" (*praecedere, parere*) knowledge of God.

Having stated that he is going to discuss the merits of beginning with self-knowledge, Calvin proceeds to buttress this claim by presenting the reader with a series of highly provocative images. These images are provocative for a number of reasons. First, they are images that Calvin seldom uses elsewhere in his text. In fact, they are drawn from a conceptual world that is very different from the conceptual world in which Calvin's rhetoric normally moves. Second, they are provocative because they draw upon and weave together several philosophical positions that are not normally woven together as tightly as Calvin's rhetoric suggests they should be. In other words, Calvin strings together several images that, on philosophical and historical grounds, appear to be unrelated, if not opposed to one another.

For example, the first image Calvin uses to describe the process of moving from knowledge of the self to knowledge of God is strongly Aristotelian and Scholastic in its emphasis. He states, "the mighty gifts with which we are endowed are hardly from ourselves; indeed, our very being is nothing but subsistence in the one God" (*Inst.*, 1.1.1, p. 35–36; OS 3:31.13–15). This "subsistence" (*subsistentia*) illustration is interesting because in the main body of the *Institutes,* Calvin usually describes the relation that human beings have with God through images that depict people as "hearing" or "seeing" God's word or acts rather than images of "remaining in," "dwelling in," or of "standing in" the Divine.[19]

Even more interesting is his next move. The Aristotelian illustration is linked to an equally surprising image of divine emanation. Calvin describes the gifts of God that are products of humanity's "subsistence in God" as flowing from heaven like "dew" and returning to the Godhead like "rivulets to a spring" (*Inst.* 1.1.1, p. 36; OS 3:31.15–16). What is surprising about this second image is that it is so tightly wedded to the first, even though it represents a philosophical tradition that is decidedly non-Aristotelian. Instead, this language of emanation is distinctly Neoplatonic. The fact that Calvin has metaphorically grafted this imagery onto an Aristotelian framework is thus extremely unusual. This second image is also unusual because, like the preceding subsistence imagery, Calvin puts forth a sustained critique of such language later in the *Institutes*. Most particularly, he argues against the implicit Platonism in the "Manichaean error" concerning knowledge of God, a critique suggesting that he considered the language of emanation suspect. Thus, in both of these opening images Calvin uses what he later considered to be questionable language and weaves together divergent philosophical positions.

From Aristotle and Plato, the list of illustrations moves on to include a third image, which is drawn chiefly from biblical sources.[20] "The miserable ruin, into which the rebellion of the first man cast us, especially compels us to look upward" (*Inst.* 1.1.1, p. 36; OS 3:31.18–20).[21] While this illustration is traditionally Calvinian in its formulation, it is further elaborated by a series of sentences that once again express a view that Calvin later questions:

> Thus, not only will we, in fasting and hungering, seek thence what we lack; but in being aroused by fear, we shall learn humility. For as a veritable world of miseries is to be found in mankind, and we are thereby despoiled of divine raiment, our shameful nakedness exposes a teeming horde of infamies. (*Inst.* 1.1.1, p. 36; OS 3:31.20–24)

In this series of images, Calvin characterizes "us" who are "fasting and hungering" (*ieiuni et famelici*) as being led to "seek what we lack" (*petere quod nobis deest*). Both the characterization of humanity's fallen state as "lack" and the suggestion that the human condition is marked by "hunger" or "famine" are not part of Calvin's common pool of images for sin. In Book 2 of the *Institutes*, he argues against using images of "lack" to define human sin because such images are too passive to capture the willful character of the Fall. Instead, Calvin more often uses active images of "prideful turning," corruption, and contagion to describe the dynamic state of sin (*Inst.* 2.1.8, pp. 251–52; OS 3:236.29–238.15). It is striking, then, that in the opening section of Book 1, metaphors that he only infrequently uses—and often critiques—are put forth as unambiguously positive evidence for the efficacy of moving from the knowledge of self to God.

The text then concludes this description of the famished, naked sinner with the summation, "Each of us must then be so stung by the consciousness of his own unhappiness as to attain at least some knowledge of God" (*Inst.* 1.1.1, p. 36; OS 3:31.24–26). Here, the text foreshadows the discussion that will soon emerge in the exposition in chapter 3 of "the conscience" (*conscientia*) as the locus of humanity's innate knowledge of the divine (*Inst.* 1.3.1, p. 44; 1.15.2, p. 184ff.; OS 3:37.14–38.19 and 174.24–176.35). Both here and in a later discussion of the natural knowledge of God afforded by this "conscience," the specific type of knowledge of the divine that one gleans from this experience is quite different from the kind of knowledge that one comes to through the revelation of God in Jesus Christ. The wisdom afforded by "the conscience" is more like the qualities espoused by "the philosophers," qualities such as "the true light of wisdom, sound virtue, full abundance of every good, and purity of righteousness" (*Inst.* 1.1.1, p. 36; OS 3:31.29–32.1). No mention is made of knowledge of "the divine benefits," such as God's providential care and redeeming love, characterizations that heavily mark Calvin's reflections on revelation from the second half of Book 1 to the end of the text. Instead, benefits of a most ambiguous and broadly appealing nature are presented as the kind of knowledge that flows from the illustrations offered thus far.[22]

Turning from classical and biblical images, the text then asks a hypothetical question in the form of a proverb, "For what man in all the world would not remain as he is—what man does not remain as he is—so long as he does not know himself . . . ?" (*Inst.* 1.1.1, p. 37; OS 3:32.4–6). Using proverbial wisdom in this manner, Calvin reveals his own humanist background once again. Along with the celebration of the vernacular, humanists such as Erasmus had promoted the careful study of the proverbial wisdom of popular culture and had advocated its subsequent use in scholarly writing.[23] Here, Calvin adopts a proverbial rhetoric; the subject of the sentence is broadened to include "all the world" and an appeal to common "experience"—not to the evidence of philosophers—verifies the legitimacy of the assertion that one moves from knowledge of self to knowledge of God. Reminding the reader that this was the task of the first series of images, Calvin concludes the paragraph with the summarizing statement, "Accordingly, the knowledge of ourselves not only arouses us to seek God, but also, as it were, leads us by the hand to find him" (*Inst.* 1.1.1, p. 37; OS 3:32.7–9).

On the basis of this reading, several observations can be made about the relation between the text and the reader in the first stage of Calvin's argument. In the series of images used to explicate the claim that persons move from self-knowledge to knowledge of God, the text appears to have extended the rhetorical strategy of the opening sentence. Using language that would have appealed to a diverse audience, Calvin draws a variety of readers into his project. Through a careful selection of imagery, he has appealed to humanists with an ear for the language of classical philosophy. He also extends a welcoming hand toward the Scholastics while appealing to a less philosophically astute audience by means of a proverbial declaration that draws from the resources of common human experience to make its point. Thus, in its use of sources, the rhetoric of the text appears to be uniquely suited to its content: to illustrate the validity of starting with self-knowledge, Calvin uses examples taken not only from biblical texts, but from a diverse pool of classical philosophical images and a mix of insights drawn from "common experience."

Yet in several instances, Calvin has made his appeal for the primacy of self-knowledge by assuming a premise or using an image that he questions elsewhere in his text. Furthermore, the unsystematic transposition of these various, often contradictory positions threatens to undermine the authority of any one position. However, while these tensions may be apparent when read in relation to later sections of the text, the rhetorical play of this paragraph is not designed to exploit these contradictions. The tone of the text is far from polemical. It is not mocking or sarcastic, nor is anyone overtly attacked. It also lacks the exhortative style that Calvin employs when he speaks polemically. In contrast, its tone is markedly subdued, more descriptive than edifying or caustic.

What then, has Calvin accomplished rhetorically in this first phase of his "argument"? He has continued to extend an open hand of invitation to a number of different audiences by pulling together a string of images that would have sparked a multitude of different interests. And each of these images depicts rather than explains the movement of knowledge as being from the person to God. The rhetoric of the text, then, does not appear to have been designed to elicit the intellectual assent of the audience by means of careful argumentation. Rather, as the reader moves through these vivid depictions, she or he is called upon to enter imaginatively the figurative world of the text and thereby to reenact the very movement the text is describing. Thus, in good humanist fashion, Calvin appears to be taking the reader through a particular kind of reflective process. However, in order to understand where Calvin is going with this "play of mind," one must move on to the second phase of the "argument" that constitutes chapter 1.

The Second Thesis: "Without Knowledge of God There Is No Knowledge of Self"

The next paragraph moves the reader to a second stage in the "argument" by providing a new set of images through which one can visualize the relation of self-knowledge to divine knowledge. Calvin begins, "Again, it is certain that man never achieves a clear knowledge of himself unless he has first looked upon God's face, and then descends from contemplating him to scrutinize himself" (*Inst.* 1.1.2, p. 37; OS 3:32.10–12).[24] While it is clear that Calvin inverts the movement of the relationship described in the preceding paragraph by stressing the fact that one must "first look upon God's face" (*prius Dei faciem sit contemplatus*) and "then descend" (*atque . . . descendet*) to self-contemplation, the connection between this statement and the preceding one is extremely ambiguous. This ambiguity centers on the word Calvin uses to connect the first paragraph to the second. He uses the Latin connective *rursum*, which can be interpreted as meaning either "again" or "on the other hand." The way one reads this word has important implications for the way one interprets the remainder of the chapter.

If one translates *rursum* as "again," then the thesis of the second paragraph appears to be a simple restatement of the thesis of the first. If this is the case, then the claim that one proceeds from knowledge of self to knowledge of God is just another way of making the claim that one should proceed from knowledge of God to self. Consequently, self-knowledge and knowledge of the divine are presented as simply two aspects of the same "wisdom." However, if *rursum* is read as meaning "on the other hand," then it appears that Calvin is alerting his audience to a shift in his approach; he is marking the fact that the content of the next paragraph represents another perspective on the topic of the relation between divine and self-knowledge, a perspective in which divine knowledge clearly takes precedence over the knowledge generated by the inward glance of the reader. If this is the case, then the images of these two paragraphs should not be read as simply a mirror reflection of one another. Rather, they are images that are meant to be held in tension, each offering a different assessment of epistemic authority in matters of divine wisdom.

Although rarely noted as a problem of translation, this ambiguity parallels an ambiguity discussed at length in the contemporary debate over Calvin's position on the relation between self-knowledge and divine knowledge.[25] The position taken by both Brunner and Tillich is supported by a reading of *rursum* as "again" because "again" suggests that self-knowledge has something positive to contribute to the search for divine wisdom. However, the position held by Barth is supported by a reading that highlights the oppositional status of the second paragraph. When one reads *rursum* as "on the other hand," the break between self-knowledge and knowledge of the divine is more decisive. In contrast to both of these positions, I want to suggest that one misses the logic of Calvin's argument if this ambiguity is viewed merely as a problem of translation that can be overcome by rendering *rursum* as either "again" or "on the other hand." When viewed from a rhetorical perspective, Calvin's argument clearly profits from this ambiguity. And the way in which he profits from it becomes more apparent when this paragraph is understood as part of a developing strategy aimed at moving the reader through images designed to effect the reader's dispositional transformation. In order to clarify what I mean, let me continue to explore the images Calvin uses as he develops this second stage of his argument.

The text employs two forms of argument to support the thesis that knowledge of God must be the starting point of self-knowledge. Following the introductory sentence where Calvin puts forth the topic to be treated, the next four sentences argue against starting with self-knowledge because of people's basic incapacity for such knowledge. He states in straightforward, expository language,

> For we always seem to ourselves righteous and upright and wise and holy—this pride is innate in all of us—unless by clear proofs we stand convinced of our own unrighteousness, foulness, folly and impurity. Moreover, we are not thus convinced if we look merely to ourselves and not also to the Lord, who is the sole standard by which this judgment must be measured. For, because all of us are inclined by nature to hypocrisy, a kind of empty image of righteousness in place of righteousness itself abundantly satisfies us. And because nothing appears within or around us that has not been contaminated by great immorality, what is a little less vile pleases us as a thing most pure—so long as we confine our minds within the limits of human corruption. (*Inst.* 1.1.2, pp. 37–38; OS 3:32.13–24)[26]

Rather than arguing positively about why one should begin with God, the text explains negatively why it is that "we" cannot begin with knowledge of ourselves. In short, tainted by sin, "we" are incapable of such knowledge. On the basis of this description, the logic of the preceding paragraph is subverted. Self-knowledge cannot accomplish the task attributed to it, that of leading "us" to knowledge of God. It is insufficient. Thus, reading *rursum* as "on the other hand" is certainly appropriate.

This subversion is accomplished, however, in a rather complicated manner. In the first paragraph, the pool of resources from which Calvin draws evidence to support the initial position is that of common experience and the sentiments of "the philosophers." As I pointed out, Calvin uses the evidence of self-knowledge to argue for beginning with self-knowledge. Thus, in the first paragraph, there exists a certain symmetry between the thesis and the type of evidence used to support it. However, in the second paragraph, this symmetry is lost. Calvin now argues against starting with self-knowledge, but he continues to fund his argument by drawing upon evidence taken from common experience and "the philosophers." For this reason, the logic of the second paragraph is much more complex and unstable than the logic of the first. Calvin uses the evidence of self-knowledge to argue against the priority of self-knowledge. Thus, in one sense, the interpretation of *rursum* as "again" appropriately denotes the fact that, at least in terms of the sources and evidence used, the second paragraph extends the logic of the first.

The peculiarity of Calvin's logic at this point is particularly apparent when one considers that later in the *Institutes* Calvin argues that human beings, blinded by self-love, are cut off from true knowledge of God and self; indeed, for this reason, he claims, they are completely incapable of fully grasping their own sinful limitation and their alienation from God on the basis of self-reflection alone (*Inst.* 2.1.2, pp. 242–43; OS 3:229.9–230.16). In the opening chapter of Book 2, Calvin explains to the reader that the evidence of common experience, when considered apart from the knowledge of faith, is unreliable, for it will never convict creatures of their sin nor will it bring them to full knowledge of God. Instead, the evidence of common experience will most likely have the opposite effect. It will convince them of their superior abilities as human beings and consequently cause them to become "puffed up" with arrogance. For this reason, Calvin argues, it is only through the knowledge of God given to them in Jesus Christ that people become convinced of their fallen nature. It is only when they compare themselves to Christ that their total depravity becomes apparent. However, in paragraph two of the opening chapter, Calvin seems to be taking a different approach. Here, he is drawing upon the evidence of self-knowledge, and not Jesus Christ, in order to convince the reader of the inadequacies of that knowledge. How would Calvin have reconciled these seemingly incongruent positions?

Again, one may discover an answer to this question if one approaches the text by looking at what it does to the reader. By using the evidence of self-knowledge as the grounds for rejecting the priority of self-knowledge, Calvin continues to appeal to those readers in his audience who would have found the argument of the first paragraph convincing. At least in terms of evidence, he is still arguing from the same standpoint. However, in the second paragraph a twist is added. The very kinds of argument that bolstered a positive appreciation of self-knowledge as a starting point are now used to undermine it. By permitting the text's symmetry to be ruptured in this manner, Calvin brings his readers into an imaginative space that is much different from the one announced in the first paragraph. The readers end up being led to affirm the priority of divine knowledge, but according to the logic of Calvin's presentation, they have been moved to this affirmation by the force of their own presuppositions concerning the adequacy of self-knowledge. In short, he uses their own evidence to convict them.

This same dynamic of arguing for the primacy of knowledge of God by internally collapsing the argument for the primacy of self-knowledge is repeated in the second form of argumentation used in this paragraph. The insufficiency of mere self-reflection is illustrated by means of an extended metaphor to which Calvin also adds his own interpretation. As several scholars have noted, Calvin describes human incapacity in terms strikingly similar to Plato's "Myth of the Cave."[27] Thus, once again, the evidence used to elevate the primacy of knowledge of the divine is itself drawn from the evidence of "the philosophers" and an appeal to commonsense experience:

> Just so, an eye to which nothing is shown but black objects judges something dirty white or even rather darkly mottled to be whiteness itself. Indeed, we can discern still more clearly from the bodily senses how much we are deluded in estimating the powers of the soul. For if in broad daylight we either look down upon the ground or survey whatever meets our view round about, we seem to ourselves endowed with the strongest and keenest sight; yet when we look up to the sun and gaze straight at it, that power of sight which was particularly strong on earth is at once blunted and confused by a great brilliance, and thus we are compelled to admit that our keenness in looking upon things earthly is sheer dullness when it comes to the sun. (*Inst.* 1.1.2, p. 38; OS 3:32.24–36)[28]

Calvin's image and Plato's myth are both constructed around the metaphor of sight, sight that illusorily assumes itself pure and perfect until exposed to the true brilliance of the sun. It is a dazzling light that compels people to admit that "our keenness in looking upon things earthly is sheer dullness." The centrality of sight metaphors and their relation to a certain conception of knowledge again places this text firmly within the realm of Renaissance humanism.[29] For this reason, this particular segment of the argument would have had a special appeal to the more erudite classical scholars of his age. In addition, its simple images would have made it comprehensible to those who did not have the education necessary to detect the Platonic reference but nonetheless embraced similar sensibilities at work in the general culture. Thus, the scope of the argument's appeal is as wide as it is in the first paragraph, but again, it has been twisted. This image, constructed on the basis of self-reflection, is deployed to refute the legitimacy of appeals to self-reflection alone.[30] The text has turned the audience's previous affirmations against them.

As if to drive this point home even more strongly, Calvin next offers a rather elaborate interpretation of this sight metaphor. Beginning "so it happens in estimating our spiritual goods," the text describes the process whereby human beings flatter themselves by unduly stressing the power of human perception alone. Calvin then concludes this stage of his argument by summarizing the force of his interpretation:

> Then, what masquerading earlier as righteousness was pleasing in us will soon grow filthy in its consummate wickedness. What wonderfully

impressed us under the name of wisdom will stink in its very foolishness. What wore the face of power will prove itself most miserable weakness. That is, what in us seems perfection itself corresponds ill to the purity of God. (*Inst.* 1.1.2, p. 38; OS 3:33.7–12)

At one level of interpretation, these concluding remarks describe again the movement from darkness to light. Recognizing one's own blindness has the reflexive effect of exposing the distortion of all that one claimed to have seen previously. When exposed to the light of God's perfections, one's own attempts at self-knowledge appear perverted. At another level, these remarks accurately describe the very process through which the text has just guided the reader. "What masquerading earlier as righteousness" points to the variety of images initially used to support the primacy of self-knowledge. It points to the place of the audience at the end of the first paragraph. "What wonderfully impressed us under the name of wisdom" sends us back to the evaluations of wisdom first presented in the chaotic play of Aristotelian, Platonic, Stoic, and Scholastic elements. Now, since the reader has been convinced by the internal subversions of those philosophical principles, these evaluations have "grown filthy." They "stink in their foolishness" and "correspond ill to the purity of God."[31] The text thus leaves the audience deflated, deflated by the force of its own assumed evidence and, consequently, in a suitable position for the next stage of Calvin's argument.

If my hypothesis that Calvin is attempting to appeal to an audience with humanist inclinations is correct, then he has accomplished a very subtle but nonetheless significant reorientation of his readers by the end of the second paragraph. In first using a series of images that would have confirmed the humanist sentiment that self-knowledge can lead to knowledge of the divine, Calvin has begun by courting their sympathies. However, in the second paragraph, he undermines the claim that self-knowledge can be theologically productive when used in the absence of divine knowledge. But he accomplishes this undermining in a clever manner. First, he does not undermine his reader's assumed position by entering into a philosophical or theological debate about the limits of self-knowledge. He will do this later in the *Institutes,* but for now, Calvin seems to have found it useful to deploy another kind of rhetorical strategy. He simply strings together a series of images that move the reader into the "self" and then he reveals the vacuous nature of the "knowledge" discovered there.

Second, Calvin pulls his humanist readers into this "inward glance" by enticing them with descriptions drawn from the philosophers and from common experience. In doing so, Calvin deconstructs their original position on the primacy of self-knowledge by using their own evidence against them. While this strategy causes a rupture in the internal logic of Calvin's position and leads to some conceptual ambiguity about whether or not Calvin values the evidence of self-knowledge, it nonetheless rhetorically positions the reader in a vulnerable position. In short, Calvin has pulled out from under the humanists' feet the ground of self-knowledge and left them destabilized. And this is precisely where he wants them to be because, in the next paragraph, Calvin intends to place their feet firmly on the ground of new territory, the ground of divine knowledge.

The Third Thesis: The Human Person Must Stand in Awe Before God's Majesty

Until this point in the chapter, Calvin has made very little use of biblical imagery, and there has been only one scriptural reference. As I have noted, the bulk of the argument has been constructed by appealing to philosophical images and commonsense testimony. However, at the beginning of the third paragraph, Calvin's rhetoric changes abruptly. Leaving behind the evidence of self-knowledge, his opening sentence pulls the reader into the world of the biblical narrative: "Hence that dread and wonder (*horror et stupor*) with which Scripture commonly represents the saints as stricken and overcome (*perculsos atque afflictos*) whenever they felt the presence of God" (*Inst.* 1.1.3, pp. 38–39; OS 3:33.13–15).

As with the previous transition from paragraph one to paragraph two, the move from the second paragraph to the third is smooth, seemingly automatic. The Latin connective *hinc*, "hence," suggests that this third stage of reflection is logically connected to the preceding one as an inference. Thus, this scriptural description is laid over the Platonic metaphor and the rhetorical leap that Calvin makes is cleverly hidden. The move from common experience to the biblical narrative is assumed as natural and the reader is taken to a new stage in the argument without an apparent rupture in its logic. The deflated reader of the previous paragraph is thus carried into this new territory without having been given the rhetorical space to protest the move.

But the new rhetorical space in which the reader now stands is decidedly different from the territory of the previous paragraph. While Calvin is still arguing the same premise, namely, that persons must begin with knowledge of God and descend from there to knowledge of themselves, his form of argumentation and the kinds of evidence and imagery he uses have changed. Unlike the previous paragraphs, this paragraph is composed almost entirely of scriptural portraits of "men who in his [God's] absence normally remained firm and constant, but who, when he manifests his glory, are so shaken and struck dumb (*quatefieri ac consternari*) as to be laid low by dread of death" (*Inst.* 1.1.3, p. 39; OS 3:33.17). Thus, the warrants used to support the claim that one must begin with knowledge of the divine have shifted. The evidence is no longer drawn from the pool of common experience or the philosophers. Instead, the evidence is now undeniably theological precisely because the evidence is drawn from the biblical narrative. With this shift in the source of his evidence, Calvin re-institutes the rhetorical symmetry that characterized the first stage of his argument. He is now arguing for the primacy of divine knowledge by us-ing the evidence of divine knowledge to buttress his claim.

In addition to reinstituting this symmetry, the rhetoric of the third stage of Calvin's argument suggests a series of other subtle shifts in his form of argumentation. For instance, in the previous paragraph, Calvin used the metaphorical image of the "cave" to make his point about the limits of self-knowledge. And he admits that this image is metaphorical because he ac-companies it with his own "interpretation" of its meaning. In this sense, the evidence of self-knowledge permits and even requires an interpretive gesture. However, when Calvin deploys scriptural evidence in this third paragraph, he simply lets it stand on its own, without interpretation. He thus presents the evidence of divine knowledge as self-authenticating. This contrast between the status of scriptural sources and metaphor sug-gests a shift in the relation between the author and the evidence he uses. The metaphor of the "cave" requires his judgment to render it intelligible and thereby useful. In contrast, the intelligibility and hence the usefulness of scripture is permitted to stand on its own merits. Its meaning is as-sumed to be self-evident.

By rhetorically granting scripture this self-authenticating status, Calvin also redefines the way in which the text engages the reader. In the first two stages of Calvin's argument, the text uses the familiar "we"; and as he moves through the various images of self-knowledge that he deploys, the presence of this "we" leads the reader to assume that she or he will find these images descriptive of some common experience. In this sense, the use of "we" has the effect of always turning the reader's gaze inward to-ward those facets of the "we" that Calvin's metaphors capture. But in con-trast to this familiar language, the rhetoric of the third paragraph shifts to the third person and thereby announces a change in the reader's relation to the material being presented. The evidence of scripture, stated in the third person, stands over and against the reader.[32] Having made this shift, the text no longer presumes that a moment of personal recognition or au-thorial judgment is needed to mediate its meaning. No inward glance is necessary. The evidence stands on its own merit and thereby judges the reader from a perspective outside of common experience. By rhetorically shaping the reader's relation to the text in this manner, the text is now per-mitted to stand as "the judgment" by which we "must be measured" and "the straightedge to which we must be shaped."[33]

The tone in which Calvin narrates these biblical scenes has also shifted in accordance with the change in the form of argument. It carries a more sermonic rhythm than the previously pedantic pace of pure exposition. This rhythm actually begins at the conclusion of the previous paragraph with the repetitive use of "what " (*quod*) to commence each sentence and the parallel construction of the phrases that follow. Then, when the witness of scripture is presented, the pitch continues to build. One biblical image after another is rapidly presented, each invoking an entire narrative to those familiar with scripture. The paragraph culminates in the doxological refrain of Isaiah, "The sun will blush and the moon be confounded when the Lord of Hosts shall reign" (*Inst.* 1.1.3, p. 39; OS 3:33.35–36). The liturgical movement of the text consequently leaves the reader with his or her attention uplifted toward the Lord, the laudatory position appropriate to the believer.

These rhetorical gestures no longer tacitly elicit the reader's assent in the form of recognition or identification with the metaphor used. Rather, Calvin's language about Job can appropriately be applied to his own work, which now "expresses a powerful argument that overwhelms men with the realization of their own stupidity, impotence, and corruption" (*Inst.* 1.1.3, p. 39; OS 3:33.25–27). And with scripture as the principal source of the argument, it is through the revelation of God that this "overwhelming" is accomplished. Thus, as with the two paragraphs before, the text is rhetorically enacting the very reality it seeks to explicate. The initial claim that human beings never achieve a clear knowledge of themselves unless they have "first looked upon God's face, and then descend from contemplating him to scrutinize [themselves]" has become a reality in the experience of the readers by the end of the third paragraph. They are judged by the word of God, which stands apart from them and toward which their gaze is now directed. As Calvin sums it up at the end, what began as "the brightest thing" has in fact become "darkness before it."

A Pedagogical Postscript: "The Order of Right Teaching"

In sharp contrast to the laudatory pitch of these lines, the last sentence of paragraph three abruptly brings the reader's attention into an entirely different sphere of argumentation. As if to bracket the entirety of the preceding discussion, it begins with the connective "yet" (*utcunque*). This bracketing and its dismissive tone are further accentuated by the phrase "however (*tamen*) the knowledge of God and ourselves may be mutually connected." This phrase seems to imply that Calvin finally has no opinion on the matter at hand, or if he does, it appears to be of little consequence. Therefore, the concluding force of his laudatory remarks is immediately defaced and thereby hidden. In its place, Calvin makes a statement that appears to give his definitive opinion on the matter: "[T]he order of right teaching requires that we discuss the former first, then proceed afterwards to treat the latter" (*Inst.* 1.1.3, p. 39; OS 3:34.2–3). Calvin offers no supporting evidence for this statement; it stands as if its legitimacy is self-evident. Hence, pragmatic questions of pedagogical effectiveness (the order of right teaching—*ordo recte docendi*) seem to have the last word in the debate.

This unusual shift in both the tone and topic of discussion raises a question about the actual purpose of the argument elaborated in the three preceding paragraphs. Why did Calvin not simply state the problem—namely, that it is difficult to discern whether knowledge of God or of ourselves takes precedence—and then proceed immediately to his conclusion that the order of right teaching requires that he begin with the first? Why develop a lengthy discussion that is later completely dismissed as gratuitous? These questions suggest that the preceding three paragraphs serve a function other than contributing to the development of an overarching textual argument about either the inadequacy of self-knowledge or, conversely, the divine image-bearing quality of human knowing. If this is the case, then focusing on the rhetorical play of the text in these sections may be of even greater significance than initially assumed. What, then, has Calvin accomplished rhetorically?

CALVIN'S RHETORICAL ACCOMPLISHMENT

To answer this question fully, I must return to an issue to which I have alluded only occasionally in the process of analyzing the text's rhetorical progression. This issue is the possible historical audiences to whom Calvin originally addressed his work. I have referred to possible historical audiences only briefly thus far because I wanted to explore first, in more general terms, how the text engages its "ideal reader." However, having accomplished this, I now wish to step back from the text and ask the historical question: how might this text have functioned in Calvin's social context? If Calvin was really the astutely pragmatic rhetorician I have depicted him as being, one may assume that he did not write this opening chapter with only an "ideal reader" in mind. Instead, it is more likely that Calvin intended this chapter to serve a practical function in the context of an actual community of readers. If so, then my rhetorical reading needs to be supplemented with references to one or more historically specific audiences in order to grasp fully the scope and function of the chapter's rhetoric.

In chapter 2 of this study, I described four of the historical audiences suggested by Calvin's prefatory remarks: Calvin's students, at first in

Strasbourg and then in Geneva; the persecuted community of French evangelicals whose cause Calvin sought to promote; the community of French humanists and certain humanistically inclined members of the French aristocracy whose financial and military support was needed to protect the French Reformers; and those hostile segments of the Roman Catholic clergy in France who were attacking the French evangelical community. With this list of Calvin's audiences as a reference, let me first determine which of these communities might have been singled out as the target of Calvin's opening chapter.

Of these four audiences, the only one that does not appear to have been directly engaged is the fourth, the perceived enemy. Their absence is testified to by the fact that the polemical language Calvin typically uses when addressing this community never makes an appearance in the four paragraphs that constitute the chapter. In contrast to more overtly polemical sections of the text, chapter 1 has a more inviting tone. The audience is "we," and for the most part, Calvin's rhetoric is quite collegial. Therefore, if this rival community is engaged, it is engaged only indirectly—by being excluded from the community of readers the text initially intends to address.

As for Calvin's students, there are several places in the opening chapter where Calvin accommodates his rhetoric to their particular needs. As I discussed in my analysis of the two opening lines, Calvin firmly positions the reader as student before teacher, and by filling the text with his own authorial presence, he establishes his authority to define the narrative of the "we" who will be led through the subsequent paragraphs. Calvin thereby makes the reader aware of the pedagogical intent of the text from the outset. He reaffirms the presence of this pedagogical intent at the conclusion of the chapter as well. When Calvin states that the "order of right teaching" requires one to commence with knowledge of the divine, his authorial identity as "teacher" is reasserted and the pragmatic requirements associated with his task of teaching are given priority, at least in terms of determining the basic structure the remainder of the *Institutes* will follow. However, apart from these two places, the rhetoric of the rest of the chapter does not seem to have been constructed to serve a pedagogical function; the text does not exhibit the kind of careful expository language Calvin typically uses when his purpose is to teach. Thus, although the text was certainly designed with his students in mind, Calvin's principal audience appears to be someone else.

Was his audience the community of persecuted Reformers in France? Undoubtedly, like Calvin's students, they remained ever before him as an audience to whom his text should speak. However, their presence in the opening chapter is not as apparent as it is elsewhere in the text. When Calvin addresses the needs of this community—particularly the pastoral needs of congregations—his rhetoric is most often either exhortative or comforting. Apart from the third paragraph, this type of language is absent from the opening chapter. Therefore, the French evangelical community, as a whole, does not appear to be a primary target of Calvin's rhetoric.

As I have suggested throughout my reading of the chapter, there is a good deal of textual evidence that points to the highly educated community of French humanists and the French aristocracy—some of whom were quite active in the above-mentioned French evangelical parishes—as the principal target of Calvin's rhetoric in this opening section of the *Institutes*. In my discussion of the first two sentences of this chapter, I described the kinds of intertextual echoes that Calvin's formulation of the twofold character of "our wisdom" would have evoked in the humanist community. I also suggested that the humanists would have been attracted to Calvin's initial argument for the primacy of self-knowledge. Fascinated with the new sorts of self-understanding and understanding of the broader world opened up by the Renaissance of classical literature, the humanists of France were focusing their attention primarily on the wonders of natural knowledge, in all its various shades and shapes. For this reason, the first stage of Calvin's argument would have been particularly appealing to them. Furthermore, the type of evidence Calvin uses in constructing the first two stages of his argument would have been appreciated more fully by the humanists than by any of Calvin's other audiences. Such readers would have noted Calvin's Aristotelian and Platonic references; for example, Calvin's use of the Platonic "Myth of the Cave" would not have gone unnoticed by this community. And given the humanists' interest in exploring the "proverbial wisdom" of vernacular culture, Calvin's proverbial comments at the end of the first paragraph would have been enticing to them as well.

However, the most compelling evidence for the primacy of this humanist audience is the strongly apologetic tone of the chapter. As I have illustrated in my analysis of the rhetorical movement of the three stages of Calvin's argument, the text is designed to reorient or convert the audience's attitude toward the efficacy of self-knowledge. It is intended to move the reader from an affirmation of the primacy of self-knowledge to an affirmation of divine knowledge as the only proper starting point in the quest for divine wisdom. Furthermore, it is designed to convert the audience, not by means of an attack, but by means of gentle persuasion, a persuasion accomplished by carrying the reader through a series of provocative images. If Calvin's principal audience had been his own students or the steadily faithful "community of believers," accomplishing such a conversion would not have been necessary. Similarly, if his target had been the Roman cleric, he most likely would not have constructed a "conversion narrative" as subtle and unpretentious as the one found in this chapter. However, if his audience was the French humanists whose allegiance to the reforming movement often vacillated, but whose steady support he intended to win, this strategy should have proved quite effective.

Having determined that this community was most likely the principal target of chapter 1, the next question is, How does Calvin rhetorically accomplish its conversion? How does he enact this apologetic gesture? To answer this question, let me return to the text and read it once again with a distinctly humanist audience in mind.

Calvin begins chapter 1 by making a broad appeal to those who, as good humanists, would laud the primacy of self-knowledge. The text then supports this position through a variety of illustrations drawn from classical philosophy and daily human experience. Using these examples, he defends the primacy of self-knowledge by turning the readers' gaze inward and commending them to reflect upon what one discovers there. In this manner, he devotes the entire first paragraph to courting the sensibilities of his humanist colleagues and convincing them that the project he has undertaken in the *Institutes* is in basic agreement with their own interests.

Having situated the humanist reader in a position of initial agreement with his text, Calvin then makes a shift in the second paragraph. He does this by smoothly advancing a thesis that may or may not be considered the inverse of his original position. The ambiguity that resides in the term *rursum* is rhetorically productive at this point. On the one hand, if it is read as "again," the text appears to be simply extending the argument of the first paragraph. If this is the case, then the humanist reader will not find her or his position challenged. On the other hand, if *rursum* is read as "on the other hand" (a reading that is probably more accurate given the subject matter of the second paragraph), the reader may correctly note that a monumental shift has occurred. The thesis that Calvin advances in the second paragraph consists of the claim that knowledge of God must precede self-knowledge as the straightedge to which "we" are shaped. The courting of the humanists continues as he offers supporting illustrations drawn from the same pool of resources as the previous paragraph. However, this evidence, by the end of the second paragraph, has been deployed to convince the reader that the former position is untenable on its own grounds. Thus, the humanists who agreed with Calvin in the beginning would be shaken, if not convicted, by the second stage of the argument.

The reader is now left in a rather interesting place. The first thesis has been dismissed and the second now stands, though it stands on the basis of evidence that seems peculiarly ill suited to its principal claim. Is the evidence of self-reflection capable of leading one to assert the primacy of divine knowledge? If so, then Calvin has accomplished nothing—except perhaps attracting the humanists' attention. In the midst of the disorientation caused by this tension, Calvin makes a move that is neither logically precipitated nor textually precedented. He simply begins to define the reader's experience in biblical terms.[34] In doing so, the biblical text itself becomes the dynamic straightedge to which the audience is shaped and formed. The reader has been brought to a new stage in the argument, one that rhetorically reenacts the claim that one should begin with knowledge of God and descend from there to contemplate oneself. Thus, if Calvin's apologetic strategy has been effective, the inward glance that was considered productive in the first paragraph and then considered vacuous in the second paragraph has now been entirely replaced by an upward glance toward God.

As for the conclusion of the chapter, the triumph of the practical and hence of the rhetorical is fittingly Calvinian. Indeed, if this rhetorical reading is considered tenable, then pragmatic considerations have driven the text from the very beginning. Furthermore, given what the text has just attempted to accomplish, the disarming effect of its reference to "the right order of teaching" and the effacing of the argument running through the three preceding paragraphs suggest that perhaps Calvin is not yet finished with the humanists.

CHALLENGING TWO ASSUMPTIONS

Throughout this rhetorical reading of chapter 1, I have tried to expand the interpretive parameters of the text by pushing beyond the limits imposed by such contemporary readings of Calvin as those of Brunner, Barth, and Tillich. In the process of pushing beyond these limits, I have indirectly challenged two major assumptions about the text held by these three theologians. The first is their assumption that Calvin's primary objective in this opening chapter was to put forth his position on "theological methodology." The second and related assumption lies in their impression that Calvin intended to put forth his position by making some strong assertions about the relation between self-knowledge and divine knowledge. In order to tease out these distinctions, these theologians attempt to dig beneath Calvin's rhetorical imagery and to uncover a deeper and purer "truth" about Calvin's view of the proper procedures for constructing a comprehensive theology.

My reading has challenged these two assumptions at a variety of levels. In the first place, it challenges these theologians' understanding of the function of the opening chapter. While it is true that Calvin treats a topic that contemporary theologians would describe as "theological methodology," he does not approach the subject in a manner typical of contemporary theologians. A rhetorical analysis of the text suggests that Calvin did not intend carefully and analytically to unfold his position on the primacy of either self-knowledge or divine knowledge. Although he does present his own position on the matter at the end of the third paragraph, the "argument" of the chapter appears to have been designed to orient the reader dispositionally toward Calvin's project rather than simply to put forth arguments in support of either self-knowledge or divine wisdom. In other words, his account of theological methodology functions to dispose or situate the reader toward the project he has undertaken rather than to discuss, in more abstract terms, the proper starting point for theology. In this sense, the text is as much if not more intended to "make the reader good" (to use Petrarch's phrase), and thereby to take the reader through an educative process of reflection, than it is to present a set of propositional truth claims about where one should begin the theological enterprise. Calvin wants to "make his readers good" by showing them the vacuousness of self-knowledge and then by bringing them under the rule of scripture so they stand in a laudatory position before the divine from whom comes all true wisdom. Accounts of Calvin's theology that fail to note these dimensions of the text and seek to analyze only its propositional truth claims risk overlooking these additional aspects of the text's meaning.

Once one comes to appreciate the kind of dispositional reorientation the text is trying to enact, then the problematic nature of the second assumption of Calvin's contemporary interpreters is exposed. This second assumption is based on several misguided notions about the character of textual meaning. First, there is the assumption that the true meaning of Calvin's text lies somewhere beneath or beyond the images and the rhetorical play that move across the surface of the text. Second, there is the correlative view that his flourishes of language serve as mere ornamental clothing to these deeper truths. From this follows a third assumption, namely that the text's rhetorical play can be interpretively bypassed in the theologian's search for the true meaning of the *Institutes*. These notions are directly challenged if one recognizes that one of the text's principal functions is to move the reader through a series of rhetorical strategies designed to convert and redispose him or her. When the text is read in this manner, one comes to see that it is precisely through the play of these images that the text's functional meaning is constituted. Through the reader's engagement with these rhetorical mechanisms, the truth of the text—the reorientation of the reader toward God—is enacted. Thus, my reading of the text suggests that instead of serving as mere ornamentation, the linguistic play of image and metaphor are an essential part of the text's structure.

In addition to challenging these two interpretive assumptions, my rhetorical reading of the first chapter has the added effect of directly challenging the substance of the interpretations rendered by Brunner, Barth, and Tillich. Without going into a detailed analysis of the positions held by these theologians, it is possible to characterize these challenges in very broad terms. First, when chapter 1 is interpreted as an extended apologetic strategy aimed at finally "converting" the reader to the position that knowledge of the divine is alone "the straightedge to which we must be shaped," then Brunner and Tillich appear to be incorrect in claiming that Calvin admits the possibility of self-knowledge playing a theologically productive role for the sinful, distorted individual. Granted, the text does admit, at certain points, the possibilities inherent in self-knowledge. As Calvin will later argue more forcefully, if one "lives in Christ," then self-knowledge can be spiritually productive. Similarly, he seems to suggest in these paragraphs that empty self-knowledge might eventually lead one, in despair and hunger, to the God who is full. But these admissions are, when viewed in the context of the chapter as a whole, only two pieces of a much broader argument aimed at eventually destroying any pretensions the audience may have toward the efficacy of self-knowledge in general. Because Brunner and Tillich do not attend to the rhetorical movement of the text and therefore do not appreciate its apologetic thrust, they mistakenly grant positive theological content to an argument that was deployed for rhetorical reasons. In other words, Brunner and Tillich fail to recognize that Calvin was courting and trying to convert a humanist audience, and that he initially put forth a positive assessment of self-knowledge to gain their attention and then eventually to collapse the argument for self-knowledge on its own internal grounds. Thus, by missing these dimensions of the text's overarching strategy, Brunner and Tillich unknowingly grant positive theological status to a claim that Calvin himself intended to reject.

For these reasons, Barth's interpretation of Calvin is much closer to the interpretation my rhetorical reading renders. Calvin does suggest, finally, that divine knowledge must precede self-knowledge and that self-knowledge is incapable of generating any theologically positive content. However, Barth does not come to this conclusion by way of an appreciation of the text's rhetorical movement. If he had, his understanding of the relationship between apologetics and dogmatics might have been much more nuanced than it is. In his now famous quip, Barth describes this relation as one in which "the best apologetic is a good dogmatics." And he asserts this on the grounds that apologetic enterprises that begin with an appeal to common human experience run the risk of implying that self-knowledge can somehow play a productive role in the theological enterprise. At one level, my reading of Calvin supports this view, because Calvin eventually asserts the singular priority of divine knowledge and consequently, the absolute limits of self-knowledge. At another level, however, Calvin adopts an apologetic strategy that, for rhetorical purposes, makes substantive use of the insights garnered through self-knowledge. Granted, he only asserts the primacy of self-knowledge for the purpose of deconstructing it. But this deconstruction is partially accomplished by the incoherence of self-knowledge itself and thus without reference to the priority of divine knowledge. In this sense, the evidence of self-knowledge appears to contribute something to Calvin's argument for the priority of divine knowledge, even if this "something" is purely negative.

Because Barth does not attend as carefully as he could have to the rhetorical dimensions of the theological enterprise, he fails to take into account that a good apologetic, quite apart from dogmatics, can serve to dispose a reader toward the task of dogmatics without necessarily carrying any "tainted notions drawn from self-knowledge" into the dogmatic sphere. This is precisely what Calvin accomplishes in the opening chapter of the *Institutes*. He puts forth the primacy of self-knowledge as an apologetic gesture aimed at converting the reader to a disposition in which divine knowledge alone is normative. However, because the function of his discussion of self-knowledge is more rhetorically than theologically substantive, it does not provide a substantive foundation upon which Calvin's dogmatic claims will be based. In short, Calvin uses apologetics in the service of dogmatics without allowing it to generate the norm for the content of dogmatics. Thus, the example of Calvin challenges the simplicity of Barth's view of apologetics and in so doing opens up new avenues for the contemporary debate over the relation between apologetics and dogmatics as forms of theological discourse.

NOTES

1. *Natural Theology: Comprising "Nature and Grace" by Dr. Emil Brunner and the Reply "No!" by Dr. Karl Barth*, trans. Peter Fraenkel (London: Centenary Press, 1946).

2. Paul Tillich, *Systematic Theology*, vol. 1. (Chicago: University of Chicago Press, 1951), 63.

3. I make reference to Barth, Brunner, and Tillich because their interpretations of Calvin are quite well known, and I want to avoid giving an extensive exposition of lesser-known contemporary theological accounts of Calvin's opening chapter. However, a number of scholars have discussed Calvin's doctrine of the knowledge of God in a much more detailed fashion. The best of these discussions is found in Dowey's *The Knowledge of God in Calvin's Theology*. In this text, Dowey offers a reading of Calvin that, although much more nuanced than Brunner's, basically supports Brunner's reading. T.H.L. Parker has also written on Calvin's doc-

trine of knowledge, and his reading supports a more Barthian interpretation. See Parker's *Calvin's Doctrine of the Knowledge of God: A Study in the Theology of John Calvin*, rev. ed. (Edinburgh: Oliver and Boyd, 1969). For a good overview of a wealth of earlier materials devoted to the study of Calvin's doctrine of the knowledge of God, see P. Lobstein, "La connaissance religieuse d'après Calvin," *Revue de théologie et de philosophie religieuse* 42 (1909): 53–110. See John Newton Thomas, "The Place of Natural Theology in the Thought of John Calvin," *Journal of Religious Thought* 15 (1957–58): 107–36. Thomas offers a review of materials pertaining to the Barth-Brunner debate up to 1958. For more contemporary discussions, see William Bouwsma's chapter "Knowing," in *John Calvin: A Sixteenth Century Portrait*, and "Calvin and the Renaissance Crisis of Knowing," *Calvin Theological Journal* 17 (November 1982): 190–211. Apart from Bouwsma's work, these treatments of Calvin basically stay within the parameters of the discussion outlined by my description of Barth's, Brunner's, and Tillich's treatment of Calvin. None of these authors investigates Calvin's doctrine of the knowledge of God and of the self within a rhetorical framework.

4. Calvin wrote literally, "nearly the whole sum of our wisdom." *Sapientia nostra* is thus literally translated "our wisdom." Following the English translation, however, I have used "we" to mark the presence of the first person plural in this sentence.

5. With regard to the question of the relationship between text and author, it is important to remember that Calvin intended the *Institutes* to be an interpretive guide for reading yet another text, sacred scripture. Recalling the discussion of the humanists' view of interpretation as digestion in chapter 1, one could argue that as Calvin digests the scriptures he interprets, they too become more "of God" (and hence true to their meaning) the more they become "of Calvin." Blending authorial/textual/scriptural identities in this manner is a topic worthy of more consideration. In this study, however, "text" will refer only to the text of the *Institutes* and not to "the biblical text," the scriptural source that the *Institutes* elaborates.

6. "The eloquence of orators has always been controlled by the good sense of the audience, since all who desire to win approval have regard to the goodwill of their auditors, and shape and adapt themselves completely according to this and to their opinion and approval." "Semper oratorum eloquentiae moderatrix fuit auditorum prudentia. Omnes enim qui probari volunt voluntatem eorum qui audiunt intuentur ad eamque et ad eorum arbitrium et nutum totos se fingunt et accomodant." Cicero, *Orator* 8.24 (trans. H. M. Hubbell, 322–23).

7. In 1536, when Calvin wrote the first version of this sentence, his reputation would have been as a young, classically trained humanist and burgeoning reformer. By 1559, however, his reputation had grown as an international churchman and political leader. In both instances—at both periods in Calvin's life—the invocation of his reputation would have played a significant rhetorical role in his work.

8. Plato, *Alcibiadaes Major*, trans. W.R.M. Lamb (Cambridge, Mass.: Harvard University Press, 1964), 132e–33c. See Charles Partee, *Calvin and Classical Philosophy* (Leiden: E.J. Brill, 1977), 30ff.

9. For example, his first explicit reference to Plato appears only two chapters later. *Inst.* 1.3.4, p. 46.

10. "Thus Natural Philosophy supplies courage to face the fear of death; resolution to resist the terrors of religion; peace of mind . . . ; self-control . . . ; and . . .

the Canon or Criterion of Knowledge, which Epicurus also established, gives a method of discerning truth from falsehood." "Sic e physicis et fortitudo sumitur contra mortis timorem et constantia contra metum religionis et sedatio animi . . . et moderatio . . . et . . . cognitionis regula et iudicio ab eodem illo constituto veri a falso distinctio traditur." Cicero, *De finibus* 1.19.64, transl. H. Rackham, Loeb Classical Library (Cambridge, Mass.: Harvard University Press, 1972), 68, 69. "No man does wrong in attempting to regain the heights from which he once came down. And why should you not believe that something of divinity exists in one who is a part of God? All this universe which encompasses us is one, and it is God; we are associates of God; we are his members." "Nemo improbe eo conatur ascendere, unde descenderat. Quid est autem cur non existimes in eo divini aliquid existere, qui dei pars est? Totum hoc, quo continemur, et unum est et deus; et socii sumus eius et membra." Seneca, *Epistulae morales* 92.30, transl. R. M. Gummere, Loeb Classical Library (Cambridge, Mass.: Harvard University Press, 1970), 466, 467.

11. See chapter 1, 18–25. For more on Calvin's relation to Stoicism, see Leontine Zanta, *La renaissance du Stoïcisme au XVIe siècle* (Geneva: Slatkine Reprints, 1975). Also see Partee, *Calvin and Classical Philosophy*, 30.

12. See Bouwsma's chapter "Knowing" and its relation to humanism in *John Calvin*, 150–60.

13. See *De transitu* 1 (*Opera*, 1.239.5f): "God willing that by every sort of teaching we be instructed in the knowledge of himself and of ourselves"; "Deus autem omni genere doctrinae ad cognitionem sui ac nostri condocefactos nos volens . . ." (*De transitu Hellenismi ad Christianismum*, Book 3, in *Omnia Opera Gulielmi Budaei* [1557 ed., reprinted Farnborough: Gregg, 1963, vol. 1, 239, lines 5–6]). The strongest argument for the influence of Budé on Calvin's opening line has been made by Josef Bohatec in *Budé und Calvin: Studien zur Gedankenwelt des französischen Frühhumanismus* (Graz: Böhlaus, 1950), 31, n. 47, 241ff. Also see Partee, *Calvin and Classical Philosophy*, 10; and Battles, *Institutes* (1536), 244.

14. Clement, *Instructor* 3.1, in *The Ante-Nicene Fathers*, vol. 2 (Grand Rapids: Wm. B. Eerdmans Publishing Co., 1979), 271. In Latin translation, "si quis enim se ipsum norit, Deum cognoscet" (J.-P. Migne, ed., *Patrologia Graeca*, 8 [Paris, 1891], col. 536a).

15. Augustine, *Soliloquies* 1.2.7, trans. Charles Starbuch, in *The Nicene and Post-Nicene Fathers of the Christian Church*, Series 1, vol. 7 (Grand Rapids: Wm. B. Eerdmans Publishing Co., 1978), 539. In Latin, the text reads, "Deum et animam scire cupio" (J.-P. Migne, ed., *Patrologia Latina* 32 [Paris, 1877], col. 872d).

16. Zwingli states, "Now, since religion involves two factors, one that towards which religion reaches out, and one that which by means of religion reaches out towards the other . . . it is God towards whom man reaches out and man who by means of religion reaches out towards Him, religion cannot be truly treated of without first of all discerning God and knowing man" (*Commentary on True and False Religion*, ed. S. M. Jackson and C. N. Heller [Durham, N.C.: Labyrinth, 1981, c. 1929], p. 58). "Quandoquidem autem religio fines duos complectitur, alterum in quem tendit religio, alterum qui religione tendit in alterum . . . Cum deus sit in quem tendit religio, homo vero qui religione tendit in eum, fieri nequit ut rite de religione tractetur nisi ante omnia deum agnoveris, hominem vero cognoveris" (Huldrici Zuinglii, *Opera*, ed. M. Schuler and J. Schulthess, vol. 3 [Zürich: Officina Schulthessiana, 1832], 155). See A. Lang's "The Sources of Calvin's *Institutes* of 1536," in *The Evangelical Quarterly* (London, 1936): 130–41. Also see Paul Wernle,

Calvin, vol. 3 of *Der evangelische Glaube nach den Hauptschriften der Reformatoren* (Tübingen: J.C.B. Mohr, 1919).

17. The statement continues ". . . all things in us insofar as they are of God are just and holy; but insofar as they are of us, we shall both acknowledge and confess them to be sin and iniquity." Martin Bucer, *Enarrationes perpetuae in sacra quatuor evangelia, recognitae nuper et locis compluribus auctae* (Strasbourg, 1530), fol. 66, v. 25–28. Translation taken from Battles, *Institutes* (1536), 244. A. Lang argues that it was the work of Martin Bucer that most decisively informed not only the shape of Calvin's opening sentence but, even more important, his understanding of piety and prayer. Lang, "Sources," 137–41. Lang's position on this matter presently finds wide support among Calvin scholars. For a fuller discussion of the influence of Bucer's *Enarrationes* on Calvin, see Ganoczy, *The Young Calvin*, 158–68, 349–51.

18. The nuance of the rhetoric that announces the commencement of Calvin's "argument" is more clearly captured if *nam primo* is read as both "in/at the beginning" and "in the first place." When read as "in/at the beginning," the sentence sounds as if it will not only offer the first piece of his argument but also describe a state of affairs that exists "at the beginning." As my reading progresses, the import of this nuance will become more evident, for I argue that Calvin is not only building an argument but is also trying to describe and invoke the active turning of the reader toward God.

Calvin's use of the verb *aspicere* (to look at) in this sentence marks the first instance of the ocular metaphors that he will use throughout this chapter. For a discussion of Calvin's ocular metaphors, see chapter 2, p. 77.

19. Even at this early stage in his "argument," Calvin is taking the Aristotelian image and rhetorically casting it in a new biblical form as well, as is evidenced by his transposition of the previous quote from Acts 17:28, we "live and move" in God (*in quo vivit et movetur* ["In ipso enim vivmus et movemur": Vulgate]), with the statement that we "subsist" in him (*in uno Deo subsist [ere]*). This transposition is conceptually provocative because Calvin's reworking suggests that "subsistence" in God and "living and moving" in God are parallel images.

20. The use of biblical imagery here represents Calvin's second reference to scripture in this chapter, the first being his reference to Acts 17:28 in the third sentence.

21. Note here that the phrase "compels us to look upward" or *sursum oculos cogit attollere*—literally translated "to lift [our] eyes upward"—once again uses an ocular metaphor to describe knowledge of God and self.

22. In this section of the text, Calvin juxtaposes a list of vices to a list of virtues in order to describe the character of the wisdom afforded by one's "conscience." The tensions exploited by these lists once again suggest a description of sin as "emptiness" or "lack" and a description of knowledge of God as "fullness." He states that when one feels one's own "ignorance, vanity, poverty, infirmity" (*ignorantia, vanitas, inopia, infirmitas*), one is then compelled to recognize in God "the true light of wisdom, sound virtue, full abundance of every good, and purity of righteousness" (*sapientiae lux, solida virtus, bonorum omnium perfecta affluentia, iustitiae puritas*). As in the previous quotation on "fasting and hungering," here "poverty" (*inopia*) could be translated as "emptiness," and, correlatively, "full abundance" (*perfecta affluentia*) could be read as "great/perfect affluence." To the list of vices, Calvin also adds his more familiar description of sin as "depravity and

corruption" (*pravitas et corruptio*), a gesture that, again, blends two forms of rhetoric. Earlier in the chapter, Calvin plays off a similar distinction when he states that "our very poverty" (*nostra tenuitas*) discloses the "infinitude of benefits" (*bonorum infinitas*) that rest in God (OS 3:31.17–18).

23. Erasmus's work on identifying and cataloguing the proverbial wisdom of popular culture had made its use commonplace in works such as Calvin's. See Erasmus, *Adagiorum chiliades tres*, in *Opera*, ed. J. Leclerc, vol. 2 (Leiden, 1703; Louvain, 1704); *Adages*, trans. M. M. Phillips (Toronto: University of Toronto Press, 1982–92), 4 vols. For a discussion of the place of proverbial wisdom in sixteenth-century French culture, see Natalie Zemon Davis, "Proverbial Wisdom and Popular Error," in *Society and Culture*, 227–67, 336–46.

24. Although the English translations of the various phrases Calvin uses in this sentence for "knowledge" and for "knowing" capture well the subtlety of his language, in Latin the movement of the text is even more complex and dramatic. He begins with the phrase, "man never achieves a clear knowledge of himself," using the term *notitio* for knowledge (previously used in OS 3:31.26), thus emphasizing the notion of "idea or conception." (In this chapter, other words used to describe "knowledge" are *agnitio* [32.7], a term that more closely resembles the notion of "recognition," and *cognitio* [31.3], a term that the translators have correctly cited as "knowledge." In contrast to these words, he uses the term *sapientia*, best translated as wisdom, to describe the fullness of the knowledge that "we" possess in God [31.1; 31.29]. He then adds that this self-knowledge must be preceded by a divine knowledge that has looked upon "God's face" (*Dei facies*), an unusual phrase that suggests a direct viewing of God's face in contrast to Calvin's more standard references to our knowledge of God's hands and feet, God's acts or benefits, and God's speech or word. This description of knowledge is then followed by the phrase, we must "descend from contemplating him," and here the verb for knowing is *contemplari* (to survey or contemplate)—a word that adds yet further nuance to his vocabulary for "knowing." The sentence then concludes with the phrase "to scrutinize himself," using yet another word for knowing, *inspicere* (to look into, view, examine, inspect), to depict the inward glance of the human person.

I include this discussion of Calvin's Latin in this opening sentence of paragraph two in order to give the English reader a sense of the complexity and force of Calvin's language. However, one would be making Calvin into a more systematic and speculative theologian than he was if one were to argue that these various linguistic distinctions reflect an underlying, carefully crafted philosophy/theology of knowledge. While it is certain that Calvin did exploit a variety of images for "knowing," they do not seem to convey distinctions whose significance lies in the logical precision of classical epistemology.

25. The ambiguity invoked by Calvin's use of *rursum* was first pointed out to me by Edward Dowey in his lecture on this chapter given in his course on Calvin at Yale Divinity School, Spring, 1989. However, Dowey only pointed to the ambiguity, and I therefore take full responsibility for the subsequent use I have made of it.

26. In the opening line, Calvin uses the term *integer*, translated as "upright," to describe how we "seem to ourselves" in pride. In the next chapter the same word, *integer*, is used, in contrast, to describe Adam before the Fall, *si integer stetisset Adam* (OS 3:34.14).

In the same opening sentence, he uses the term *argumentum*, translated as "proof," to describe what it will take to convince us "of our own unrighteousness" (OS 3:32.14). When translated as "argument," this term more clearly captures the forensic nature of Calvin's project in this section. He is trying to argue or to prove his point to his reader. This forensic quality is further highlighted in the next phrase by his use of the term *convincere*, translated "convinced," to describe what the "arguments" do to "us" (OS 3:32.16). In Latin, the juridical force of *convincere* is more evident if it is translated as "convicted" or "proved mistaken." Again, in the next statement, Calvin drives the forensic force of his point home when he describes God as the "sole standard by which this judgment must be measured." Here, the terms *exigere* (to regulate) and *iudicium* (a legal judgment) directly evoke the juridical rhetoric of law courts and legal decisions. The significance of this collection of legal images will become more apparent in my concluding discussion of the role played by apologetic discourse in this chapter.

27. Plato, *The Republic*, trans. P. Shore, ed. E. H. Warmington (Cambridge, Mass.: Harvard University Press, 1966), 514ff. Also see Bouwsma, *John Calvin*, 99, and Partee, *Calvin and Classical Philosophy*, 105–16.

28. In this short series of images, Calvin rhetorically blends a number of ocular metaphors with metaphors that play off notions of contamination and pollution. For ocular language, note his repeated use of *oculus* (eye) and his words derived from ocular verbs: *observare, hallucinari, despicere, intueri, videre*.

29. Bouwsma, *John Calvin*, 150–60, esp. 158.

30. Calvin's use of phrases and words suggesting "ocular inadequacy" are complemented later by his description of scripture as "the spectacles" that allow human beings "to see" God's benefits in creation and to understand themselves as God creatures. See *Inst.* 1.6.1, p. 70.

31. Here, Calvin's use of metaphors related to pollution and contamination becomes most evident in his use of the term *sordescere* ("grown filthy") and his references to evaluations that *pro stultitia foetere* ("stink in their foolishness") and *divinae puritatis male respondere* ("correspond ill to the purity of God").

32. This sense of "scriptural judgment" is strengthened further in this third paragraph by Calvin's repeated invocation of biblical references in which the presence of God is described as forcefully encountering persons. For example, in the opening two sentences alone, those who stand in God's presence are depicted as being "afflicted and overcome" (*perculsos atque afflictos*), "shaken" (*quatefieri*), "overwhelmed" (*absorberi*—passive, to be swallowed, gulped up, or engrossed by), "laid low" (*concideri*—passive, to be cut up, cut down, destroyed), and "almost annihilated" (*pene nulli esse*—to be made nonexistent, nullified, or ruined). Although the violence of these images is unmistakable, note that the Latin intimates a sense of awe, reverence, and amazement as well.

33. *Inst.* 1.1.2, p. 37; OS 3:32.18; and *Inst.* 1.1.2, p. 38; OS 3:33.6. Each of these phrases highlights a different dimension of the relationship Calvin is describing between knowledge of God and of ourselves. In the first phrase, "we" are "measured" (*exigeri*—passive, to determine or regulate) by "the Lord who is the sole standard of this judgment." Here, the emphasis is laid upon the act of measuring, an act in which our "self knowledge" is "assessed" by the divine but not transformed. In the second phrase, however, the relationship described is one in which we are shaped (*conformari nos oportet*) by knowledge of God. Here, the movement between God and persons is more dynamic, active, and forceful. "We" are

"made," "formed," or "put together" by our knowledge of God. This shift from an image of "measuring" to an image of "shaping" parallels the rhetorical shifts that are occurring in the text. In paragraph two of chapter 1, Calvin attempts to "judge" the reader by exposing the inadequacy of self-knowledge. In paragraph three, however, he undertakes to remake the reader by allowing the scriptural word to form the positive context for shaping self-understanding in the presence of the Divine.

34. It should be noted that given their interest in "ancient texts," Calvin's humanist colleagues would have found this shift to scripture appealing not only for overtly theological reasons but for textual, philological, and historical reasons as well.

4

ELOQUENCE IN SERVICE OF PIETY

A Reading of Chapter 2 of Book 1 of the *Institutes:*
"What It Is to Know God, and to What Purpose
the Knowledge of Him Tends"

For God will have His people to be edified; and He hath appointed His Word for that purpose. Therefore, if we go not about the salvation of the people, that they may receive nourishment by that doctrine that is taught them, it is sacrilege; for we pervert the pure use of the Word of God. . . . whatsoever draweth us to the kingdom of heaven, or taketh our affections from the world, and leadeth us to Jesus Christ, that we may be grafted into His body, is called holy.

Car Dieu veut que son peuple soit edifié, et a ordonné sa parole a cest usage. Si donc nous ne taschons au salut du peuple, et qu'il reçoyve bonne substance de la doctrine qu'on luy propose, c'est un sacrilege, car on pervertit le pur usage de la parole de Dieu. . . . tout ce qui nous attire au Royaume celeste, tout ce qui nous destourne du monde, et qui nous conduit à Jesus Christ, afin que nous soyons bien incorporez en luy, cela est nommé sacré.

John Calvin

At the end of chapter 1, Calvin leaves the reader with eyes riveted upon the divine and ears open to receiving the word of God as it is presented in scripture. Having cast aside the dubious project of seeking God through knowledge of the self, he has unveiled the glory of divine wisdom and called the reader to enter a world where all things are shaped against the straightedge of revelation alone. It is a world where the reader is beckoned to awe and fear, to adoration and praise of the One whose light overwhelms all darkness. And it is a world where the chatter of self-indulgent and narcissistic rhetoric is silenced by the thunderous rhetoric of divine oration. Standing in this posture of reverence and wonder, the reader is thus prepared to move into the rhetorical world of the text's second chapter.

What will Calvin do next? What "play of mind" or "twist of logic" will he take the reader through now? A partial answer to this question lies in the title of the chapter, "What it is to know God, and to what purpose the knowledge of him tends." Having positioned the reader before the divine, Calvin is going to describe more fully the kind of "knowing" one experiences when the object of knowledge is God. In this sense, it appears that chapter 2 is going to extend and develop the rhetorical logic played out in the opening chapter. If one can imagine the first chapter as a process of clearing a path toward the divine, then chapter 2 would seem to be a description of what one should know and how one should feel having reached the end of that path. One should experience, Calvin will explain,

121

a disposition best captured by the term *pietas;* in common Christian parlance, one should emerge illumined by the light of true godliness or piety.
   It should not be surprising, however, to discover that Calvin develops
a number of clever rhetorical devices to describe this disposition. At one
level, he offers a rather straightforward, propositional exposition of the
nature of *pietas;* he simply provides the reader with a useful definition of
true godliness. At another level, he engages in a series of rhetorical maneuvers designed to provoke directly this disposition in the reader. In this
sense, he is interested not only in telling the reader what she or he should
experience but also in making "the reader good" by rhetorically eliciting
the very disposition he describes. Discerning the means by which he accomplishes this end is the task of my analysis of the rhetoric in chapter 2.
   One of the most challenging aspects of reading Calvin rhetorically
arises from the ever-changing pace and texture of the *Institutes.* The style
and form of argumentation Calvin uses shift from chapter to chapter.
Thus, one of the first things the reader will notice upon entering the world
of chapter 2 is that even though it extends the project of chapter 1, it employs a very different style and form of presentation. In contrast to the
steadily building and evenly paced tone of chapter 1, this chapter seems
more choppy and uneven. It consists of a mix of several rhetorical forms;
it uses the explicative voice quite frequently; it refrains from using a flour-
ish of figurative images; and it often lapses into short sermonic and polemical exhortations. Thus, one cannot make rhetorical sense of this chapter
by simply applying the pattern of argument used in the previous one. An
entirely different tack must be taken.
   Again, it is not surprising to discover that the rhetorical pattern that
governs the flow of this chapter's logic corresponds to the task Calvin has
undertaken: it is a pattern designed to invoke the disposition *pietas.* The
image of waves best captures the pattern's movement. By mixing and
blending a series of rhetorical forms, Calvin constructs waves of appeal
that wash over the reader. These waves begin in the calm voice of exposition. They then build in intensity as the temper of sermonic and polemical passion takes over. At the climactic moment of the discussion, they
crash upon the reader in a wondrous display of doxological elation. And
finally, having moved the reader to the heights of *pietas,* the waves recede
into the steady tone of exposition. But in the course of this one short chapter, Calvin is not content to sweep the reader away only once: As if to drive
home the power of godly piety and familiarize the reader with its force,
Calvin repeats the wave pattern four times, creating the rhetorical effect
of a relentless play between turbulence and rest, between affective exalta-
tion and intellectual assent.
   In the following pages, I will be tracing the movement of these four
waves as they build and break across the surface of the text. However, if

one is to appreciate the full array of rhetorical agendas that Calvin negotiates in this context, it is necessary to examine the way he exploits other
discursive gestures as well; for as I have shown in my analysis of the prefaces, Calvin does not write to an anonymous audience. He always has a
readership in mind, and he never ceases to accommodate his rhetoric to
catch their attention and to meet their needs. Thus, as I follow the ebb and
flow of these rhetorical waves, I will ask about the shape and nature of the
historical audiences he hopes to convert or strengthen through this exercise. For whom were these waves intended to be uplifting? I will suggest
that his faithful followers were not the only people in need of such an exercise. In fact, I will argue that these waves are designed to strengthen the
resolve of some while breaking against and knocking over others. But I
shall let the text itself tell this part of the story.

RHETORICAL READING OF BOOK 1, CHAPTER 2

Calvin's Introductory Comments

"What It Is to Know God, and to What Purpose the Knowledge of Him
Tends."

Now the knowledge of God, as I understand it, is that by which we not
only conceive there is a God but also grasp what befits us and is proper
to his glory, in fine, what it is to our advantage to know of him. Indeed,
we shall not say that, properly speaking, God is known where there is
no religion or piety. (*Inst.* 1.2.1, p. 39; OS 3:32.6–10)

In the same manner as in chapter 1, Calvin begins chapter 2 with a series of propositions that introduce the reader to the topic at hand and spec-
ify the terms of its treatment. Having previously determined the epistemological scope of this project, its dual object, and the pedagogical
precedence that divine wisdom takes over self-knowledge, he now turns
to the task of more carefully delineating the character of "our knowledge
of God." As the chapter title suggests, this knowledge is first described as
a knowing that has a purpose. As such, it is a functional or practical
knowledge; it does something; it "tends" (*tendere*). Calvin further develops this sense of purpose in the opening sentence as he informs his audience that this knowledge has the peculiar quality of being both "advanta-
geous" and "expeditious" (a single Latin verb, *expedire*). He also observes
in the following sentence that it is a knowledge that cannot be held apart
from the disposition he refers to as religion (*religio*) or piety (*pietas*). It is
therefore a knowledge that situates one in the world in a very specific way.
      Having thus laid out the purpose, usefulness, and distinctly disposi-

tional quality of this knowledge, Calvin uses the remainder of the chapter to elaborate further his understanding of this knowledge called *pietas*. The most immediately striking aspect of the various terms Calvin employs to explicate the unique character of this knowledge is the rather stark contrast between these terms and the language used by the Scholastics on the same topic. Instead of simply "conceiving" (*concipere*) and "knowing" (*cognoscere*), Calvin portrays a type of knowledge that "grasps" (*tenere*) and shapes. In contemporary treatments of this chapter, the peculiar quality of this knowledge has been assessed frequently through the lens of existential phenomenology. It is thus characterized as "deciding knowledge" or "practical knowledge." However, based on my preceding discussion of Calvin's background in rhetoric, it is also possible to situate these terms within the framework of Renaissance humanism. When read in this light, Calvin's opening description of the unique form of "knowing" associated with "knowledge of the divine" portrays it as a decidedly effective and active form of knowing. Indeed, while this knowing intellectually conceives a propositional truth-content, it is also practically useful and purposeful. But most importantly, it is a knowing that involves the dispositional reorientation of the one who holds it. When *pietas* is viewed in this manner, one cannot help but hear the echoes of Cicero and Petrarch reverberating throughout these opening lines.

In addition to introducing the central theme of the chapter, this opening set of propositions also accomplishes a series of other "situatings" similar to those outlined in my analysis of the opening lines of chapter 1. As rhetorical gestures, the two sentences cited above locate and thereby negotiate a set of relationships between text, context, audience, and author. The most notable of these negotiations occurs in the first sentence, where Calvin once again deploys a rhetoric that establishes a relation of familiarity between text and audience. The use of the inclusive "we," "us," and "ours" serves to create a textual identity shared by both author and reader. It thereby positions the reader in a posture of implicit agreement with the text by assuming a bond between the reader's voice and that of the text.

Furthermore, the fact that this use of "we" is accompanied by a rhetoric that is straightforwardly expositional in character suggests that the relation between text and reader is the relationship of teacher and student. The rhetoric of these opening lines thus alerts the reader to the distinctively pedagogical intentions of the discussion that follows. It positions Calvin as teacher and marks the text as the vehicle for his instruction. These textual dynamics suggest that Calvin most likely designed this chapter, just as he designed the book as a whole, with an audience of students in mind.

In addition to a suggested readership of students, another audience makes an appearance in these opening lines. While functioning as an inclusive gesture, these two sentences also posit a space beyond the text to which those readers who do not agree with Calvin's position are exiled. The text thus announces the presence of an underlying polemical agenda. For this reason, it appears that Calvin is not simply going to teach his students in a straightforward expository manner; rather, he is going to teach them by polemicizing against an opponent who, on the topic of the "knowledge of God," holds a position different from his own. The presence of this exclusionary dynamic is signaled by Calvin's approach to defining *pietas*. He formulates his definition by illustrating how this understanding of "knowledge of God" extends beyond an "alternative definition" to which he alludes but which he never explicitly identifies. In the first sentence, Calvin contrasts a positive knowledge that "grasps" and is "befitting" with a knowledge that simply "conceives" of God's existence. Using a similar strategy, the second sentence defines *pietas* negatively by stating that one cannot claim to have true knowledge apart from it. The reader is told what not to "claim" and thereby positioned vis-à-vis an adversary who would speak otherwise.

This dialectical form of argumentation situates the movement of the discourse between two polarities. In terms of identity, it is a polarity between "us" (the implied author and the compliant audience) and "them" (the yet unnamed other). Thematically, this polarized movement is played out in the tension between "useful" knowledge on the one hand and "useless" knowledge on the other; between true and false religion; between piety and its yet unidentified opposite. For the reader who agrees with Calvin, this rhetoric alerts her or him to the fact that she or he is standing with the reformer on contested ground. And for those who do not share Calvin's position, the text has rhetorically constituted the battlefield, drawn the lines, and commenced to sound the battle cry.

While it is easy to imagine the face of Calvin's students, it is more difficult to tell toward whom Calvin aims this opening polemical gesture. Fortunately, a series of helpful historical clues allows one to reconstruct speculatively the particular dispute in which Calvin deployed this polemic. The most useful of these clues comes at the beginning of the second paragraph of chapter 2, where Calvin openly names his antagonist as Epicurus.

In the classical world, the Epicureans were a philosophical school known to the sixteenth century primarily through Cicero's dialogue *De natura deorum*.[1] Scholars generally accept Calvin's familiarity with this particular text given the strong parallels between the language and structure of Cicero's argument and the reformer's own language and argument in chapters 3 through 5 of the *Institutes*.[2] Cicero's text is also strongly echoed in the opening lines of chapter 2. In the introductory propositions, Calvin defines his topic as *religio et pietas*. In defining his topic in this manner, he employs a verbal construction almost repeating Cicero's *"pietas, sanctitas, et religio.*"[3] Furthermore, Cicero initially directs the scope of his dialogue to a treatment of God's providence, taking up the question of whether or not "the gods are entirely idle and inactive." He states that he wants to direct his discussion to this question because this topic alone involves issues that are immediately beneficial or useful for one to know.[4] Calvin's opening sentences reflect a similar interest, particularly when he assesses "our knowledge of God" in terms of its useful and beneficial nature. On the basis of the strong similarities between the two texts, it appears as if chapter 2 intends to engage, at least on one level, an audience educated in the classics. As I have noted in chapter 1, this audience would have included a number of humanists and French aristocrats whose support Calvin was seeking. Thus, given the textual evidence, it seems that Calvin will continue the apologetic appeal he initiated in the first chapter.

It is highly unlikely, however, that the humanist movement, broadly conceived, would have suddenly become the target of Calvin's polemical attack. As I have noted, Calvin was intent upon securing their support for the reforming movement in France and probably would not have risked alienating them by attacking them as harshly as he does the opponent he posits in this chapter. It is also unlikely that Calvin's polemical target in this chapter was only the ancient school of Epicureans. His attack on his opponent is much too vicious and sustained to have been prompted solely by his disagreements with a school of thinkers who lived hundreds of years before his time. It is much more likely that his target was a contemporary. And in fact there was a group of thinkers in sixteenth-century Europe who had earned for themselves the distinguished title of "Epicureans." In Calvin's polemical treatise *Concerning Scandals,* he attacks, under the name of "the Epicureans," a small group of humanist scholars whom he considers to be "atheists." In this company he lists Agrippa, Dolet, Servetus, Rabelais, Deperius, and Gouvéa.[5] Calvin characterizes their theology as dangerous because

> [they] break through to the point that all religions have their origins in men's brains, that God exists because it pleases men to believe so, that hope of eternal life has been invented to deceive the simple, and that the fear of judgment is childish terror.[6]

In addition to grouping them together on these theological grounds, grounds that actually have striking similarities to the original Epicureans, Calvin also identifies them as a group that wielded considerable power in the French courts. He states, "[Epicureanism is] rampant everywhere throughout the world, and in fact chiefly holds sway in the courts of kings and princes, in courts of justice, and in other distinguished walks of life."[7]

On the basis of information provided by Calvin in his correspondence with the French court in Navarre during the 1550s, it seems this particu-

lar "heretical sect" was competing with Calvin for the aristocracy's attention and support. This small group represented an elite and considerably
more radical offshoot of the larger humanist movement. Because they had
launched very direct attacks against the French crown and the French Roman church in their writings, they had been forced, like Calvin, to depend
on the generosity of certain highly placed figures in the French court who
could offer them economic support and political sanctuary. However, unlike Calvin, the basis of their attack upon the dominant powers in France
was as antiauthoritarian as it was religious.[8] In this regard, they were
known to have had as harsh a critique of the Reformation's "authoritari-
anism" as they had for the tyranny of the French state and the Roman
church. For these reasons, one can understand why Calvin might have felt
compelled to polemicize against their position early in the *Institutes*. If he
was determined to court the sympathies of the more moderate humanists,
he would have had to distinguish his position from the position of those
factions within the humanist movement that had the potential to turn the
aristocracy against the cause of the French evangelical community.

If these men are the target of the polemical undercurrent I have identified in Calvin's chapter 2, why does Calvin offer only subtle clues to their
identity? Why does he identify them only under the broad title "Epicureans"? To answer this question, it is necessary to consider once again how
Calvin might rhetorically profit from some textual vagueness. Given the
vast range of positions covered by the group he calls "Epicureans," nar-
rating their identities into a single ancient character with whom they each
have at least some intellectual affinity makes them as a whole a much more
unified, easily caricatured, and hence, vulnerable target. It also invokes the
weight of classical opinion against them: the Epicureans do not fare well
in Cicero's dialogues.[9] Furthermore, by so naming his opponent Calvin
creates a distance between himself and his adversary that makes his attacks less pointed and therefore "safer," while simultaneously allowing
him greater latitude in his polemical maneuvering. Thus, as a rhetorical
gesture, the invocation of the "Epicureans" of Cicero's *De natura deorum*
provides an excellent arena for fighting a more immediately pressing battle, one that may not be strictly theological but is nonetheless essential to
the life of the growing Reformed community in France and Geneva.

On the basis of textual evidence, I have identified the presence of at
least three rhetorical agendas that are implicitly invoked in these opening
sentences. First, there is Calvin's pedagogical agenda in relation to his students, those he instructed in Strasbourg and then in Geneva as well as
those students who studied his work in their homes, at work, or in small
local churches scattered throughout France. Second, there is Calvin's
apologetic agenda aimed at courting the sympathies of the moderate humanists whom Calvin first engaged in the opening chapter, an audience

in need of persuasion and conversion. And third, there is a strong polemical undercurrent that appears to have been directed at the small group of radical "Epicureans" whom, for reasons that are not quite clear but most likely related to the complex politics of France at the time, Calvin felt compelled to attack and marginalize as his textual foe. As I continue to move through the rhetoric of this chapter, I will be returning to these three audiences and agendas and analyzing the subtle ways in which Calvin's discussion of *pietas* continues to address all three groups simultaneously.

In addition to stating the purpose of the chapter and identifying the chapter's various audiences, the rhetoric of these opening sentences also introduces a third kind of textual posturing. This posturing involves the way Calvin inhabits his authorial identity and establishes the terms of his power vis-à-vis his audiences. At this early stage in the chapter's argument, the author assumes several significant positions. First, by qualifying the opening sentence with the clause "as I understand it" (*intellegere*),[10] Calvin marks the text as a product of his own interpretive activity.[11] This gesture brings to the discussion a sense of authorial humility by implying that the content of the discourse to follow simply represents his own personal understanding of the issue at hand. In addition to disarming the audience in this fashion, this same clause rhetorically contributes to the construction of the polemical space previously outlined: by qualifying the text as his own interpretation, Calvin implicitly admits the possibility of other ways of understanding.

However, the identification of author and text, its humble tone, and the admission of possible difference do not themselves provide fortification of Calvin's own authority. This move comes in the second sentence where the proposition that there can be no knowledge of God apart from *pietas* is qualified by the adverbial phrase, "properly speaking" (*proprie loquendo*). By immediately following his assertion of authorial rights over the text with the claim that the text speaks "properly," Calvin cleverly legitimates his own voice alone in a field of possible voices. Consequently, the reader must affirm both Calvin's humility and his unquestionable authority. In sum, by entering the text as "I," Calvin identifies his role as an interpretive one; he thus humbly marks the text as his own while simultaneously admitting a diversity of interpretations, which he then subverts with his own claim to "speak properly."

As a way of concluding this discussion of the first two lines of Calvin's second chapter in the *Institutes*, let me briefly review a list of the functions this chapter appears to have been designed to serve. First, its most obvious function is to examine the unique type of religious disposition known as *pietas*, a term that Calvin sets in a distinctly rhetorical framework. Second, the rhetoric of these opening lines suggests that Calvin will develop his examination of *pietas* with respect to three different audiences: he will pursue a pedagogical agenda with regard to his students; he will continue his apologetic engagement of the more moderate humanists; and he will launch a polemical attack against a certain group of fringe humanists whom he identifies as "Epicureans." Third, it appears that Calvin will use his rhetorical skills to establish the character of his own authorial power and position.

The First Wave

The first "rhetorical wave" of chapter 2 begins with the two introductory sentences I have just examined. In these sentences, Calvin introduces his definition of *pietas* for the first time. Following this short definition, Calvin continues in an expository mode as he directs the reader's attention away from the effects of the knowledge "on us" and toward the "object" of the knowledge, God. In one long sentence, he speaks of two basic types of knowledge of the divine: one that had as its original source "the very order of nature" (*genuinus naturae ordo*) but is now lost on us, "the accursed" (*maledicti*); the other, a knowledge in which we "apprehend God the Redeemer in Christ the Mediator" (*Deum redemptorem in Christo mediatore apprehendere*). Calvin writes:

> I do not yet touch upon the sort of knowledge with which men, in themselves lost and accursed, apprehend God the Redeemer in Christ the Mediator; but I speak only of the primal and simple knowledge to which the very order of nature would have led us if Adam had remained upright. (*Inst.* 1.1.1, p. 40; OS 3:34.10–14)

By shifting from a discussion of "our disposition" to a discussion of the "divine object" that evokes this disposition, the text accomplishes several things. First, the reader is presented for the first time in the *Institutes* with a short narrative of the story that will structure the remainder of Book 1 and Book 2: the story of creation, fall, and redemption.[12] Similarly, by bracketing all present knowledge of God under the revelation in Christ, the text is laying important groundwork for Calvin's discussion of human sin in Book 2. However, given its explicative tone and the presence of directional comments that invoke the identity of Calvin the pedagogue, one may infer that the text's principal concern is that of further explaining to the reader the source of this knowledge called *pietas* and the nature of its content. This second sentence thus follows as a logical extension of the two preceding introductory sentences. In addition, by moving the reader's gaze from self to God, it serves a transitional function as Calvin prepares the reader for the next phase of his argument.

Beginning with the adverb "nevertheless" (*tanem*), the following sentence decisively initiates the second phase of Calvin's first rhetorical "wave." It begins,

> Nevertheless, it is one thing to feel that God as our Maker supports us by his power, governs us by his providence, nourishes us by his goodness, and attends us with all sorts of blessings—and another thing to embrace the grace of reconciliation offered to us in Christ. (*Inst.* 1.1.1, p. 40; OS 3:34.17–21)

The use of "nevertheless" informs the reader that this new stage of Calvin's discussion should take precedence over the first one, and it is distinguished from the former in several ways. First, the tone of the text has changed from a tone of explication to one of exhortation. (This is particularly apparent in the sermonically repetitive rhythm of its syntax.) The reader is thus drawn into a different relation to the text. Gone are the sporadic third-person references of the previous statements; gone are the more explicative references to God as "the Redeemer" (*redemptor*) and the "author of salvation" (*salutis author*). Here, God is identified as "our Maker" (*fictor noster*) and depicted not in the propositional language of the introduction but through a series of confessionally generated images. Through these shifts in vocabulary and tone, Calvin moves the reader from the position of student into the play of a distinctly edifying rhetoric. Conversely, if the reader is identified as the text's polemical adversary, this movement encourages his or her increased marginalization as the tone of the text mocks any attempt at atheistic posturing.

Paralleling these changes in tone is an equally remarkable shift in the actual content of the images deployed and the "arguments" they present. The text moves from a simple definition of the quality and conditions of true knowledge to an actual enactment of its terms. Given that Calvin has already told the reader that the disposition of *pietas* involves being convinced of the personal benefits one gains from God's love and care, he is now ready to persuasively induce the disposition of *pietas* by enticing the reader with a list of those benefits. God "supports us by his power, governs us by his providence, nourishes us by his goodness and attends us with all sorts of blessings." Moreover, in this series of descriptive comments, "we" are depicted in the active role of receiving them, of being convinced and thereby "feeling" (*sentire*) and "embracing" (*amplecti*) the knowledge offered. Thus, Calvin not only presents the reader with the "benefits" of such knowledge, he also delineates the response appropriate for one who receives such understanding. If his audience has followed Calvin's directives, then the play of mind now induced is one of doxological awe.

Having taken the reader to the heights of *pietas,* this wave of appeal begins to recede. Continuing to focus on God, the next two sentences remind the reader of the threefold source of this knowledge: "First, as much in the fashioning of the universe as in the general teaching of Scripture the Lord shows himself to be simply Creator. Then, in the face of Christ he shows himself the Redeemer" (*Inst.* 1.2.1, p. 40; OS 3:34.21–24). However, in contrast to the previous statement, the tone and language of the text have now shifted back into the more pedantic pace of the explicative. In the next sentence, this becomes even more apparent. "Of the resulting twofold knowledge of God we shall now discuss the first aspect; the second will be dealt with in its proper place (proper place—*suus ordo*)" (*Inst.* 1.2.1, p. 40; OS 3:34.24–25). Thus, having moved from a rhetoric of explication to one of exhortation, then returning to the initial activity of defining and explaining, the first wave of Calvin's argument has concluded.

The Second Wave

The sentence following this explicative comment begins "moreover" (*autem*), thus indicating a continuation of the chapter's central "argument." Calvin then states,

> Although our mind cannot apprehend God without rendering some honor to him, it will not suffice simply to hold that there is One whom all ought to honor and adore, unless we are also persuaded that he is the fountain of every good, and that we must seek nothing elsewhere than in him. (*Inst.* 1.2.1, p. 40; OS 3:34.30–37)

With this statement, the text once again returns to the discussion that initiated the chapter. Calvin's concern here, as in his introductory sentences, is to explicate a definition of the religious disposition *pietas*, and, in doing so, he again alludes to the text's polemical undercurrent. Taking up the argument presented by Cotta the philosopher against Vellius the Epicurean in Cicero's *De natura deorum*, Calvin argues that honor and adoration of the divine are predicated upon some sense of God's providential care.[13] In addition to echoing this Ciceronian subtext, the use of the verb "persuade" (*persuadere*) to portray the activity of religious knowing recalls Cicero's *Orator* and its emphasis on persuasive dimensions of understanding. However, this second way of defining *pietas* moves beyond Calvin's initial definition by adding a new term to the list of dispositions that characterize true piety. Here, Calvin equates effective persuasion with obedience. This new emphasis on obedience will become more fully developed as the force of the second wave continues to build.

In the following sentence, the second wave begins to grow in intensity:

> This I take to mean that not only does he sustain this universe (as he once founded it) by his boundless might, regulate it by his wisdom, preserve it by his goodness, and especially rule mankind by his righteousness

and judgment, bear with it in his mercy, watch over it by his protection; but also that no drop will be found either of wisdom and light, or of righteousness or power or rectitude, or of genuine truth, which does not flow from him, and of which he is not the cause. (*Inst.* 1.2.1, pp. 40–41; OS 3:34.30–37)

The statement's beginning, "This I take to mean" (*Hoc ita accipio*), again signals the text's status as interpretation and thereby heightens its polemical tone by suggesting the possibility of other interpretations of the same issue. What Calvin then proceeds to interpret, however, is not a further insight into the nature of *pietas*, but rather a description of actions of the God whom "we" must "honor and adore" (*colere et adorare*). Thus, the reader's attention is once again turned away from his or her own disposition and riveted upon the object of knowledge itself. As before, this shift coincides with a change in tone. With the rhythm and images of doxology, Calvin praises the powers of God. At length, he draws out eight specific virtues of the divine and their particular benefit "for us": "boundless might," regulating "wisdom," preserving "goodness," judgmental "righteousness," "mercy," "protection," "truth," and "rectitude," all of which highlight the scope and strength of God's rule (*regere*).[14] This emphasis on God's sovereign authority represents a step beyond the scope of predominantly "merciful" virtues praised in the first wave and corresponds to the emphasis on obedience and submission just introduced. Continuing in the doxological voice, the next two sentences then depict the disposition appropriate to the one persuaded, both by the breadth of God's reign and by Calvin's textual disclosure of it. "We" are to "learn to await and seek all these things from him, and thankfully ascribe them, once received, to him" (*Inst.* 1.2.1, p. 41; OS 3:34.37–39). In this movement from explication to exhortation, Calvin has once more turned from simply defining *pietas* to rhetorically enacting the conditions of its emergence.

As in the preceding wave, the high-pitched tone of his rhetoric slowly begins to wane as he returns the reader to the initial task of elaborating a definition of *pietas*, which now incorporates the insights generated by the previous doxology. Summarizing the use to which the audience should put their knowledge of God's virtues, Calvin inaugurates this stage with the claim that this sense of "the powers of God" is for us "a fit teacher of piety" (*idoneus pietatis magister*) from which "religion is born" (*Inst.* 1.2.1, p. 41; OS 3:35.2–3). This statement also serves as a summary of what the text itself has just attempted to enact, a teaching aimed at invoking *pietas*. Then, in the following sentence, the reader is presented with a concise definition of the term at issue. Entering the text once again as author, Calvin writes, "I call 'piety' that reverence joined with love of God which the knowledge of his benefits induces" (*Inst.* 1.2.1, p. 41; OS 3:35.3–5).[15]

In the two sentences that conclude the first paragraph, Calvin reiterates one last time the underlying anthropological assumption upon which he has constructed his conception of "our knowledge of God." He explains,

For until men recognize that they owe everything to God, that they are nourished by his fatherly care, that he is the Author of their every good, that they should seek nothing beyond him—they will never yield him willing service. Nay, unless they establish their complete happiness in him, they will never give themselves truly and sincerely to him. (*Inst.* 1.2.1, p. 41; OS 3:35.5–10)

The assumption here is that one will render honor to God only if one is persuaded of God's sovereign rule and providential care. The necessity of grasping this particular type of knowledge appears to stem from a prior assumption that persons are most aptly persuaded by appeals to self-interest and that a description of God's providence most effectively makes such an appeal. This assumption of self-interest is, incidentally, in direct line with Cicero's teaching on the matter; and it gives further insight into aspects of Calvin's anthropology that are not addressed in his more explicit discussion of human nature but nonetheless inform his understanding of the motives and tensions that shape the human will and hence shape his rhetorical attempts to persuade this will.

In the process of constructing this second wave of appeal, Calvin continues to play with language in some rather interesting ways. As I have previously suggested, Calvin frequently uses the vocabulary of "rhetoric" to describe God's relation to the world. In this chapter, the dramatic blending of a narrative of God's communication with a narrative of rhetorical appeal is readily apparent. For instance, Calvin works out his description of "the way we come to knowledge of God" in language suggesting the scene of a public oration. In this oratorical scene, Calvin depicts God as primarily relating to people as the giver of knowledge, as the one who speaks. Furthermore, the knowledge that is directed toward people has as its goal eliciting not only a passive understanding but also a dispositional transformation. This knowledge thus represents a "useful knowledge" (*expedire* + *notitia*), deployed to "compel" (*oportet*), "persuade" (*persuadere*), "induce" (*conciliare*), and thereby "teach" (*magister*) people.

Viewed in these terms, God appears as the Grand Orator and "we" (the readers) become God's captive audience. Moreover, Calvin describes the actual content of the rhetoric by which persuasion is accomplished as the "powers of God" (*virtutes Dei*) and, consequently, as the history of God's acts on humanity's behalf. But the persuasive force of God's rhetoric, according to Calvin, is not immediately apparent to people. It must be accommodated to human limitations and needs. Thus, as Calvin describes it, this speech comes to its human audience in the tangible forms of scripture, creation, and Christ the Mediator. When viewed through the lens of classical rhetoric then, the "powers" represent the content of the orator's argument, or *inventio*, and the three mediating sources of scripture, creation, and Christ the Mediator appear as the ornamentation of God's actual rhetoric. In other words, these mediating sources represent the style, rhythm, tone, and texture of God's discourse.

God's accommodation to humanity also includes God's willingness to persuade by promising gifts and benefits. In this case, the presentation of the breadth of God's providential rule is precipitated by Calvin's belief that such an argument is necessary to persuade a self-interested audience to turn everything over to the divine.[16] Similarly, the discourse is driven by a very particular goal. Calvin addresses "us" with a specific end in view, namely, the turning of ourselves over to God, "to yield him willing service," "to establish our complete happiness in him," and "to seek nothing elsewhere than in him" (*Inst.* 1.2.1, p. 41; OS 3:35.7–9). This concern to transform the audience dispositionally in the process of addressing them also finds its parallel in the civic context of Cicero's discussion of oration. For him, an orator never simply conceives a speech in a vacuum but instead shapes it with his eye carefully fixed on the public actions toward which his discourse will move its appraising recipients. Thus, when considered alongside Cicero's views, the images and arguments that structure this second wave support the claim that rhetoric is not just descriptive of Calvin's activity in constructing the text; it is also determinative of the conceptual arena from which his doctrine of God emerges.

In the context of this second wave of rhetorical appeal, Calvin also continues to work out the persona he intends to assume as author through a series of clever and subtle moves. These gestures revolve around the slippery task of identifying "the orator." As stated above, at one level, God is depicted by Calvin as "the orator," and the scriptures, creation, and Jesus Christ are imaged as the language through which God's oratorical "argument" is adorned and mediated. However, as I have also illustrated, the text itself engages in repeated attempts to induce the reader into a position of obedience and praise. In this way, the text is rhetorically mimicking the activity of divine persuasion. And throughout this enactment, who is depicted as the orator? It is Calvin who enters the text. "I understand," "I take to mean," "I speak," and "I call" all describe his presence as the one who has generated "the rhetorical waves" that now persuade. Whose authority, then, does the text really invoke?

The ambiguity produced by this overlay of Calvin's identity with that of the divine appears most clearly in one of the pivotal statements of this section. Having described the wealth of God's powers and benefits, Calvin states: "For this sense of the powers of God is for us a fit teacher of piety." Here, a surface reading first points to God as the teacher toward whom the student of divine knowledge is called to turn. However, the qualifying phrase, "for this sense," complicates matters. The reference to "this sense" implies the possibility of other "senses" of the topic at hand while simultaneously marking the particular "sense" rendered in the text as an interpretive product. And it is Calvin as interpreter and author who has just rendered for the audience this instructive "sense." Following the logic of this reading, the student is thus induced to take as *magister* both the textual author and the Author of salvation and creation. And this confusion of identities in turn causes a series of other displacements to occur. Much to the textual author's advantage, the previous equation of effective persuasion and subservient obedience secures for Calvin the dutiful allegiance of his readership just as it secures for the divine author their "willing service." In other words, whether or not the logic of the tradition allows it, this rhetorical interfacing permits both "orators" to profit from the claim to power belonging to the One who providentially rules all.

The significance of the authorial power seized by Calvin through these discursive workings becomes apparent when viewed in the context of the historical audiences to whom he was speaking. By weaving together divine and authorial identity, Calvin has performed a clever double play with regard to the audience of the already-committed: his students, his Swiss and German colleagues in the reforming movement, and his comrades in the French evangelical community.[17] The first part of this double play concerns Calvin's depiction of God's power and rule. By invoking divine authority in terms of sovereign rule, the text implicitly subverts all competing claims for allegiance or power. This would have been particularly important for those persons in the reforming movement who were being persecuted under the rule of the king of France. As the rhetoric of the second wave implies, it is to God alone that all obedience should be rendered. By asserting this in the manner he does, Calvin cleverly makes a rhetorical space in which resistance to the dominant authorities of church and crown could be justified.

Yet there is another side to this double play. While Calvin may have wished to undermine the authority of the Roman church and the French crown, he had to be careful not to undermine inadvertently the grounds for his own authority as a political and ecclesiastical voice for reform. The way in which he constructs the rhetoric of the chapter allows him to accomplish both things simultaneously. By blending the rhetoric of divine rule with a rhetoric that supports his own authorial power as the one who speaks and thereby disposes the audience toward obedience, Calvin establishes both the sovereignty of God (and hence the undermining of all other authorities) and the terms of his own claims to the audience's allegiance. In this manner, Calvin is able to hold together both his concern to thwart the claims of a hostile power by invoking divine sovereignty and his concern to deploy a rhetoric that protects his own social location.

In addition to appealing to his faithful followers, Calvin also continues to work out both his apologetic agendas in this second wave of appeal. In terms of Calvin's attempt to court and convert the sympathies of moderate humanists in the French aristocracy, the rhetoric of this wave suggests he is continuing his quest to garner their approval and support. The presence of the Ciceronian subtext, *De natura deorum*, would have appealed to those humanists who might have been impressed by Calvin's subtle wrestling with this highly honored classical text. Similarly, the description Calvin gives of the divine in his doxological interlude is couched in a "rhetorical" language that Cicero himself could have embraced. It is entirely void of distinctly biblical imagery, and the "powers" of God that Calvin applauds are powers any Stoic philosopher would have eagerly affirmed. Thus, through language such as this, Calvin continues to court his humanist colleagues.

The Third Wave

What is God? Men who pose this question are merely toying with idle speculations. (*Inst.* 1.2.2, p. 41; OS 3:35.11–12)

Up to this point in the chapter, Calvin has largely carried out his attack on the Epicureans through the subtle echoing of Cicero's dialogue combined with smatterings of dialectical argumentation. But even those who are unacquainted with Cicero or unimpressed by the subtlety of Calvin's dialectic thus far will have no doubt about the polemical nature of this discussion after reading the opening sentence of the second paragraph. Bringing the battle to the surface of the text, Calvin begins the third wave of his argument by mockingly asking his audience, "What is God?" Since Calvin has just repudiated the kind of religious knowledge that remains content with simply conceiving of God's existence, the reader is immediately alerted to the ironic thrust of this obviously hypothetical question. Further, in asking a question that only his opponent would have asked, Calvin invites the voice of the adversary to enter the text. The entrance of this voice suggests an opponent close enough to engage in the debate. Hence, the faces of Calvin's contemporary foes come to mind. Yet, even as he brings these faces into focus, he rhetorically gains the advantage. Insofar as the adversarial voice is heard only as it is mockingly echoed through the voice of the author, Calvin deploys a rhetorical gesture that itself enacts a textual conquest of the formerly implied and now admitted adversary.

In the following sentence, the intensity of this attack is heightened as Calvin begins to chastise the enemies whose question he has just sarcastically asked. He refers to them in the third person as "men" who in asking such questions are merely "toying with idle speculations." Using one of Seneca's favored adjectives to describe the hedonistic frivolity of the Epicureans, the author belittles his opponents' philosophizing as "toying" (*ludere*). He further characterizes their speculations as "idle" (*frigidus*), a term used frequently by Cicero to describe language that lacks energy and vigor or, more precisely, rhetorical arguments that fail to produce the intended effect. Thus, even in the heat of this attack, the conceptual arena of rhetoric serves as the measure against which the enemy's position is assessed. Their speculations are mocked, not because they are misdirected or false, but because they lack persuasive force.

In the next sentence, the focus of Calvin's argument shifts. Changing from the third-person language used in his direct assault to the first-person appeal used when addressing his comrades, he states, "It is more important for us to know what sort he is and what is consistent with his nature" (*Inst.* 1.2.2, p. 41; OS 3:35.11–12). The juxtaposition of this proposition aimed at the "we" with the preceding attack on the more distanced "men" reemphasizes the combative nature of the discourse. It thus contributes to the now overtly polemical agenda of the paragraph by positioning the reader on Calvin's side while further marginalizing his opponent.

However, in addition to extending Calvin's polemical agenda, the clearly propositional and therefore instructive tone of this statement also suggests a shift to a more distinctly dogmatic and pedagogical agenda. When viewed in this way, the preceding polemic appears to function not only as an assault but as an effective pretext for clarifying his own constructive project. Against the contrasting backdrop of "idle speculations," Calvin is able to explicate more clearly his definition of true knowledge of God, an explication constructed for the benefit of the faithful. With regard to these two different ways of reading the rhetorical movement of the text at this point, Calvin offers the reader no clear evidence as to which agenda takes precedence, the polemical or the dogmatic/pedagogical, the rhetoric of attack or the rhetoric of appeal. And as the argument of chapter 2 progresses, this is an ambiguity Calvin will continue to exploit.

In contrast to the propositional form of the preceding statement, the fourth sentence resumes the paragraph's tactic of frontal assault. Resorting once again to his interrogative voice, Calvin now pulls his readers into the assault upon the Epicureans by directly asking them a question in which their suggested "profession" of the enemy's position is denounced. Finally revealing the identity of his opponent, he inquires, "What good is it to profess with Epicurus some sort of God who has cast aside the care of the world only to amuse himself in idleness?" (*Inst.* 1.2.2, p. 41; OS 3:35.14–15).[18] The lack of explanatory statements surrounding Calvin's reference to Epicurus leads one to believe that the name was quite familiar to the sixteenth-century academy. And although on the surface his reference harkens back to the classical world of Cicero and the Epicureans, this implied familiarity contributes to the sense that Calvin is engaging in a contemporary debate. Rehashing the point of his question in the following sentence, he continues, "What help is it, in short, to know a God with whom we have nothing to do?" (*Inst.* 1.2.2, p. 41; OS 3:35.16–17). As with his previous denunciation, Calvin critiques the opposition on the basis of a conception of religious knowledge formulated within the conceptual arena of rhetoric. He argues against the Epicureans that a God without a providential relation to the world is of no "help" (*iuvare*) to humanity and hence lacks the qualities necessary to persuade people to belief. In *De natura deorum*, Cicero similarly claims that people need to believe in a benevolent God who interacts with the world in order that they might be compelled to worship.[19] Thus, Calvin relies on his knowledge of rhetoric as well as his reader's familiarity with its history to advance his own position in the current debate.

Having just brought the face of the enemy clearly into focus, Calvin once more juxtaposes this obviously polemical gesture with a rhetoric of a more instructive and confessional character in the following sentence:

> Rather, our knowledge should serve first to teach us fear and reverence; secondly, with it as our guide and teacher, we should learn to seek every good from him, and, having received it, to credit it to his account. (*Inst.* 1.2.2, pp. 41–42; OS 3:35.17–20)

Turning to "us," Calvin again exploits the technical language of oratory to describe a contrasting form of knowledge that serves as "our guide and teacher" (*dux ac magister*) and thereby "teaches us fear and reverence" in the hope that "we should learn to seek every good from him."[20] The instructive tone of this assertion is quite apparent when contrasted with his previously ironic tone. Deploying a common pedagogical device, the author carefully numbers the points he is making. Further, the confluence of the assertion that "our knowledge teaches us reverence and fear" and the text's unspoken but obvious rhetorical intention to "teach us" (*instituere*) contributes to the productive confusion of authorial and divine identity. Thus, once again, Calvin secures a certain degree of authority for himself by describing God's action in terms that simultaneously represent the nature of his own present textual relation to the audience.

With this last sentence, the first stage of Calvin's argument in this third "rhetorical wave" concludes. As with the initial stages of the two preceding waves of appeal, he introduces the third wave of his address by returning the audience's attention to the task of the chapter, namely, defining the character of "our knowledge of God." Using the same strategy as in previous paragraphs, he develops this definition against the backdrop of an opposing position. However, in contrast to the subtlety of his former argument, in this third wave the opponent is explicitly named. Subsequently, the polemical agenda of the discussion is brought into clear focus. At the same time as he sharpens the focus of this agenda, however, he also continues to advance, through a succession of short and pointed contrasts, a rhetoric that appeals more directly to the sentiments of those he considers allies and students. His swift movement back and forth between a polemical agenda and this more instructive and dogmatic interest heightens the sense of the double-edged character of his discourse. At the conclusion of this initial phase of the third wave, the audience has thus been positioned before a textual orator who speaks both to his ever-faithful body of believers and to a more ominous group of Epicurean adversaries hovering somewhere outside, but nonetheless nearby, the world of the text and the reader.

The text then moves on to the second phase of its appeal. As in the earlier waves, a series of more exhortative pronouncements follows on the heels of the opening explicative comments. Here, Calvin puts before his audience both the beneficial attributes of God and the disposition appropriate to one persuaded to worship. In this section, the exhortation takes the form of an extended rhetorical question in which Calvin repeatedly asks the reader, in an aggressive tone, how one could conceive of God but not simultaneously render God total obedience. He demands,

> For how can the thought of God penetrate your mind without your realizing immediately that, since you are his handiwork, you have been made over and bound to his command by right of creation, that you owe your life to him?—that whatever you undertake, whatever you do, ought to be ascribed to him? (*Inst.* 1.2.2, p. 42; OS 3:35.20–24)

In a form of address rarely found in the text, Calvin here directly engages his readership as "you." Given both the offensive and sermonic qualities of the interrogation, it is not immediately apparent whether these remarks are directed at friend or foe. Either possibility is rhetorically plausible in light of both the polemical and pedagogical agendas of his previous comments. In relation to the Epicurean opponent, the question could be interpreted as an extension of Calvin's attack, thus moving against the reader with the force of a hostile cross-examination. For the faithful, on the other hand, it would more likely resound with the passion of a pastoral plea, thereby advancing the reformer's dogmatic agenda. Once again, the ambiguity of the text at this point is quite suggestive.

Equally provocative is the legal language that Calvin now uses to define the relation of "you" to the divine. Recalling the vocabulary of his earlier work on Seneca and hence drawing directly from the field of Roman jurisprudence, he describes people as being "made over and bound" (*addictus et mancipatus*) to God's "command" (*imperium*). In classical Latin, *addictus* refers to an act of enslavement or surrender, and *mancipatus* in the language of Roman property law denotes a legal transference of ownership. Both terms describe "your" relation to God's *imperium*, traditionally understood as the supreme administrative power held by a king or emperor alone. And this command is described further as God's *ipso creationis iure*, "according to the law of creation."

How one assesses the impact of these images upon the audience depends on whether one reads Calvin's questioning as a hostile cross-examination or a pastoral appeal. On the one hand, to transfer language reserved for king's rights to the rights of the divine might work to subvert the political rhetoric that supported the rights of earthly kings. If so, Calvin is advancing his polemical agenda by challenging the rhetoric implicated in the political maneuvering of his Epicurean opponents. On the other hand, when viewed from the perspective of the faithful, a community in which many pastors were being imprisoned for treason, Calvin's depiction of the believer's enslavement to and ownership by the divine and not the king may have served as a renunciation of similar "enslavements" by lesser powers. The legal language would have thereby functioned to support and comfort those whom the text portrays as being oppressed by the actions of earthly kings.

In the next sentence, Calvin begins the third and final phase of this wave of appeal. He steps away from his previous exhortative interlude and begins to summarize the points he has made:

> If this be so, it now assuredly follows that your life is wickedly corrupt unless it be disposed to his service, seeing that his will ought for us to be the law by which we live. Again, you cannot behold him clearly unless you acknowledge him to be the fountainhead and source of every good. From this too would arise the desire to cleave to him and trust in him, but for the fact that man's depravity seduces his mind from rightly seeking him. (*Inst.* 1.2.2, p. 42; OS 3:35.24–36.5)

Calvin uses this series of remarks to generate further insights into the nature of *pietas*. His beginning, *Id si est* (If this be so), signals the audience that the previous statement is to serve as evidence. He then proceeds to explicate further his definition of religious knowledge in language that engages the reader through both an aggressive assault and a supportive affirmation. Given the force of his previous polemic, Calvin's first statement resounds with the denunciatory tone of a direct attack—here aimed at the Epicurean adversary: "It now assuredly follows that your life is wickedly corrupt." Then, returning to his larger audience of committed followers, he qualifies this statement to give discursive space to their affirmation and support. He allows that the pronouncement of wickedness holds "unless [your life] be disposed to his service, seeing that his will ought to be the law by which we live." The following sentence follows a similar structure. Beginning with the negative claim "you cannot behold him," Calvin severely reprimands his opponent and then returns to his allies with the qualifier "unless you acknowledge him to be the fountainhead and source of every good." On this note, he concludes the final expository phase of the third wave of appeal and thus leaves his readers either emotionally castigated and blinded to knowledge of God (if they happen to be among the Epicureans) or affectively uplifted by the promise of true vision (if they are among the blessed and pious).

The Fourth Wave

Thus far, this reading of chapter 2 has suggested that the structured waves that constitute the text's argument are one of the central rhetorical motifs of Calvin's appeal. In this final section of the chapter, this same wave structure operates yet again, but in this fourth instance, it moves through the three stages with a clarity and directness not found in earlier discussions.

The first stage of this wave begins with a lengthy description of the contemplative activities proper to a truly "pious mind" (*pia mens*):

> For, to begin with, the pious mind does not dream up for itself any god it pleases, but contemplates the one and only true God. And it does not attach to him whatever it pleases, but is content to hold him to be as he manifests himself; furthermore, the mind always exercises the utmost diligence and care not to wander astray, or rashly and boldly go beyond his will. (*Inst.* 1.2.2, p. 42; OS 3:36.5–10)

In its initial stage, the pedagogical and explicative focus of the text is made manifest by the series of directional comments that carefully guide the reader through a set of new insights into the ever-expanding definition of *pietas*. Adopting the "pious mind" as the subject of his explication, the author portrays an ideal instance of appropriate religious disposition. Such a mind does not conjure up a God suited only to its own needs and desires, but rather endeavors to behold God through God's chosen act of self-revelation. And if such contemplation is always constrained by the limits of God's revelatory act, it reflects the workings of the pious mind that avoids the temptation to speculate "rashly and boldly" about God's will or being.

Following these expository comments, the text offers a summary statement that serves as a transition between the explicative and the exhortative. Calvin tells the reader that the pious mind "recognizes God because it knows that he governs all things; and trusts that he is its guide and protector, therefore giving itself over completely to trust in him" (*Inst.*

1.2.2, p. 42; OS 3:36.10–12). In both tone and content, the sentence extends the expository agenda that is characteristic of the first stage of the argument. But it also serves as a prototype for the four exhortative descriptions that follow. In these sentences, the reader is once again moved out of the classroom and positioned before the pulpit of a preacher who proclaims passionately,

> Because it understands him to be the Author of every good, if anything oppresses, if anything is lacking, immediately it betakes itself to his protection, waiting for help from him. Because it is persuaded that he is good and merciful, it reposes in him with perfect trust and doubts not that in his loving-kindness a remedy will be provided for all its ills. Because it acknowledges him as Lord and Father, the pious mind also deems it meet and right to observe his authority in all things, reverence his majesty, take care to advance his glory, and obey his commandments. Because it sees him to be righteous judge, armed with severity to punish wickedness, it ever holds his judgment seat before its gaze, and through fear of him restrains itself from provoking his anger. (*Inst.* 1.2.2, pp. 42–43; OS 3:36.12–23)

The use of a repetitive syntax and grammar gives this series of remarks a patently sermonic quality. Further, the text forfeits any pretense of careful explication. Instead, it imports a vast array of images to build its emotive appeal. In each sentence, Calvin draws from a different pool of theological metaphors and images, each connected to the other in its rhythm and structure. In this manner, the author once again shifts from an exposition of the nature of *pietas* to a rigorous attempt to evoke rhetorically the attitude just described.

Just as this stylistic form aims to move the reader into the disposition of *pietas*, the actual content of these four descriptive exhortations is presented in a way that not only explains the nature of God but also attempts to invoke the reader's praise of this God. In each of these sentences Calvin describes the powers of God in terms that emphasize their beneficial or useful character, thus accommodating his appeal to the self-interested temperament of the reader. God, as Author of every good, protects people from oppression; as a God of mercy, God provides a remedy for people's ills; as Lord and Father, God rules over all things; and as righteous judge, God has the authority and power to punish.[21] Calvin depicts each of these acts of God as being accommodated to a specific human condition. He depicts the pious mind as being effectively persuaded by these powers. It acknowledges (*agnoscere*) him, it is persuaded (*persuaderi*) by him, it understands (*intelligere*) him, and therefore it truly sees (*videre*) him. If the reader finds herself or himself reflected in these activities of the pious mind, then the normative force of Calvin's description is clear: "we" are to be likewise.

Finally, in addition to highlighting the benefits of God's power and people's effective persuasion by them, Calvin rehearses the corresponding disposition of one thus affected. One "reposes in him with perfect trust"; "the pious mind also deems it meet and right to observe his authority . . . and obey his commandments"; and "it ever holds his judgment seat before its gaze." In each of these instances, Calvin moves beyond a simple explanation of "what it is to know God" and takes up the task of exhortation in order to make this knowledge a reality in the life of the one who holds it. Once again, this utterance fully exploits the rhetorical power of both style and content to accomplish its ends.

As with the previous waves, the exhortation abruptly ends, and the text now shifts back into the expository mode. Calvin concludes the argument of the entire chapter by offering a summary definition of *pietas:*

> Here indeed is pure and real religion: faith so joined with an earnest fear of God that this fear also embraces willing reverence, and carries with it such legitimate worship as is prescribed in the law. (*Inst.* 1.2.2, p. 43; OS 3:37.7–10)

In the light of the rhetorical logic that has driven the text through the preceding two paragraphs, it is now apparent that the argumentative case upon which this culminating definition rests is of a peculiar sort. Calvin has not brought the reader to this conclusion only by means of a carefully reasoned argument, complete with warrants and supporting evidence. Nor has he crafted an argument based principally on an appeal to common experience. Rather, his concluding definition of *pietas* rests primarily upon the evidence offered in Calvin's own exhortative interludes. It is the textually proclaimed "powers of God" (*potentia Dei*) that convince the reader that pure and real religion requires faith joined with "earnest fear" (*serius timor*). Similarly, it is Calvin's exhortative description of the obedient disposition appropriate to one persuaded of God's authority that justifies his claim that *pietas* requires "such legitimate worship as prescribed in the law." Thus, it is Calvin's sermonic description of the life of faith, rather than an argument grounded in propositional logic, that decisively funds his final theological assertion.

Having traced the three-phased wave structure of this section, I shall now return to the three other textual functions that have been traced throughout the previous sections and see how they are played out in the context of Calvin's fourth wave of appeal. In terms of the first textual function, the function of defining *pietas,* I have already highlighted the various ways in which Calvin continues to focus his understanding of *pietas* through a distinctly rhetorical lens. In addition, my analysis of this wave has shown how Calvin continues to focus his depiction of God's revealing activity through the lens of rhetoric as well. He portrays God as reaching out to compel and persuade the creature to obedience through the promise of divine benefits. He also depicts God as accommodating these benefits to the specific needs of the creature, needs such as security, wellness, and protection. Similarly, he characterizes the creature's response in terms of the disposition evoked by God's rhetorical outreaching. The pious creature is portrayed as obeying, trusting, waiting, seeking, and rendering praise to the One from whom these benefits have come. In all these ways, Calvin continues to develop his notion of God as the Grand Orator and believers as God's receptive audience.

In terms of the second textual function, the more political and concrete social function of the text, Calvin continues to deploy a rhetoric that is capable of simultaneously negotiating the terms of his pedagogical, polemical, confessional, and apologetic agendas. At the conclusion of the third wave of appeal, I noted that by rapidly alternating his attack on the Epicureans with a rhetoric of appeal and comfort directed to a more friendly community, Calvin accustoms his readers to the double-edged nature of his pronouncements. Now, in this fourth and final wave of appeal, Calvin continues to utilize the double-edged appeal as he attempts both to strengthen the faithful with promises of God's mercy and protection and to frighten the unfaithful with the announcement of God's wrath.

In the first two of the four statements that constitute his impassioned appeal, the author uses a language of comfort and promise. He portrays God as merciful protector and defender of the oppressed. The virtues of divine loving-kindness and steadfastness are emphasized, and the providence of God is depicted chiefly as evidence of God's ability to protect. In response to these powers of God, the pious mind, as Calvin describes it, waits for help from God, reposes in him with perfect trust, and, finally, finds in him a "remedy" for all its ills. As such images suggest, this description of God's care and protection would have resonated powerfully in the context of a community that perceived itself as under assault and in need of defense. In this regard, it employs a language best suited to the community of evangelical readers who faced the continued threat of persecution in the French provinces and in exile.

In contrast to the promise and shelter provided by the rhetoric of these two sentences, the two sentences that follow represent a radical shift in both the tone and texture of Calvin's language. While still respecting the exhortative form of the earlier sentences, his rhetoric is now cast in a decidedly harsher mold. Here, Calvin deploys the same legal images used in his previous attack on the Epicurean humanists to portray God as Lord and Righteous judge. The virtues of God's omnipotence and majesty come to the fore and the Sovereign appears as easily provoked to anger and armed with severity to punish wickedness. Further, the breadth of God's providential rule now serves as evidence of the strength of God's wrath.

And in the shadow of these images, the pious mind is described as taking care to advance his glory, as obeying his commandments, and most important, as restraining itself from exciting God's rage. Given the previous vituperative encounters with Calvin's textually invoked adversary, this language immediately suggests an Epicurean audience as the target of attack. It thus serves the polemical agenda Calvin has been developing since the beginning of the chapter.

As if to emphasize the double-edged character of his exhortation, Calvin follows these pronouncements with a series of clarifying comments that distinguish between two kinds of activity undertaken by God in relation to the creature. Insofar as God's activities or powers are for Calvin the rhetoric of God, these activities can also be understood as two distinct forms of divine persuasion. Calvin begins by describing the pious mind as embracing God, first, as "the punisher of the wicked," and, second, as "the benefactor of the pious." With this distinction, he makes it clear that the rhetoric of judgment is not to be directed toward the pious, the category within which he has taken care to place his sympathetic readership. Rather, it is the hope of life eternal that works to persuade them. Similarly, the rhetoric of promise and comfort must not be mistakenly applied to those who oppose God. For them, a rhetoric of punishment and wrath is unquestionably the appropriate one.

Calvin reiterates the same point in the following sentence, "For the pious mind realizes that the punishment of the impious and wicked and reward of life eternal for the righteous equally pertain to God's glory." On the basis of Calvin's previous attempts to expose the impiety of his Epicurean adversary, it is not difficult for the reader to provide a historical face for Calvin's threat at this point. Nor is it difficult to supply a historical referent for those persons to whom the promise of eternal life applies. Thus, by reaffirming the twofold agenda of his discourse, the author textually militates against a reading that would have either the faithful threatened with God's wrath or the enemy embraced by God's promise. Consequently, if the reader is not attentive to these distinctions, the theological thrust of the entire chapter risks being radically misunderstood. However, when read with these distinctions in mind, both the pastoral and political acuity of the *Institutes* can be more fully appreciated.

THE CHARACTER OF CALVIN'S THEOLOGY

After a rhetorical reading of the second chapter of the *Institutes*, is it now possible to step back from the text and these insights in order to glean the character of Calvin's theology from such an analysis of his writings? A useful way of answering this question is to compare several of the more popular interpretations of this chapter to my own reading of Calvin. Four of the best-known readings of Calvin's definition of *pietas* are found in the works of Paul Lobstein, Richard Stauffer, Edward Dowey, and T.H.L. Parker.[22] Although I do not intend to give a comprehensive assessment of their interpretations of *pietas*, I will make some general comments about them for the purpose of comparing them to the reading I have given.

In each of these four interpretations, the author makes assumptions about Calvin's discussion of *pietas*, assumptions that my reading challenges. These assumptions are of four basic sorts: (1) the textual coherence of chapter 2; (2) the overarching purpose of the definition of *pietas* in chapter 2; (3) the relationship between the meaning of the chapter and its audience; and (4) the most appropriate analytic lens through which to view the chapter's epistemological claims.

The first of these assumptions entails that the textual coherence of this chapter resides in its propositional presentation of a definition of *pietas*. As in Barth's, Brunner's, and Tillich's approach to chapter 1, each of the four interpretations mentioned above assumes that the central purpose of chapter 2 is to present the reader with a well-reasoned, carefully executed, logically constructed analysis of the character of "religious knowledge." On the basis of this assumption, these interpretations mainly attend to the propositional components of the rhetoric in the chapter. And in doing so, they overlook the great wealth of textual activity that occurs in this chapter but resists the limits of propositional analysis. Their analysis of the text thus misses a full appreciation of the complex theological capital Calvin has invested in his discussion of *pietas*.

Part of the difficulty involved in approaching the text as these theologians do lies in their presupposition of a certain degree of textual coherence. They assume the text is analytically structured so that the logic of the chapter is unified around a central organizing argument. However, my reading challenges this assumption on two levels. At one level, if my analysis does nothing else, it should convince the reader that there is no central argument that neatly ties the chapter together. Quite to the contrary, there are many different arguments taking place all at once. Because of this complicated interweaving of several different arguments and agendas, the text's structure appears quite chaotic in places. In addition to having no unified argument, the text also resists any attempt to locate its unity in terms of its style or genre. Its tone and texture shift frequently. At one moment it is denouncing an opponent and in the next, uplifting and exhorting its audience to render God glory. At one moment it is carefully teaching and in the next it is declaring war on the ever-threatening adversary, and so it continues throughout the chapter. Thus, in contrast to the stable and unified version of the *Institutes* read by Lobstein, Parker, Dowey, and Stauffer, the text that I have explored is extremely complex.

It moves in several directions; it engages several diverse audiences; and it deploys a multitude of textual strategies as it negotiates a complex series of authorial agendas.

In addition to challenging overly simplistic assumptions of textual coherence, my reading also takes to task these four theologians regarding a second assumption, namely, that the purpose of the chapter is to give a straightforward definition of *pietas* and to present the reader with arguments in support of this definition. While it is true that one of the text's functions lies in an expository analysis of *pietas*, my rhetorical reading has attempted to uncover other functions that the chapter serves as well, and when these additional functions are taken into consideration, a very different picture of Calvin's theology as a whole begins to emerge.

At the most general level, my analysis of Calvin's four waves of appeal in chapter 2 has shown that Calvin is not concerned only to define *pietas* for the reader, but also to invoke in the reader a pious disposition. His attempts to invoke this disposition come in the second stage of each of his waves of appeal. Having presented the definition of *pietas* in the first stage of each wave, Calvin then consistently shifts into a more sermonic mode of presentation in which he extols the virtues of God and the benefits God promises to those who behold God's majesty and render God praise. In these sermonic interludes, it is obvious that Calvin is no longer simply defining *pietas*. Instead, he is trying to persuade the readers of God's great mercies in order that they might actually experience the very disposition he has previously set forth. Given Calvin's decidedly practical description of *pietas*, it follows that he would attempt to invoke a pious disposition in this manner. According to his definition, true knowledge of God does not consist of a simple intellectual assent to God's existence. Rather, it involves trust, obedience, and worship. Thus, if Calvin wanted to define for his readers the meaning of *pietas* in terms that move beyond the realm of simple conceptual knowledge, then he would have had to use a language that would elicit such things as trust, obedience, and worship. In this sense, the rhetoric of chapter 2 serves the practical function of "making the reader good" by inducing a "play of mind" designed to make the reader pious.

In addition to this function, I have indicated the various ways in which this chapter also speaks to and attempts to affect the disposition of several historical audiences: Calvin's students, his faithful (and persecuted) followers, his moderate-minded friends in the humanist circles in France and Germany, and his opponents, the Epicureans. I have also illustrated the various rhetorics Calvin uses to engage these different audiences. I have traced the interweaving of pedagogical, consolatory, apologetic, and harsh and pointed polemical agendas. And throughout my analysis, I have explored the ways in which each of the communities might have interpreted Calvin's discussion of *pietas*. One of the most interesting insights that has followed from this part of my analysis has been the recognition that one sentence or set of images may well serve different social functions depending on where one stands in relation to the text. If the reader identifies herself or himself as the text's opponent, then the rhetoric of the chapter moves across the reader with the force of an assault. On the other hand, if the reader identifies herself or himself as one of the faithful, the very same rhetorical gesture may reach out to embrace and comfort. In this way, the meaning of the chapter varies according to whom it speaks.

By situating the text in its historical context and discerning its meaning through the politics of its interactions with Calvin's various readers, I have indirectly challenged a third set of assumptions that undergirds the interpretations given by Dowey, Parker, and Lobstein. The assumption I have challenged is that the text speaks to a general, ahistorical audience and, consequently, that the text's meaning can be discerned apart from the terms of its social engagement. All three of these theologians interpret Calvin's definition of *pietas* without reference to his implied audiences. In doing so, they seem to embrace implicitly a view of language that holds that the words of this text point unambiguously to a static, extralinguistic idea or reality that the interpreter must discern and rearticulate in order to offer the modern reader the "true meaning of the text." In opposition to this view, I have read Calvin's text with a more pragmatic notion of what language is, a notion that has strong affinities with the rhetorical tradition in which Calvin was trained. The meaning I have sought is consequently one that resides somewhere between the text and its audience, a meaning that is historically as well as socially and politically functional.

When the text is viewed from this perspective, what may have appeared at first glance to be a straightforward theological discourse on *pietas*, presented to an entirely ahistorical audience, now appears as a rather complicated textual terrain upon which a variety of theological and political agendas are being discursively negotiated. This is not to say that the discussion of the character and nature of the knowledge of God is simply a pretext for fighting other, more significant textual battles. As my discussion of Calvin's definition of *pietas* has revealed, he approaches the question of the knowledge of God with great seriousness, both as a theologian and as a student of scripture and the tradition. Nonetheless, this rhetorical analysis does expose the unavoidably political nature of Calvin's theological language. It shows that Calvin's theological enterprise cannot be easily disentangled from the context within which he conceived it. His definition of *pietas* was not wrought in a vacuum but emerged in the midst of a pressing social crisis, and the terms with which it was elaborated constituted a position within this crisis.

Furthermore, this historical situating also exposes the depth to which these contextual concerns mark the text. Questions of politics and power are not questions that Calvin reserves for Book 4, where he discusses social and ecclesiastical polity. Rather, in the rhetorical movement of each theological pronouncement, in this chapter and throughout the *Institutes*, the discourse is shot through with the conflicts and tensions of his shifting contexts. And the traces left by these conflicts are far more than secondary or accidental aspects of the chapter's argument. Indeed, the images and language that describe "our knowledge of God" are shaped according to their rhetorical effectiveness and hence gauged by the social positions they inscribe. Thus, in Calvin's writings there is not one language of theology and another language of the political or social; they are inextricably knotted together. As to which language takes precedence, the question itself presupposes distinctions that this reading has suggested are difficult to make.

This exposure of the multiple agendas that drive the chapter not only challenges theological readings of Calvin that avoid questions of history and practice in favor of more abstract assessments of his thought; it also expands the framework within which discussions like the Barth-Brunner debate attempt to determine whether Calvin's theology represents an apologetic or a more decidedly dogmatic agenda. As this reading has shown, the discourse of his theology is not of one type or form. What may appear at one level as a set of strictly dogmatic assertions may also appear, when read in the context of the Epicurean controversy, as an extended apology aimed at the Stoics. Similarly, a discussion that seems to have been occasioned by purely polemical intentions could be serving both apologetic and edifying ends as well. Hence, textual distinctions between the rhetoric of dogmatics and the language of apologetics break down and in their place one finds the emergence of a different set of distinctions, distinctions that are determined on the basis of the social functions the text may have served in the shifting and complex landscape of its conception and delivery.[23]

There is a fourth and final way in which my reading of chapter 2 challenges and expands on the more popular interpretations of the text put forth by Dowey, Lobstein, and Stauffer. It concerns the conceptual lens through which these interpreters have focused Calvin's definition of *pietas*. Because it ostensibly takes up the topic of "knowledge," chapter 2 has proved fertile ground for exploring Calvin's theological epistemology. In their analyses of this unique aspect of Calvin's theology, these three theologians have assessed his position by using conceptual categories found in contemporary schools of thought that outline the foundations of a general theory of knowledge. The two schools of thought upon which these theologians have drawn are the Kantian school and the school of existential phenomenology. For example, the French scholar Paul

Lobstein draws upon the epistemological framework of Kant's *Critique of Practical Reason* to describe Calvin's understanding of that unusual sort of "knowing" called *pietas*. According to Lobstein, Calvin's notion of *pietas* is intimately tied to the moral life. It is best portrayed, he claims, as a sort of "practical knowing" that, in contrast to merely speculative or theoretical knowledge, engages the believer's conscience and heart and hence exhibits an inescapably transformative quality.[24] Along similar lines, Richard Stauffer also depicts *pietas* in terms of its principally moral character.[25]

Closely related in substance, but nonetheless distinguishable in approach from these views of *pietas*, are the interpretations of "religious knowledge" offered by theologians drawing from the resources of the more contemporary insights of existential philosophy. Subsuming *pietas* under the heading of "faith," Edward Dowey credits Kierkegaard with the term "existential" and then defends its relevance to Calvin's theology. "One need scarcely prove," he argues, "that Calvin's concept of religious knowledge belongs to those who can be classified as existential."[26] For Dowey, the phrase "existential knowledge" refers to a type of nonspeculative knowing that engages the hearer in such a way that the very existence of the hearer is recognized as depending on it.[27] Dowey further compares this knowledge to Tillich's notion of "deciding knowledge," a knowledge that concerns one ultimately, and to H. R. Mackintosh's sense of a knowledge that "concerns one infinitely here and now."[28]

While there are certainly many similarities between the content of these definitions of *pietas* and Calvin's own definition, there are also several problems involved in approaching Calvin's text through the lenses of Kant and the existentialists. Both the Kantian and the phenomenological assessments of *pietas* delineate the subjective inner workings of an understanding that has the divine as its object. In doing so, each brings to this discussion of *pietas* its own theory of knowledge and its antecedent anthropology and through these lenses discerns the working of a "universal understanding" that is uniquely grasped by the divine. In both cases, Calvin's text is viewed as answering the question of how the believer as "a subject" comes to know the divine. And, in attempting to answer this question, these readings impose on the text Enlightenment categories such as "the subject" and "consciousness," and even the notion of "a theory of knowledge," all of which were terms quite unfamiliar to sixteenth-century theologians.

In contrast to this approach, I have used the conceptual world of the rhetorical tradition as the lens through which to focus and analyze Calvin's understanding of *pietas*. This approach has several advantages, the most obvious one being that it does not require one to impose on the text distinctly modern notions like "the subject." When viewed through the lens of rhetoric, Calvin's discussion of religious knowing is shown to be more concerned with the mechanism through which this knowledge is disseminated, or "orated" as the case may be, than with the inner workings of a subjective understanding. A rhetorical conceptualization of *pietas* thus shifts the focus away from the subject and toward the one who is speaking, God. Similarly, my discussion of *pietas* as a form of effective persuasion highlights the fact that Calvin was more interested in delineating the kinds of disposition that follow from true piety than in explicating the internal workings of the intellect or conscience.

In this sense, reading *pietas* through the lens of rhetoric has the advantage of avoiding distinctly modernist "theories of knowledge," and contemporary assumptions about the general nature of the human creature, for the most part, are thus held at bay. Consequently, by harkening back to a pre-Enlightenment epistemological scheme, this reading is able to avoid many of the Enlightenment snares in which these other readings of Calvin become entangled. Ironically, in so doing, it also opens the door to viewing Calvin's theology in relation to a set of issues that are more postmodern in character, a topic to which I shall return in the last chapter.

NOTES

1. Cicero, *De natura deorum*, trans. H. Rackham, ed. E. H. Warmington, The Loeb Classical Library (Cambridge, Mass.: Harvard University Press, 1967).

2. Egil Grislis, "Calvin's Use of Cicero in the *Institutes* I:1–5: A Case Study in Theological Method," *Archiv für Reformationsgeschichte* 62 (1971): 5–37.

3. "Sunt enim philosophi et fuerunt qui omnino nullam habere censerent rerum humanarum procurationem deos. Quorum si vera sententia est, quae potest esse pietas, quae sanctitas, quae religio?" "For there are and have been philosophers who hold that the gods exercise no control over human affairs whatever. But if their opinion is the true one, how can piety, reverence or religion exist?" Cicero, *De natura deorum* 1.2.3 (4–5).

4. Ibid., 1.1.2 (4–5).

5. John Calvin, *Concerning Scandals*, trans. John W. Fraser (Grand Rapids: Wm. B. Eerdmans Publishing Co., 1978), 61; OS 2:201.6, 11–12.

6. Ibid., 62; "eo tandem perrumpunt, religiones omnes ex hominum cerebro natas esse: Deum esse, quia sic credere libeat: futurae vitae spem lactandis simplicibus inventam esse: metum iudicii puerile esse terriculamentum" (OS 2:202.10–14).

7. Ibid., 63; "quum in toto mundo passim grassatur, tum vero in regnum et principum aulis, in tribunalibus, in splendidis aliis vitae generibus praecipue regnat" (OS 2:202.28–31).

8. Each of these figures represented quite distinct and eccentric—by sixteenth-century standards—theological and political positions. On Agrippa, see Charles G. Nauert, Jr., *Agrippa and the Crisis of Renaissance Thought* (Urbana: University of Illinois Press, 1965); and Francis Yates, *The Occult Philosophy in the Elizabethan Age*

(London: Routledge & Kegan Paul, 1979). On Dolet, see Richard Copley Christie, *Etienne Dolet, The Martyr of the Renaissance, 1508–1548: A Biography* (London: Macmillan & Co., 1889); and John Charles Dawson, *Toulouse in the Renaissance: The Floral Games; University and Student Life; Etienne Dolet* (New York: Columbia University Press, 1923). On Bonaventure Des Periers, see Christie, *Dolet*, 228–29. On Rabelais, see Michael Screech, *Rabelais* (Ithaca, N.Y.: Cornell University Press, 1979).

9. Cicero, *De natura deorum* 1.21.57–60 (56–59).

10. The sentence literally reads, "Now I understand knowledge of God [as that] by which we not only conceive . . ." Note that the English clause is a single Latin word.

11. See Marjorie O'Rourke Boyle, *Erasmus on Language and Method in Theology* (Buffalo: University of Toronto Press, 1977); and Cave, *The Cornucopian Text: Problems of Writing in the French Renaissance*. This notion of the text as interpretation and author as interpreter once again displays Calvin's own strong humanist proclivities.

12. For this reason, scholars often view these two sentences as the key to the overarching structure of the *Institutes* as a whole, dividing the text into a treatment of knowledge of God the Creator in Book 1 and then knowledge of God as Redeemer in Book 2.

13. Cicero, *De natura deorum* 1.21–24.57–68 (54–67).

14. "Boundless might" (*immensa potentia*), regulating "wisdom" (*moderari + sapientia*), preserving "goodness" (*conservare + bonitas*), judgmental/ruling "righteousness" (*iudicium + iustitia*), "mercy" (*misericordia*), "protection" (*praesidium*), "truth" (*veritas*), "rectitude" (*rectitudo*).

15. Note that "induces" (in Latin, *conciliare*) can be translated also as "brings about" or "wins over," thus highlighting again the active, persuasive dimensions of God's relation to the creature.

16. Battles, "God Was Accommodating Himself to Human Capacity," 19–38.

17. As to the exact historical face of his audience, it must be noted that large segments of chapter 3 originated with the 1539 edition of the *Institutes*, which was written in the early stages of Calvin's theological career while he was teaching at Sturm's school in Strasbourg. Additional parts were added in Geneva for the 1559 edition and hence were most likely crafted with a more international audience of reformers, evangelical lay persons, and theological students in mind. At both the early and late stages of his career, however, questions of authorial authority would have been an important issue to consider in the process of writing "persuasive" theology.

18. Note Latin: "to profess" (*fateri*), "cast aside" (*abicere*), "the care of the world" (*cura mundi*), "to amuse himself in idleness" (*se otio oblectare*).

19. "Sin autem dei neque possunt nos iuvare nec volunt, nec omnino curant nec quid agamus animadvertunt, nec est quod ab iis ad hominum vitam permanare possit, quid est quod ullos deis immortalibus cultus honores preces adhibeamus?" "But if on the contrary the gods have neither the power nor the will to aid us, if they pay no heed to us at all and take no notice of our actions, if they can exert no possible influence upon the life of men, what ground have we for rendering any sort of worship, honour or prayer to the immortal gods?" Cicero, *De natura deorum* 1.2.3 (pp. 4–7).

20. Note Calvin's pedagogical vocabulary: "guide and teacher" (*dux ac magis-*

ter), "teaches us fear and reverence" (*ad timorem ac reverentiam nos instituat*), "we should learn to seek every good from him" (*omne bonum ab illo petere . . . discamus*).

21. Note the force of the Latin vocabulary deployed in this series of images: protects (*praesidium*), oppression (*premere*), provides a remedy (*parare + remedium*), ills (*mala*), all things (*omnia*), authority (*imperium*), punish (*vindicare*).

22. Paul Lobstein, "La connaissance religieuse d'après Calvin," 53–110; Richard Stauffer, *Dieu, la création, et la providence dans la prédication de Calvin* (Berne: Peter Lang, 1972); Edward A. Dowey, Jr., *The Knowledge of God in Calvin's Theology;* and T.H.L. Parker, *Calvin's Doctrine of the Knowledge of God.*

23. Several discussions of Calvin's theology have come to similar conclusions in their readings of his corpus, most particularly with regard to determining the theological principles that organize his writings. Most notable in this respect is the work of Jean-Daniel Benoit, *Calvin, Directeur d'âmes* (Strasbourg: Oberlin Press, 1947). Drawing upon a vast range of material, from Calvin's letters to his sermons and commentaries, Benoit argues that Calvin was first and foremost concerned with nurturing pastorally the life of faith and that his work is most appropriately assessed in terms of the type of dispositions it fosters, and not whether its logic is consistent. Referring to the *Institutes* as "le livre de piété," Benoit convincingly traces the various instances where Calvin's writings explicitly claim that pastoral concerns serve as the governing intention of the work.

In a similar manner, Brian Armstrong has rightly criticized contemporary scholars who read Calvin as if he were a professional university theologian who felt compelled to structure his thought around certain organizing topoi or loci. Against this view, he argues that Calvin was primarily concerned with the spiritual nurture of "the saints"—hence the antispeculative bent of the text, its practical emphasis, and the edifying thrust of its rhetoric. See Armstrong, "The Nature of Structure of Calvin's Thought according to the *Institutes:* Another Look," 55–81.

24. Lobstein, "La connaissance," 53–110.

25. Stauffer, *Dieu, la création, et la providence.*

26. Dowey, *The Knowledge of God in Calvin's Theology,* 26.

27. Ibid.

28. Paul Tillich, *Systematic Theology,* vol. 1; and H. R. Mackintosh, *Types of Modern Theology: Schleiermacher to Barth* (New York: Charles Scribner's Sons, 1937), 219. Although he is not as phenomenological as the others, T.H.L. Parker comes close to Dowey's position when he describes the all-encompassing nature of "grasping" and being "grasped by" the revelation of God in Jesus Christ (Parker, *Calvin's Doctrine of the Knowledge of God,* 137).

5

DIVINITATIS SENSUS AND "BOUNDARIES OF OTHERNESS" IN CHRISTIAN IDENTITY

A Reading of Chapter 3 of Book 1 of the *Institutes*:
"The Knowledge of God Has Been Naturally Implanted in the Minds of Men"

Although figurative expression is less precise, it expresses with greater significance and elegance what, said simply and without figure, would have less force and address. Hence figures are called the eyes of speech, not because they explain the matter more correctly than simple, proper language, but because they win attention by their propriety, arouse the mind by their luster, and by their lively similitude so represent what is said that it enters more effectively into the heart.

Quamvis loquutio figurata minus aperta sit, significantius tamen et splendidius exprimere quod simpliciter et absque figura dictum minus haberet efficaciae et ornatus. Itaque figurae vocantur orationis lumina: non quod facilius rem declarent quam nudus et vulgaris sermo, sed quia attentionem conciliant elegantia, et splendore expergefaciunt mentes, vivaque similitudine repraesentant quid dicitur, quo melius penetret in animos.

John Calvin

Displaying the power of true eloquence, Calvin has accomplished a good deal by the time he arrives at the beginning of chapter 3. In the prefaces he ushers in, by special invitation, a diverse but faithful audience of students and parishioners, and he greets them with a humble promise: to the best of his ability he will instruct them, exhort them, comfort them, and defend them as he struggles to present a true account of the foundations of the faith they share. At the same time, he extends a warm welcome to those readers who may be a bit more skeptical about his project; he urges them to listen carefully and to be open to the possibility that his account may convince them of the legitimacy of the theological perspective he will narrate. In this group of readers, he appears to acknowledge especially the presence of the well-educated, classically trained, and moderately minded humanists in France.

In recognition of the controversial nature of his project, he also calls the audience's attention to uninvited spectators who occupy the fringes of his textual theater. In this group he identifies the presence of several hostile factions that include the Roman Catholic clerical establishment of France, the more radical sectors of the humanist movement, and the unruly Anabaptist sects, who have been mistakenly identified with his cause. To these spectators, he fires off a few caustic remarks and then warns that in the following pages, he will not let their presence go unnoticed. To the contrary, he promises to continually assault and disarm the rhetorical weapons they have aimed at him and his faithful comrades.

After using the prefaces to identify the competing expectations and backgrounds that comprise his audience, Calvin then devotes the opening two chapters of the *Institutes* to delineating the subject matter and the order of presentation he will utilize for the remainder of his project. While introducing these topics and demarcating the overarching content of his project, Calvin also pulls the reader into the discursive world of the text by deploying a number of rhetorical strategies designed to interact with the various segments of his audience. In the first chapter, he appears to engage in an extended apology directed to those humanists he hopes to convert to his theological program. In the second chapter, he shifts his focus slightly and attempts to inculcate in his faithful readers an attitude appropriate to *pietas.* In the process of doing so, he also offers his faithful followers a word of comfort and assurance that God's benefits have been and will continue to be poured out upon them. To his opponents, however, he describes the wrathful punishment that awaits them. In particular, he singles out, as special recipients of this wrath, a group of controversial humanists, the Epicureans. Thus, by the end of chapter 2, if his rhetorical calculations are correct and his introduction effective, his audience should stand ready for the main body of the oration to commence.

In chapter 3 of the *Institutes,* Calvin finally turns to the task he sets for himself and begins to describe the foundations of the Christian religion. Here, he begins his discussion of Christian doctrine with a description of the "awareness of divinity" that is implanted in all persons and from which flows an innate sense of God the creator. Over the years, Calvin's treatment of this "divine sense" has stimulated much controversy among Calvin scholars. The most heated of these controversies have revolved around disagreements about whether or not Calvin actually believed it was possible for human beings to have a "natural or innate knowledge of God." As with many of Calvin's doctrines, his discussion of the innate "awareness of divinity" is ambiguous enough to permit a well-argued defense on either side of the issue; consequently, countless books and articles have been devoted to untangling Calvin's "real" position on the matter. As I have done in the two previous chapters, I will argue that a rhetorical reading of Calvin's position can shed new light on this debate by providing additional insight into why Calvin formulates the doctrine in the manner he does. Through a careful study of his explanatory examples and his figurative language, I will argue that Calvin is negotiating a complex series of social agendas that may not be immediately apparent but are nonetheless crucial for understanding the weave of signification within which the text acquires its theological "meaning."

AN UNRESOLVED PUZZLE

The first textual clue to the presence of this complex weave of "meanings" appears when one analyzes the peculiar function played by this chapter in relation to the rest of the *Institutes*. Chapter 3 is the first part of an extended argument on the nature of "our knowledge of God the Creator" that runs through his next five chapters. In these chapters, Calvin discusses the different avenues through which knowledge of God the creator is made known to the creature. According to Calvin, these avenues are threefold: (1) the creature's innate sense of divinity; (2) the splendor and order of creation; and (3) the witness of scripture. In the process of developing his discussion of God the creator, Calvin explores each of these avenues in order to determine both the content of the knowledge they present and the viability of their testimony in the life of the creature.

The unusual thing about this discussion, however, is that Calvin eventually comes to the conclusion that the inborn knowledge he describes in chapter 3 is useless if left solely to its own intuitions. To use his own words, there is no one "in whom it ripens—much less shows fruit in season" (*Inst.* 1.4.1, p. 47; OS 3:41.1–2).[1] With this conclusion—which first appears in chapter 4—Calvin seems to suggest that the knowledge described in chapter 3 plays little if any constructive role in articulating the positive content of "our knowledge of God." If this inborn knowledge is truly as useless and as quickly "smothered or corrupted" as Calvin asserts, then one cannot help but wonder why he has included such an extended discussion of it in the first place. Is it a topic that is going to play an important role later in the *Institutes?* Perhaps. But at this early stage in the text's development, Calvin does not offer his readers clues about its future function.[2] Instead, he not only leaves the topic hanging, he leaves many questions unanswered. To get a sense of the oddity of the relation of chapter 3 to the rest of the text, let me examine more carefully the role it plays in the text's broader argument.

Topically, chapter 3 initiates the discussion of the sources of "our knowledge of God as Creator." The source in question here is a knowledge of God that inheres in the hearts of all humanity. Referred to as "an awareness of divinity" (*divinitatis sensus*), the "seed of religion" (*religionis semen*), and "a religious inclination" (*ad religionem propensio*), it consists of an inborn knowledge of divine majesty that God continually replenishes. As a natural instinct, this "sense" permits Calvin to argue in this chapter for the universality of the perception that there is a God and that "he is our maker." To do so, he enlists a series of examples drawn from other cultures and religions as well as some from the "pagan philosophers." Calvin also illustrates, in his most extended proof, how this sense unceasingly stirs the conscience of even the most ardent unbeliever. Working from this premise, he then concludes that "no one can take refuge in the pretense of ignorance" of God. Thus, on the basis of the universal presence of the *divinitatis sensus*, the false pretensions of those who forthrightly deny knowing God are revealed.

Having established the inherent and sustained presence of this "divine sense" and its judgment against the unbeliever, Calvin quickly limits the scope of this natural knowledge in the next chapter, by claiming that in fact no one, neither the unbeliever nor the religious person, is able to know God correctly through this medium alone. Because all creation has degenerated from this knowledge, "so it happens that no real piety remains in the world" (*Inst.* 1.4.1, p. 47; OS 3:41.5).[3] Wandering off into empty speculation, most persons "do not therefore apprehend God as he offers himself, but imagine him as they have fashioned him in their own presumption" (*Inst.* 1.4.1, p. 47; OS 3:41.14–15).[4] He supports this contention by illustrating that many of those who claim to believe in the divine actually display in their actions a fundamental disregard for the one true God. This pervasive impiety is clearly present in the superstition, idolatry, and hypocrisy of supposedly "pious men." However, Calvin does not include his "faithful followers" in his examples of idolaters, and he hints at the end of the chapter that the confused knowledge of the impious differs from the piety that takes true religion as its source (*Inst.* 1.4.4, p. 50; OS 3:43.33–44.3).[5] Thus, although he claims that absolutely no one can come to know God through the evidence of the "conscience alone," the primary target of his condemnations appears to be those who practice "false religion" and not the truly faithful.

Yet there remains a peculiar element at play at this point in Calvin's argument. This peculiarity lies in the fact that the evidence that in chapter 3 acts as positive proof for the universality of an innately religious sense now serves in chapter 4 as evidence that no one actually has what Calvin considers to be an appropriate form of religiosity. In other words, the idolatry that he first champions as evidence of a pervasive sense of divinity instilled in all human creatures Calvin now uses as evidence to expose the pervasive corruption of these same creatures. Here it seems that Calvin is arguing at cross-purposes and hence effectively undermining the warrants upon which the argument of chapter 3 is constructed: by exposing the "emptiness" of all forms of religion that spring from the "seed of religion," he destroys the very foundations of the position he has just so carefully explained. One hears in this unusual play of argument echoes of the rhetoric that framed chapter 1. And in light of this self-subversion, one wonders, again, why Calvin meticulously builds an argument that he then proceeds to tear down. Interpretations of this section that attend only to the logical structure of his argument have difficulty answering this question. But from a rhetorical perspective, this "logical" inconsistency serves as a warning signal that Calvin may have purposes other than strictly logical ones in thus framing his topic.

In the fifth chapter of the *Institutes*, Calvin introduces the reader to the second source of "our knowledge of God the creator": the knowledge displayed for all to see in the splendor of God's creation, both in its fashioning and its continued governance. In the vast and beautiful expanse of the universe as well as in the ingenious composition of the human body, God "has engraved unmistakable marks of his glory, so clear and so prominent that even unlettered and stupid folk cannot plead the excuse of ignorance" (*Inst.* 1.5.1, p. 52; OS 3:45.6–8).[6] As with the *divinitatis sensus*, the revelation of creation also serves a double function in Calvin's argument. First, as in chapter 3, it bears witness against those unbelievers who would claim either that God is nature, a pantheistic viewpoint, or that there is no God, the perspective of an atheist. The conspicuous presence of the revelation of God in creation therefore convicts both the pantheist and the atheist of a willful turning from God by exposing the false pretensions of their assumed ignorance. In its second function, the witness of creation also reveals the impious hypocrisy of those who claim to believe in a sovereign God and yet continue to practice superstition and idolatry. Calvin argues that if they truly believed in God, then their lives would fully reflect the persuasive force of their faith. This segment of chapter 5 thus parallels the argument of chapter 4.

Chapter 5 also parallels chapter 4 in terms of the logical morass into which Calvin wanders. He uses the evidence of creation to argue first, in a positive manner, that "a sense of divinity" accompanies the reflections of anyone who beholds the splendor of creation. Then, in direct opposition to this first use, Calvin deploys it as evidence against those who claim to see God's presence in creation but practice impiety nonetheless. Like the evidence afforded by the "divine sense," these different uses of creation appear to cancel out one another. Yet Calvin does not seem to be troubled by this tension, a fact that again prompts the question, What purpose might this chapter be serving other than its most apparent argumentative purpose?

Against the backdrop of these two forms of natural knowledge, Calvin turns to scripture as the third source of divine wisdom concerning God the Creator. Empowered by the Holy Spirit as it works upon the hearts of its readers, scripture serves as the lens through which the previously blinded creature can see the presence of God in creation and in the depths of one's own conscience. As with his discussion of the previous sources, Calvin attends in great detail to a variety of proofs for both the scope and validity of this source's witness. Describing how the work of the Spirit authenticates the truth of scripture, Calvin once again exposes the willful neglect of both unbelievers and the impious who reject its prescriptions. And yet, as he powerfully presents the breadth and force of scripture's revelation, Calvin leaves a further trail of ambiguities and silences that historically have given rise to innumerable controversies over the relation of the witness of scripture to the witness of nature.

One of the most obvious difficulties here concerns the importance of the three chapters that precede Calvin's discussion of scripture. In asserting the singular authority of scripture as the witness to God the creator, Calvin once more effectively cancels out the evidence upon which the arguments of the previous chapters are predicated. In light of this negation of the substantive content generated naturally by the *divinitatis sensus* and creation, it seems that as far as the overarching structure of Calvin's discussion of natural knowledge is concerned, he could have simply begun with the announcement that through scripture alone the blinded creature beholds the splendor of its creator. But he did not; and the interesting question from a rhetorical standpoint is, Why not? For many of Calvin's present-day interpreters, the answer to this question lies in solving what they believe to be a complicated but logical riddle that undergirds and drives his whole discussion of natural knowledge. For others, this ambiguity is simply identified as a paradox and left hanging. For still others, the answer to this question rests in determining which strands of the Christian tradition concerning natural knowledge he comes closest to affirming. However, what these interpreters seldom consider is the possibility that Calvin intended these chapters on "natural knowledge" to serve rhetorical functions that are not necessarily wedded to concerns for logical precision, conceptual clarity, or systematic rigor. In order to determine what these rhetorical functions might be, let me return now to chapter 3 and explore once again those "other fields of play" into which the rhetoric of the Genevan reformer invites his reader.

CONSTRUCTING THE BOUNDARIES
OF CHRISTIAN IDENTITY

The Opening Paragraph

In the opening sentence of the chapter, Calvin asserts the central principle upon which he constructs the argument of the next three paragraphs: "There is within the human mind, and indeed by natural instinct, an awareness of divinity" (*Inst.* 1.3.1, p. 43; OS 3:37.16–17). This proposition's explicative and straightforward tone immediately suggests to the reader the pedagogical agenda of the discussion to follow. Hence, Calvin stands as teacher before an audience that he places, as previously, in the position of students. Then, reemphasizing the force of this statement, he follows it with the claim, "This we take to be beyond controversy" (*extra controversiam ponimus*). Using his familiar "we," he gathers the weight of the community of the faithful behind his assertion, thus making it evident from the outset that all who disagree stand outside the text's embrace.

Given the popularity of the notion of *divinitatis sensus* in both the Scholastic and humanist circles in the sixteenth century, Calvin's assertion that its universal presence is "beyond controversy" would have been a fairly safe assumption. Further, on the basis of the long and varied history of its definition and use, this notion would have been familiar to most of Calvin's Protestant contemporaries, although the term would not have sparked the same degree of attention and debate as it would in centuries to follow. Indeed, Augustine's famous explication of the universal presence and function of the *divinitatis sensus* would have come immediately to the mind of scholars well versed in the canons of the Christian tradition.[7] And as for the student of the theology of Calvin's day, works ranging from Thomas Aquinas to Melanchthon would have been seen to lend at least tacit support for Calvin's position.[8] In addition to these theological references, students of Renaissance humanism would have also noted classical affinities with his assertion. Such students would have heard quite clearly in Calvin's work the textual echoes of Cicero's famous dialogue, *De natura deorum*.[9] In fact, many scholars have noted that, in addition to providing a subtext for chapter 2, this particular work by Cicero undergirds the bulk of the argument of chapter 3 as well.[10]

But beyond conveying an appeal of obvious breadth, the second sentence has another interesting effect: by stating that the presence of the "divine sense" is "beyond controversy," the text rhetorically evokes, if only to dismiss, the very atmosphere of controversy it disclaims. The reader soon finds that such a framing is entirely appropriate because the remainder of the chapter constitutes a defense of this supposedly uncontroversial claim. That Calvin missed this irony is highly unlikely given that Cicero's Academic philosopher Cotta makes the same observation about his Stoic interlocutor's "unnecessary defense" of the innate divine sense in the dialogue after which Calvin models his own.[11] Thus, for the reader familiar with the classical origins of the discussion as well as for the less erudite, this chapter commences with the same level of tension marking the preceding chapter. The audience is informed that a debate will ensue—a debate, ironically, over an "uncontroversial" topic.

Having introduced this topic, Calvin, in the following sentence, sets forth the terms in which he will elaborate the notion of *divinitatis sensus*. In a pragmatic fashion indicative of his humanist background, he begins by focusing on the practical function it serves:

> To prevent anyone from taking refuge in the pretense of ignorance, God himself has implanted in all men a certain understanding of his divine majesty. Ever renewing its memory, he repeatedly sheds fresh drops. (*Inst.* 1.3.1, pp. 43–44; OS 3:37.18–21)

By attending solely to the function or purpose served by this divine sense, Calvin makes a significant departure from the medieval Scholastics' treatments of the *divinitatis sensus* in that he omits a detailed ontology of its origin and nature. While it is possible to cull from this chapter some insight into the content of the seed's revelation and its location in the creature's conscience, the text does not provide enough information to construct a systematic account of either. At times it appears to rest in the believer's "mind" (*mens, animus*); at others, it inheres deep in one's "heart" (*cor, viscera*) or "marrow" (*medulla*).[12] Similarly, as far as describing the nature of the knowledge this seed provides, the text remains unsystematic. Calvin most frequently implies that the seed simply testifies to God's existence. However, he adds that it also testifies to God's majesty and power as well as God's concern to continue to shed "fresh drops" (*novae guttae*) that renew God's relation with humanity. He also joins to this list the claim that the content of the knowledge provided by this seed consists of an awareness of good and evil. This broad and rather loosely defined conjunction of descriptions makes it clear that Calvin's interests in the *divinitatis sensus* are not primarily Scholastic. Instead of exploring what this innate sense *is*, he is going to focus on what it *does* or what functions it serves. Calvin thus remains consistent with his previous disavowal of all theologically speculative enterprises.

In addition to the unsystematic character of Calvin's definition of the *divinitatis sensus*, his treatment of this topic differs from traditional discussions in yet another significant way. In most classical discussions, the concept of the "divine sense" is not treated as an isolated topic but is woven into the fabric of theological doctrine as a whole. For example, in the writings of Augustine and Thomas, this innate sense is carefully defined and then brought into the development of doctrines ranging from the nature of the human person to the function of the sacraments and the character of faith. However, in a rather startling contrast to this integrated approach to the concept of "divine sense," Calvin addresses the theological function of the *divinitatis sensus* solely in his discussion of natural knowledge in chapters 3 and 4 of Book 1 and not elsewhere in the *Institutes*. And its absence from the remainder of the *Institutes* is notable. For example, at the end of Book 1 of the *Institutes*, one might expect to find reference to the *divinitatis sensus* included in Calvin's general anthropology, but any such reference is conspicuously absent here. This is likewise true for the first five chapters of Book 2, where Calvin supplements his anthropology with an account of the creature's fallen nature. Again, in the context of this discussion, the term never occurs.[13] Similarly, it would seem to find an appropriate place in Calvin's later discussion of the life of faith in Book 3. However, he here discusses the notion of the *semen fidei* (the seed of faith) at length but does so without explicitly referring to the conception of the *religionis semen* he developed in chapter 3.[14]

On the basis of these absences, it appears that the discussions of chapters 3 and 4 do not provide an obvious or well-defined foundation for doctrines developed later in the *Instiiutes*. Given the term's lack of sustained conceptual development, one can appreciate the conceptual contortions theologians, particularly the Reformed epistemologists, go through in their attempt to weave the notion of *divinitatis sensus* into a systematic account of the whole *Institutes*.[15] Evidence suggests that this attempt to systematize will not succeed precisely because Calvin does not elaborate a systematized epistemology with respect to this notion of "innate knowledge." This does not mean, however, that the notion is unimportant. Calvin clearly thought it was. The interpretive task is thus to explore what specific purpose or purposes this functional but rather loosely defined discussion of "innate knowledge" is serving.

The initial statement of the formal function of the *divinitatis sensus* offers the first clue regarding its role. The purpose of God's implanting the "seed of religion" in the minds of all persons is stated negatively: "to prevent anyone from taking refuge in the pretense of ignorance" (*Inst.* 1.3.1, p. 43; OS 3:37.18). On the basis of this statement, it is clear that the presence of the *divinitatis sensus* serves the purpose of exposing some form of willful or intentional ignorance. At this point, however, the text leaves ambiguous the specific nature of the reality of which one might claim to be ignorant. Is Calvin claiming that the presence of the "seed of religion" prevents one from claiming ignorance of God's existence? Or does the seed admonish those who, having already affirmed God's existence, nonetheless claim to be ignorant of the kind of response God requires of them? In other words, is Calvin trying to undermine the position of the "atheist" or the "idolater"? Or perhaps both? In terms of a rhetorical analysis, the importance of these distinctions is not to be underestimated. If the notion serves to convict the atheist, then the chapter serves one type of function. But if it is also directed at those who practice false religion, then a different social and theological agenda is likely.

This opening paragraph offers several additional clues indicating which of these audiences Calvin intends the presence of the seed to convict. In the fourth sentence of the chapter, a generally religious but impious humanity is suggested as the target:

> Since, therefore, men one and all perceive that there is a God and that he is their Maker, they are condemned by their own testimony because they

have failed to honor him and to consecrate their lives to his will. (*Inst.* 1.3.1, p. 44; OS 3:37.21–24)

This statement implies that for those "men one and all" (*ad unum omnes*) who readily acknowledge the existence of God, the principal sin of which "they" are convicted is that of inappropriately honoring or worshiping God and thereby refusing to follow God's will. Those convicted by the presence of an innate knowledge of God are not persons lacking in knowledge, but rather those who know God yet fail to turn their lives over to "him" in worshipful obedience. If this description accurately characterizes the beginning of the chapter, then its polemical target appears initially to be all persons whose religious practice is found lacking—a large audience, to say the least.

However, in the next sentence, Calvin shifts his focus toward a smaller audience, those who claim ignorance of God or who say that there is no God, the atheists. Garnering the support of Cicero, he argues against such a position by claiming: "[T]here is, as the eminent pagan says, no nation so barbarous, no people so savage, that they have not a deep-seated conviction that there is a God" (*Inst.* 1.3.1, p. 44; OS 3:38.1–3).[16] Here, it appears that Calvin is using the universal presence of the "seed of religion" specifically to counter the arguments of those who deny "there is a God" (*Deum esse*). And in the sentences that immediately follow, he continues to argue that the presence of the *divinitatis sensus* testifies to God's existence and not necessarily to the form of praise appropriate to God. In one example after another, Calvin argues on anthropological grounds that a fundamental ignorance of God's existence is impossible. It is impossible because the people of every civilization in history have witnessed to the existence of God in their construction of various religious practices. In these examples, Calvin shows little interest in evaluating these practices as idolatrous, a critique he would surely include if the target of his attack were those who practice "false religion." Given the length and force of this discussion, one may thus conclude that countering "the atheist's position" remains the central task of the chapter. Nonetheless, this does not imply that Calvin has rejected the possibility that the *divinitatis sensus* also serves to convict those who believe in God but practice impiety. In the following chapter, this group of "idolaters" returns as the central focus of his attack. But, for the purposes of chapter 3, these "idolaters" fade into the background while the willful ignorance of the unbelievers, the atheists, comes into the foreground.

Having determined that one function of this chapter is to convict the so-called atheist of a willful rejection of God's existence, a number of additional questions immediately arise about how this "convicting of the atheist" might work toward other functions the text is designed to serve. From a rhetorical perspective, an interesting question to ask of the text is, Why does Calvin launch his discussion of "our knowledge of God the

Creator" with an attack on these atheists? To answer this question, one needs to explore some subsidiary questions as well. Can one assume that the purpose of this chapter is strictly polemical, or might Calvin be using his polemic in the service of his pedagogical or apologetic agenda? Given the evidence presented in his prefaces, the possibility that Calvin has a number of agendas woven into this polemic is not at all unlikely. One must also ask about the historical face of the atheist he wants to convict: who might these "unbelievers" have been, and why does Calvin endeavor to undermine the legitimacy of their claims to "unbelief"? To resolve these questions about Calvin's atheist audience as well as the issue of his agenda, let me turn back to the text and see what clues Calvin offers.

The third chapter's style of argumentation provides one means of discerning the text's underlying rhetorical agendas. This chapter differs stylistically from chapter 2: in contrast to the meandering logic and mixed genres that typify the latter, Calvin now presents the reader with a central thesis, namely, that it is impossible for anyone to claim ignorance of God, and having presented his thesis, he then proceeds to offer evidence in its support. Calvin expounds this evidence in a straightforward manner and gives careful attention to the internal logic that holds his supporting examples together. He employs an unusually tight form of reasoning and appeals frequently to the findings of scholarly investigation. Thus, he executes his argument with a dialectical precision not found in the rhetoric of the two previous chapters.

An excellent example of this style of argument lies in the first paragraph of the chapter. As the first warrant for his claim that the "seed of religion" is universally implanted in the minds of persons, he submits: "If ignorance of God is to be looked for anywhere, surely one is most likely to find an example among the more backward folk and those more remote from civilization" (*Inst.* 1.3.1, p. 44; OS 3:37.24–38.1). Following this statement, he draws supporting evidence from a not-so-surprising classical source, Cicero.[17] Calvin states (as partially cited above):

> Yet there is, as the eminent pagan says, no nation so barbarous, no people so savage, that they have not a deep-seated conviction that there is a God. And they who in other aspects of life seem least to differ from brutes still continue to retain some seed of religion. So deeply does the common conception occupy the minds of all, so tenaciously does it inhere in the hearts of all! Therefore, since from the beginning of the world there has been no region, no city, in short, no household, that could do without religion, there lies in this a tacit confession of a sense of deity inscribed in the hearts of all. (*Inst.* 1.3.1, p. 44; OS 3:38.1–11)

Continuing to garner evidence in support of his thesis, Calvin draws on yet another source. He offers empirical "proof" (*documentum*) for his position:

Indeed, even idolatry is ample proof of this conception. We know how man does not willingly humble himself so as to place other creatures over himself. Since, then, he prefers to worship wood and stone rather than to be thought of as having no God, clearly this is a most vivid impression of a divine being. (*Inst.* 1.3.1, p. 44; OS 3:38.11–16)

Having laid out his evidence, Calvin then concludes the first paragraph by restating his opening thesis in even stronger language:

So impossible is it to blot this from man's mind that [his] natural disposition would be more easily altered, as altered indeed it is when man voluntarily sinks from his natural haughtiness to the very depths in order to honor God! (*Inst.* 1.3.1, p. 44; OS 3:38.16–19)

In terms of assessing Calvin's rhetorical agenda in this chapter, the presence of this carefully reasoned and well-defended argument for the universality of the *divinitatis sensus* suggests several things about his intended audience. In the first place, this type of argumentative strategy effectively serves Calvin's pedagogical interests. As such, it would have appealed especially to his student readership because it is clear, precise, and unabashedly scholarly in its execution. Second, this form of appeal would have found an attentive audience in the highly educated community of humanists who were the first target of Calvin's apology in the opening chapter, particularly in light of the "copious" genius he displays in the structure of his central thesis. Thus, one may assume that Calvin is continuing to pursue his apologetic purposes as he did previously. Third, the absence of the exhortative voice and the gentle pastoral appeals that Calvin uses most frequently when he speaks to his French parishioners suggests that this audience is not, at the moment, in the foreground of his targeted audiences.

That Calvin has most likely structured this chapter to speak to the interests of his students and humanist scholars gains further support from the kinds of evidence he uses. As I have argued in the previous chapters, when Calvin intends to nurture, exhort, or comfort a community such as the French parishioners, he typically uses biblical imagery and direct biblical quotations in his appeal. However, in this chapter, there is only one brief reference to scripture. Instead of drawing upon biblical evidence, Calvin repeatedly appeals to evidence provided by classical "pagan" texts. In constructing his argument, he draws upon the testimony of such diverse figures as Diagoras, Dionysius, Plato, and Plutarch. The use of this evidence suggests that Calvin is engaging an audience who would find the testimony of these classical texts intelligible as well as convincing. Once again, the communities of readers who immediately come to mind are humanist scholars and Calvin's own students, who were required to read extensively in both the Roman and Greek classics.

The presence of these pedagogical and apologetic agendas points to an interesting ambiguity about the role played by the polemical agenda implied by the posture of his argument as a whole. In chapter 2, it was easy to identify Calvin's polemical gestures because he used an explicitly caustic and mocking rhetoric to attack his Epicurean foes. By using this type of language, Calvin gave his readers a sense that the enemy was standing right before them and that he was dismantling their pretensions publicly, for the sake of his more faithful readers who may have found this particular enemy threatening. However, in this chapter, Calvin never resorts to this type of language. His tone is steady and controlled and the absence of these vituperative gestures suggests that his "enemy" occupies a much more distant position in relation to the rhetorical world of his text. In fact, the absence of Calvin's usual polemical devices leaves one with the sense that the text is not designed to attack an immediate and threatening opponent. Instead, it appears that the "polemic" implied by his description of the seed's "convicting" function is a polemic designed to feed his more obvious pedagogical and apologetic agendas. In other words, even though the content of the chapter's argument points to polemical intentions, the rhetoric of the chapter signals agendas more appropriately described as "teaching" and "persuading for the purposes of conversion."

Another aspect of the peculiar use to which Calvin puts his polemic against the "atheist" comes into view when one tries to determine the historical face of this opponent based on the evidence provided by the first paragraph. In the process of constructing his defense of the presence of the *divinitatis sensus,* Calvin makes reference to several groups whose diverse religious practices offer positive evidence in support of the universal presence of the sense. The odd thing about Calvin's use of these groups is that the "savage" barbarian, the testimony of the "eminent pagan" Cicero, and the idolatrous worshipers of "wood and stone" all represent communities and religious perspectives that Calvin explicitly denounces later in the *Institutes.* Yet, they are employed here, without apparent critique, as witnesses in defense of his position. While the terms he actually uses to characterize these groups are admittedly far from laudatory—the barbarians remain uncivilized "brutes," Cicero remains a "pagan," and the idolaters remain precisely that—the force of his comments is clearly not directed against these audiences. Quite to the contrary, they are used as favorable evidence and hence rhetorically placed on Calvin's own side of the debate. He thus lines up his usual enemies and embraces them by valorizing their religious experience. In this way, he cleverly constructs a polemic that accomplishes its marginalizing intention by incorporating its own margins, the margins being those who, for the bulk of the *Institutes,* occupy in some form the position of "other." Given the breadth of this embrace, one wonders who is left to fill the space of the "unbeliever"? The absence of an obvious opponent further supports the contention that this chapter is designed with more pedagogical and apologetic than directly polemical purposes in mind.

At the close of my analysis of this first paragraph, what conclusions may be drawn about its rhetorical function? I have argued that Calvin's discussion of the presence of the *divinitatis sensus* does not serve a conceptually systematized or foundational function in relation to the remainder of the *Institutes* but rather appears to serve an agenda of a different sort. The question, then, is what might this other agenda be? First, given the propositional form of the paragraph's introduction and the carefully structured form of its argument, the agenda initially appears to be pedagogical. The reader meets Calvin in his nonthreatening role as teacher and is positioned before the text as student. Second, the notion of the *divinitatis sensus* is introduced topically as "beyond controversy"; and I have illustrated its historically noncontroversial character. However, in making such a claim, Calvin also rhetorically sets the discussion in the context of a debate. And when he first elaborates the term *divinitatis sensus* in terms of the function it serves—denying anyone the excuse of claiming ignorance of God—the polemical thrust of the discourse is further revealed. Thus, in treating a theological notion central to the tradition, Calvin pursues a pedagogical agenda that adopts a strategy of polemic to make its point.

Compared to his previous polemics, however, the character of this polemic is highly unusual. First, in contrast to the discussions of previous theologians, his polemic does not revolve around a debate regarding the seat or content of the "seed of religion." The ad hoc treatment of these issues reveals that this is not Calvin's concern. Rather, his polemic rests in the negative or convicting function that the seed serves, particularly with regard to those who would be "atheists." Second, the tone he adopts to pursue this attack lacks the caustic force of his previous polemical sections. Here, it is more suggestive of a distanced or perhaps absent target. Third, in both the logic of his argument and his use of sources, Calvin succeeds in embracing many of his usual enemies. The barbarians, idolaters, and pagans all provide him with positive evidence. Thus, Calvin puts to use the theological notion of *divinitatis sensus* as the central component of a polemic that intends to embrace rather than to exclude. And the embrace extends to an audience who would find cautious reasoning, noncaustic language, and a wide range of classical and ethnographic resources appealing—in short, an audience of theological students and humanist scholars.

Paragraphs Two and Three

In the course of the next two paragraphs, Calvin does not deviate significantly from either the topical or rhetorical agenda set forth in the opening paragraph. He continues to develop his defense of the universality of the *divinitatis sensus* by arguing against an unnamed opponent who supposedly denies the existence of God. He thus continues to give his readers the sense that he is debating someone, but it is "someone" whose identity only slowly emerges as his argument advances. In example after example, he describes how even the impious cannot claim ignorance of the divine because no matter how hard they strive to deny God's existence, they remain haunted by a deep and abiding sense of God's presence. Then, after each of these examples, he returns to the central thesis of the chapter and states once again that a truly atheistic disposition is not only indefensible but, more importantly, it is an anthropological impossibility. Calvin's position implies that those who deny God's existence are simply lying; and in doing so, they fundamentally "degenerate from the law of their creation" (*Inst.* 1.3.3, p. 46; OS 3:40.16).

However, as Calvin continues to invoke the presence of the unnamed opponent whom he is supposedly debating, he persistently avoids using the caustic rhetoric he normally reserves for polemical attacks. His tone and pace remain steady and his argument advances with logical precision. Given this textual temper, it seems Calvin is still more interested in teaching and persuading than he is in convicting or disarming. This dynamic again raises a question about the peculiar rhetorical role played by the ever-present "opponent." If Calvin simply intends to teach his students about the universal presence of an awareness of divinity, why does he posit an "enemy" to do so? Similarly, if his concern is to persuade the humanists of the legitimacy of his theology, why does he invoke a textual opponent in order to construct his defense of the universal presence of the *divinitatis sensus*? Is it part of a clever rhetorical strategy designed to teach by means of positing an "unspecified enemy?" If so, are there perhaps yet unnamed rhetorical undercurrents moving through the text of this chapter?

One way to begin sorting through these questions is to try to identify possible historical faces for this textual "other." In the second and third paragraphs, Calvin offers several subtle clues that help locate the plausible sixteenth-century referents for his supposed atheist. Most of these clues are imbedded in the argument of the second paragraph. Here, Calvin invites this apparently formidable opponent to enter the debate. Prefacing his comments with the dismissive assertion "therefore it is utterly vain for some men to say," he presents to the reader an account of his opponent's position:

> [They say] that religion was invented by the subtlety and craft of a few to hold the simple folk in thrall by this device and that those very persons who originated the worship of God for others did not in the least believe that any God existed. (*Inst.* 1.3.2, p. 44; OS 3:38.20–24)

Having stated their position, he then proceeds to dismantle it through a series of clever retorts. First, he partially concedes the opposition's point:

I confess, indeed, that in order to hold men's minds in greater subjection, clever men have devised very many things in religion by which to inspire the common folk with reverence and to strike them with terror. (*Inst.* 1.3.2, pp. 44–45; OS 3:38.24–27)

Then, as Calvin often does with his opponents, he takes his enemies' position and turns it against them:

But they would never have achieved this if men's minds had not already been imbued with a firm conviction about God, from which the inclination toward religion springs as from a seed. (*Inst.* 1.3.2, p. 45; OS 3:38.27–30)

He next attributes this firm conviction not only to the simple folk but to the crafty inventors of religion as well:

And indeed it is not credible that those who craftily imposed upon the ruder folk under pretense of religion were entirely devoid of the knowledge of God. If, indeed, there were some in the past, and today not a few appear, who deny that God exists, yet willy-nilly they from time to time feel an inkling of what they desire not to believe. (*Inst.* 1.3.2, p. 45; OS 3:38.30–39.1)

To support this contention, he draws out at length the example of Gaius Caligula, "the boldest despiser of God," who despite his professed unbelief trembled at the slightest sign of God's wrath:

One reads of no one who burst forth into bolder or more unbridled contempt of deity than Gaius Caligula; yet no one trembled more miserably when any sign of God's wrath manifested itself; thus—albeit unwillingly—he shuddered at the God whom he professedly sought to despise. You may see now and again how this also happens to those like him; how he who is the boldest despiser of God is of all men the most startled at the rustle of a falling leaf. (*Inst.* 1.3.2, p. 45; OS 3:39.1–8)

After the example of Caligula, Calvin moves on to a series of more general reflections on how the presence of God in the "seed of religion" works upon the conscience of all who try to flee it; and he concludes with an appeal to a broadly conceived notion of the "anxiety of conscience" (*conscientiae anxietas*) as a manifestation of the *religionis semen* and its final, inescapable conviction of the unbeliever:

If for these there is any respite from anxiety of conscience, it is not much different from the sleep of drunken or frenzied persons, who do not rest peacefully even while sleeping because they are continually troubled with dire and dreadful dreams. The impious themselves therefore exemplify the fact that some conception of God is ever alive in all men's minds. (*Inst.* 1.3.2, p. 45; OS 3:39.14–20)

Thus, by the end of the paragraph, the opponent's argument has not only "self-destructed," but the impious are also exposed for the reader as haunted and trembling before the divine.

In the process of dismantling his opponent's position, Calvin has also given the reader a clearer picture of the identity of this textual "other." First, in his opening statement about religion as the invention of "crafty men," Calvin alerts the reader to the fact that the position he is critiquing belongs to persons of power and education. This disclosure immediately rules out the possibility of attributing the atheism he is attacking to incipient "pagan" elements among the general population. On the contrary, Calvin portrays the simple or common folk as victims of those who hold them in "greater subjection." As such, these common folk are incorporated into the audience he seeks to affirm.

Second, for the reader well-versed in the classical tradition, the characterization he gives of his opponents' position would immediately bring to mind similar characterizations of the "atheists" found in the writings of Aristotle on religion.[18] Here as elsewhere, the classical "atheist" is depicted as a crafty political opportunist who nonetheless still trembles in the face of God's wrath. At this point in the text Calvin is also quoting, once again, almost verbatim from Cicero's *De natura deorum*. In that dialogue, the Skeptic philosopher Cotta calls religion an invention in his argument to counter the defense of a *sensus religionis* put forth by the Epicurean philosopher Vellius and the Stoic philosopher Balbus.[19] Thus, Calvin has invoked an opponent imbued with the weight of classical conceptions of "atheism." However, the text does not allow "these men" to appear before its readership as simply a literary reference to an impious group of the past. Later in the paragraph, he pulls Cicero's skeptical philosopher into the present by noting, "[i]f, indeed, there were some in the past, and today not a few appear, who deny that God exists . . ." (*qui Deum esse negunt . . .*). With this statement, Calvin identifies his real opponents as contemporaries, as men of "today." In this manner, Calvin informs his readers that the space of his textual other is occupied by presently living men of power whose philosophical inclinations are similar to those of the classical Skeptics who appear to deny any knowledge of God.

The Historical Face of Calvin's "Atheist"

Unfortunately, in terms of identifying the historical face of Calvin's opponent, chapter 3 offers no more evidence than that which I have just examined. Therefore, to determine who these powerful and crafty "atheists" may have been, let me step back from chapter 3 and look at some of Calvin's other writings to see if he elsewhere provides a more historically specific referent for this group. The most informative sources in this regard are the reformer's polemical tracts, which cover a period of over thirty years. Throughout these writings, Calvin frequently and quite loosely uses the term "atheist" to describe his opponents. In most cases, it is coupled with the terms "Epicurean," "Libertine," and "Skeptic." Quite surprisingly, however, in these polemical texts, the term "atheist" is seldom associated with persons who actually question the existence of God. Rather, it functions as a broad category describing many people whom Calvin considered "dangerous to the faith" for a variety of reasons, such as their position on the character of divine activity, the nature of the Trinity, the theology of the Eucharist, and the status of infant baptism.[20] These persons range from "papists," "Nicodemites," "Epicurean humanists," and "astrologers" to Genevan "Libertines," "soul sleepers," and Anabaptists.[21]

Of these groups, the two that share the most similarities with the "atheists" described in the argument of chapter 3 are the Epicurean humanists and the Genevan Libertines. One may infer that these people—or people like them—are the supposed atheists of this chapter because they are the only ones whose philosophical inclinations could have been typified according to a distinctly classical scheme like Cicero's. And they are also the only two groups in the above list whom Calvin considered both "crafty" and "powerful." Although both "the papists" and "the Nicodemites" represent groups that had accumulated great social and political power, Calvin seldom refers to them as "crafty" and he never identifies them with characters drawn from the world of classical philosophy. In contrast, the "Epicureans" (a term commonly directed at the group of humanists I discussed in the previous chapter) and the "Libertines" (a name used to signal the party of Calvin's opponents in Geneva) represent for Calvin two groups of persons who not only fit this chapter's classical description of the philosophical atheists but who also wielded enough social power to pose a threat, real or imagined, to the theological cause of reform.

To determine further if the "Epicureans" and the "Libertines" are the implied targets of accusations of "atheism" in chapter 3, one must look more closely at the descriptions Calvin offers of both groups elsewhere in his writings. They are discussed respectively in Calvin's 1550 treatise *De scandalis* and in his correspondences concerning the Caroli controversy of 1537, the Bolsec affair of 1551, and the letters to Monsieur Falais on the Gruet affair of 1547.[22] In looking at these tracts, letters, and events, note that most of chapter 3 was first penned by Calvin in 1539, a period shortly after the Caroli affair but before the writing of *De scandalis*, before his letters concerning the eruptions of the Bolsec and Gruet affairs, and before his polemics at the height of the Perrinist "Libertine" conflict in Geneva. The later dates of these events make it clear that Bolsec, Gruet, and the

Perrinist Libertines are not the specific target of Calvin's attack in this chapter because his encounter with them had yet to unfold. But, as is the case with many of Calvin's opponents, these people represent a "type" against whom Calvin would rigorously polemicize throughout his career. Thus, exploring how these letters and tracts characterize the "Epicureans" and "Libertines" who "deny that God exists" helps to identify the particular "type" of historical character Calvin may have had in mind when crafting "the atheist" with whom he argues in this chapter.

Written to strengthen the faithful with "the kinds of weapons with which the Lord usually equips his people for resistance, whenever he summons them to battle," *De scandalis* identifies the Epicurean position as one of the strongest opponents met on the battlefield of faith.[23] Describing them as "rejectors of the gospel" and "those who spread atheistic views," Calvin lists a now familiar group: Agrippa, Servetus, Dolet, Rabelais, Deperius, and Gouvéa.[24] Again, in language reminiscent of chapter 3, he describes them as men of power who take pride in their "sharpness of mind," thus paralleling his depiction of the impious as "crafty and subtle men." He characterizes them further as men who "turn to the empty pleasures of the world," an image that also recalls his portrayal in chapter 3 of the impious as the moral equals of Caligula. There is one significant point, however, where *De scandalis* and chapter 3 diverge in their descriptions of this "atheistic" opposition. In *De scandalis*, Calvin calls his opponents "atheists," but he never associates the term "atheist" with the questioning of God's existence; however, in chapter 3, the denial of God's existence— "those who deny that God exists"—appears to be one of the principal accusations directed toward his polemic's opposition. What does this ambiguity about the content of the charge "atheism" reveal about both the historical face of Calvin's target and the rhetorical shape of discussion in chapter 3?

With respect to the men attacked in *De scandalis*, historical evidence suggests that had Calvin lodged this complaint against them—denying God's existence—it would have been without warrant. While these men represented a spectrum of theologically unpopular opinions, they remained faithful to the Roman Catholic Church throughout their careers, and as far as their surviving texts indicate, they never even approached the position of "atheism" if it is understood as the questioning of God's very being.[25] The closest they would have come to embracing unorthodox theological views would have been their various attempts to reconceptualize the character of God's providential rule, as did the Epicureans among the ancients. It may well be that from Calvin's perspective, to challenge God's providence was equivalent to questioning God's existence. However, in the theological writings of these men, the question of God's existence not only remains unchallenged, it is not even engaged as an issue. Therefore, if sixteenth-century "Epicureans" such as these are the target of Calvin's attack, his accusation of "denying God's existence" would appear to be either a historical exaggeration or a lively fabrication. The possibility that the accusation of "atheism" was a lively fabrication on Calvin's part, however, does not rule out the possibility that he found it rhetorically useful to give this particular group such a caricatured identity.[26] As to why he may have deployed such an exaggerated gesture, let me continue to look to Calvin's own writings for an answer.

In addition to *De scandalis*, Calvin's letters concerning the Caroli affair of 1537, the Gruet affair of 1547, and the Bolsec incident of 1551 reveal that accusations of "atheism" were also part of the rhetorical arsenal deployed by the reformer in his prolonged and often violent confrontation with oppositional elements within Geneva referred to under the broad heading "Libertines."[27] Although separated by a period of ten years, Caroli and Gruet were both perceived as ideological allies of the Perrins, a leading family who over a period of twenty years came into repeated conflicts with Calvin and the ruling Genevan Consistory.[28] And although neither of these two men were themselves powerful political figures in the city of Geneva, for Calvin they represented oppositional forces that threatened the cause of reform.[29]

The arsenal of terms that Calvin directs at these men is frequently similar to the terms used to describe the "atheists" of *De scandalis*. For example, in his personal correspondence during the Gruet trial, Calvin states that the charge against Gruet is "unbelief," which he further describes as "a radical denial of the existence of God," an accusation that parallels his description of the opponent in chapter 3.[30] As with the Epicureans, however, historical evidence suggests that Gruet (as well as Caroli and Bolsec) did not deny the existence of God; at most, he questioned traditional Trinitarian formulations. Thus, in terms of Calvin's dealing with a "Libertine" such as Gruet, one finds, once again, that the charge of "atheism" may have been fabricated by the reformer and then rhetorically deployed in order to marginalize a figure or a group that threatened the cause of religious and political reform in Geneva. If this is in fact the rhetorical strategy of chapter 3, then what light does it throw on Calvin's discussion of the *divinitatis sensus?* Again, a bit more historical background may be helpful in moving the reader closer to a potential answer to this question.

The absence of any modern "atheism" in either of these groups, the Epicurean humanists or the Genevan Libertines, confirms the conclusions of a well-known debate among historians in the French Annales school on the presence of atheism in the sixteenth century. Led by the work of Lucien Febvre and later supported and expanded by the writings of Paul Oskar Kristeller, Jean Wirth, and François Berriot, early Renaissance scholars have argued at length that despite nineteenth- and early–twentieth-century protestations to the contrary, the predominant medieval cosmology that still held sway at the time of the Reformation did not provide a conceptual framework within which questioning the existence of God would have been possible.[31] They have further demonstrated that in contrast to contemporary understandings of atheism, in the sixteenth century the term is best understood as a rhetorical tool, gleaned from the classics and deployed in theological polemics. When put to polemical use, the term "atheist" thus served as a broadly derogatory description of a vast array of opponents who either offered theologically unorthodox opinions or threatened existing ecclesiastical structures in both Rome and the various reforming movements.[32] In either case, they have argued that no one, not even the more radical Italian humanists, challenged the necessary existence of some form of deity.[33] On the basis of this evidence, it appears that Calvin may have adopted the style of theological polemics described by Kristeller and Febvre and, following the literary conventions of his day, attributed the title "atheist" to his opponents for the purpose of sheer rhetorical effectiveness.

While the Annales school debate throws much light on the nature and function of Calvin's "atheistic" foe in chapter 3, it should be noted as well that the fictional atheism that Calvin attributes to his opponents is anomalous in one important respect: contrary to the Annales school's thesis that no one in the sixteenth century actually questioned the existence of God, Calvin suggests in the third chapter that the opponent he is debating *does* question God's existence. Even though Calvin may have fabricated this identity, he nonetheless accuses this "atheist opponent" of denying God's existence, a claim that the Annales debate, as I have shown, suggests was not plausible in the sixteenth century.[34] How, then, is one to interpret Calvin's claim that he is responding to a group of persons—albeit, a group that is a rhetorical creation—that historical evidence suggests was outside the conceptual framework of the sixteenth-century intellect?

In answering this last question, all I can offer is a brief and speculative remark. Could it be that in the process of invoking this exaggerated polemical foe, Calvin textually fashions a historically unprecedented "atheistic" identity and, in doing so, inadvertently both challenges and expands the conceptual framework of his age? If this is the case, then chapter 3 may be serving a rhetorical and social function that has been neglected by Calvin's interpreters over the years. Calvin may have textually generated, in his grand rhetorical fashion, an identity that had as yet no explicit historical referent but would soon be occupied by one of modernity's most interesting characters, that very alive and popular foe known to later generations of Enlightenment theologians as the intellectual atheist. Would it not be one of history's ironies if here, in the *Institutes*, one could trace the conceptual roots of not only Puritan, Presbyterian, and

Dutch Reformed identities, but the emergent identity of contemporary culture's great religious skeptic as well?[35] With this question, I admittedly have moved far beyond the scope of the present study, but when one begins to "imagine with" an orator as "subtle" and "powerful" as Calvin himself, such speculative ruminations are hard to resist.

The Rhetorical Function of "Otherness"

Although I have determined something of the social functions that may have been served by the polemical debate moving through chapter 3, the most important question still remains unanswered. My rhetorical analysis of the three paragraphs that constitute this chapter has demonstrated that Calvin's style, tone, and form of argumentation all suggest that the polemical agenda was constructed primarily for the purpose of supporting his pedagogical and apologetic interests. For this reason, it seems that even though his construction of this textual "atheist" may have served rhetorically to buttress Calvin's disputes with the Epicureans and the Genevan Libertines, this function is a secondary one. The more important functions are those of teaching and persuading an audience that was far from hostile, Calvin's students and the moderate elements within the humanist movement. In this regard, the question that remains unanswered concerns the peculiar way in which this textually posited "other" rhetorically serves to advance two agendas that are not polemical but constructive in nature. To answer this question, one must again consider the general context in which Calvin's text was being deployed.

As evangelist, apologist, and confessional leader of a marginal but growing community of faith in Geneva and France, the task of carving out the character of his community's identity remained a central one for Calvin. In my analysis of Calvin's "Prefatory Address to King Francis I of France," I explored the narrative world within which Calvin attempted to define the unique identity of the faithful. In this same context, I also argued that the task of generating a communal identity for the faithful was particularly difficult and yet enormously important. It was difficult because the evangelical communities in France whom Calvin was attempting to define were religiously, politically, and socially outside many of his age's more traditional structures of cultural valuation. In this sense, the dominant culture's appraisal of their identity was not only insufficient but also dangerous because it constituted one of the means by which their marginalization was enacted rhetorically. It was therefore extremely important for Calvin to generate textually a robust and theologically solid identity that could function to bolster and empower this community rather than contributing to its oppression. In order to accomplish such a feat, Calvin had to reconceive the systems of signification through which the community of the faithful would come to understand and identify itself.

In terms of constructing a new language of identity, the question of limits and boundaries became a central one for Calvin.[36] For a socially marginal community who had already been given a "seditious and treasonous" identity by the dominant culture, the process of generating an alternative identity inevitably included the task of fending off the forces assaulting them. Under such circumstances, the question "Who are we?" becomes entangled with the question "Who are we not?" One can see this dynamic at play in Calvin's preface to the king. Here, he identifies the community of truly faithful Christians as the saints and martyrs who are being persecuted by the "evil" Roman clerics. In order to identify the faithful in this way, Calvin rhetorically profits from the construction of a polemical foe whose contrasting identity reveals the "purity" and "godliness" of the people he seeks to support, teach, and theologically edify.

A similar dynamic may be at work in the third chapter as well. If so, it would help to account for the rather strange role Calvin's polemic plays in the construction of his argument. As I stated earlier, Calvin's polemic is odd in that it appears to function as an embracing gesture designed to advance his pedagogical agenda, rather than as a gesture aimed only at attacking an enemy. Through this rhetorical gesture, Calvin may have been using the presence of a fictional or exaggerated foe to promote the construction of a positive communal identity. If this is the case, then the question of whether or not the atheist actually existed becomes superfluous because the rhetorical function of this discussion lies in constituting an identity that is "other than itself." In this sense, Calvin's textual "other" points beyond itself, and in its negative reflection, the identity of "that which this other is not" is established.[37] The "atheist" thus becomes a rhetorical device designed not only to teach but also to invoke an identity suitable for Calvin's students in Geneva. Similarly, the "atheist" may function as a rhetorical trope intended to promote Calvin's apologetic agenda by making his own position more appealing when contrasted to the fictionalized or exaggerated other he has posited.

An Interweave of Agendas

As I pointed out at the beginning of this chapter, Reformed theologians have had a difficult time giving a coherent account of Calvin's view of "natural knowledge" because his overarching discussion of the subject is seemingly confused and often inconsistent. Evidence of this confusion can be seen in the fact that Calvin effectively cancels out the entire argument of chapter 3 by the time he gets to his treatment of scripture in chapter 6. In an effort to throw some light on this particular confusion, I have sug-

gested that perhaps Calvin's discussion of "natural knowledge" was designed to do more than simply present his position on the possibility of
such knowledge. I have suggested also that a reading that attends to the
rhetorical play of chapter 3 may help to discern what this "more" might
be.

Now, at the end of my close reading of the text, what can be said in summary about this "more"? What kinds of rhetorical functions has this chapter been designed to serve and what has Calvin accomplished in terms of
socially positioning his readers? As with the two previous chapters, the
answer is complex. At the most obvious level, the chapter provides a context in which Calvin can discuss a doctrine that has long been included in
the canons of Western Christian theology, the doctrine of the *divinitatis
sensus*. Because of its history and because of Calvin's own desire to stay
within the doctrinal boundaries marked by patristic theology, Calvin
could not have avoided treating this topic without leaving a glaring hole
in his own theology. Similarly, Calvin wanted to give his students a comprehensive account of the foundations of the Christian faith, and he could
not have done so without at least mentioning the "seed of religion." However, as a clever rhetorician, Calvin also uses the discursive space provided by this doctrine to pursue a number of additional goals.

One of these goals was to continue to carve out the terms of his own authority as a leader in Geneva and in the growing international Reformed
movement. In this chapter, Calvin may have pursued this goal by using
the discursive space provided by the "seed of religion" as a battleground
upon which he could launch attacks at two formidable opponents, the Epicurean humanists and the Genevan Libertines. He may have accomplished this assault by giving each of these groups a fictional identity, the
identity of "the atheist." Rhetorically positioning them as his textual
"other," he could then proceed to disarm them discursively by depicting
them as liars and as morally decrepit, crafty men. Thus, through this
rhetoric of "otherness" and its accompanying polemic, Calvin may have
managed, once again, to advance a complex political and social agenda in
the context of a theological discussion.

However, I have suggested that this polemical agenda is only a secondary one and that Calvin's principal agenda most likely remained that
of building up the community of the faithful by teaching his students and
by apologetically courting the sympathies of moderate French humanists
and their supporters in the French aristocracy in order to garner their support for the cause of the evangelical church in Calvin's homeland. In this
third chapter, he seemingly accomplishes both these agendas by constructing a textual "other" over and against which the emerging identity
of the Reformed movement could take shape. By positing this fictional
"other," Calvin may have created a rhetorical space within which the

purity and godliness of the faithful could become all the more apparent. Similarly, in this same rhetorical space, he could also advance his apology to the humanists by making his own position appear irresistible and indisputable. In both cases, the textually invoked "other" serves not only to exclude his opponents, but more importantly, to define and embrace his colleagues, friends, and faithful followers. This insight into the way in which Calvin might have profited rhetorically from the presence of a discursive "other" is particularly crucial for understanding the theology of the remainder of the *Institutes*, for this "other" will continue to emerge, in a variety of forms that are calculated to move and dispose Calvin's audience in particular ways.

THEOLOGICAL CONCLUSIONS

I began my analysis of chapter 3 with the suggestion that one's understanding of the complexities at work in Calvin's doctrine of "natural knowledge of God the Creator" might be productively supplemented with insights into the broader social function of the text. As I now bring to a close my investigations into just a few of those social functions, I hope the reader can begin to see new possibilities for reading Calvin and to envision unprecedented avenues for interpreting Calvin's theology. However, opening up these possibilities and envisioning these avenues far from simplifies the interpretive task. Instead, this analysis, if it has succeeded, raises more questions than it answers—questions related both to how Calvin's text should be read as a historical document and to how it might be used in the context of contemporary constructive theology.

For instance, what does one do with a doctrine whose rhetorical success is predicated upon an argument that constructs and then excludes "the other"? The answer to this question is neither simple nor clear. On the one hand, the rhetoric of otherness in this chapter can lend itself to a positive or sympathetic reading of Calvin's theology. Such a reading will most likely occur if one focuses on the function his rhetoric would have served for the "we" of the chapter. For this community, the language of the text appears to intend the teaching, uplifting, and encouraging of the faithful living in a marginal situation. The "argument" thus seems designed as "good news" for persons who were being persecuted daily. It is crafted to articulate the character of their piety by defining the boundaries of their emergent identity as a reforming movement. When one looks at the rhetorical gestures Calvin uses to accomplish this task, one finds that it is precisely through the countermarginalization of "the other"—the atheist—that a foundation is laid for the construction of this still nascent communal identity. In this manner, Calvin's rhetoric of "otherness" can be interpreted as a rhetoric designed to establish theological/linguistic boundaries that strengthen the weak, bolster the besieged, and give shape to the shattered.

On the other hand, theological assessments of Calvin's rhetoric must look not only at his doctrine's original social function but at its present-day possibilities as well. And here the issue becomes more complex. While it is one thing to describe the original social function of such a gesture, it is quite another to decide what present-day churches standing in the Reformed tradition should do with this kind of rhetoric. In this context, Calvin's example requires that one ask if there are parallels to this rhetoric in contemporary Calvinist theology. Does the Reformed tradition continue to invoke a language that creates and then marginalizes "the other" in order to circumscribe the boundaries of its beliefs and practices? If so, who are the present-day "others" and what is the social cost of their exclusion? Here, one cannot help but call to mind those moments in the history of the Reformed tradition when such a rhetoric was used for destructive purposes. For example, Reformed theologians continue to struggle with the often violent rhetorics of "otherness" that typified some forms of Calvinist Puritans' views of indigenous peoples in colonial New England. Similarly, it is hard for persons in Reformed traditions to avoid the all-too-recent memory of how Calvinist distinctions between "us" and "them" were used to facilitate the construction and perpetuation of an apartheid ideology in South Africa.

But these examples alone do not settle the question of contemporary use. In terms of assessing this rhetoric of otherness, one must continue to push the question by asking if it makes a difference whom one puts in the position of Calvin's "other." Could there be contemporary situations that parallel Calvin's insofar as the space of "the other" is reserved not for the socially marginal but for the powerful and privileged? And if this occurs, could it be that such a rhetoric serves a liberative rather than oppressive social function when deployed by persons whose identities have been historically eclipsed or oppressively distorted by the dominant culture? Here, many examples from history come to mind as well: the struggle of Reformed communities in South Africa who resisted apartheid policies on Calvinist grounds; the theology of Reformed theologians who actively resisted the rise of National Socialism in Hitler's Germany; and the many small resistances of Reformed Christians in North America who struggle to live faithfully in the context of the dominant culture's often oppressive value systems. These examples lead one to ask if it is possible to speak with the political and theological boldness of a figure like Calvin and not construct norms and boundaries that exclude and judge. If it is possible to avoid drawing lines and positing "others," what would such a rhetoric be like? Would it be a "boundless" identity? If so, who would profit from its enactment?

As these examples suggest, this reading of chapter 3 also raises a series of questions related to the character of theological meaning. How does one, as a contemporary reader, assess it? If my analysis of the multiple functions that this doctrine served in the sixteenth century shows how the *Institutes* accrues its theological meanings, then it is clear that textual meaning is far from stable or static. Rather, as my reading suggests, these meanings shift and turn as quickly as the weight of popular language shifts and changes, following the ever-fluctuating movement of culture, power, and the play of theological images. At one moment, the text appears to be teaching. Then, with only a slight turn in the angle of vision, the text cuts back against an unnamed foe. At one moment, it embraces the "pagan" philosopher; at the next, it attacks the natural religion of classical philosophy. At one moment it claims that all persons know God; at the next, "not one in a hundred" is described as having a sense of God's presence. In this manner, the text fluctuates between discursive logics that are often as hard to track rhetorically as they are difficult to map historically.

How certain can one be that the text actually served these multiple and shifting functions with regard to its historical audiences? Again, the answer to this question is complex. Just as I, as this text's interpreter, cannot presume to know the mind of Calvin, I cannot reenter the sixteenth century and experience the force that Calvin's rhetoric accrued as it intermingled with the language of popular culture and struggled to forge this new evangelical identity. In this sense, its effect cannot be measured precisely. But to push the question even further, even if I could measure its sixteenth-century force, would this allow me to stabilize and pin down the meanings of the text? Most probably not, for even in the present context, I cannot map precisely the multiple functions served by a *divinitatis sensus* rhetoric. In a time of intensifying cultural wars over the canonical status of traditionally privileged discourses of "otherness," it would be difficult to find a single meaning that defines the implications of Calvin's construction of and attack on his textual "others," the "impious."

But the fact that static interpretations of this doctrine cannot be produced, be they interpretations of its meaning in the sixteenth century or today, need not prevent one from struggling to construct historically and socially plausible accounts of the functions of his theology. And in the process of doing so, Calvin's readers are not left simply to their own imaginative devices. Numerous clues can assist in marking the limits of plausibility: the advice of historians, the insight of social scientists, the creative work of literary critics, and of course, present-day experiences of the relationship between meaning, context, and the language of "otherness." There are also the clues of numerous "prefaces," all of which suggest boundaries of plausibility. These "prefaces" may take the form of letters, as in Calvin's work, or they may be prefatory phenomena that come in the form of institutions, ecclesial practices, theological creeds, political movements, or simply the internal rules of a given communal discourse. And if one stands in the culture of a Reformed Christian community that seeks to make constructive use of Calvin, then one also has the concrete prefatory materials of individual and collective identities that continue to be deeply shaped by the rhetoric of Calvin's theology. Those "seeds of religion" and the many lives in which they grow are still flowering into new dimensions of plausibility, and in these dimensions the rhetoric of piety continues to thrive and sow yet more "seeds" of Christian identity.

NOTES

1. "[I]n quo maturescat tantum abest ut fructus appareat suo tempore" (OS 3:41.1–2).

2. As I will later argue, the actual term *"divinitatis sensus"* appears to play no significant role in shaping the doctrines Calvin treats in the remainder of the *Institutes*. The fact that the term does not appear to serve an explicit function, however, does not mean it does not play an implicit role in his theology. Based on Calvin's description of the Christian life in Book 3, one can assume that when human beings are "imbued with the grace of Jesus Christ," this innate sense, along with all the faculties of the human person, becomes an enlivened part of Christian knowledge and action.

3. "Ita fit ut nulla in mundo recta maneat pietas" (OS 3:41.5).

4. "[N]on apprehendunt qualem se offert, sed qualem pro sua temeritate fabricati sunt, imaginantur" (OS 3:41.14–15).

5. "This, however, is but a vain and false shadow of religion, scarcely even worth being called a shadow. From it one may easily grasp anew how much this confused knowledge of God differs from the piety from which religion takes its source, which is instilled in the breasts of believers only" (Inst. 1.4.4., p. 50); "Sed quando inanis ea est et mendax religionis umbra, vix etiam digna quae umbra nominetur: hinc rursus facile elicitur quantum ab hac confusa Dei notitia differat quae solis fidelium pectoribus instillatur pietas, ex qua demum religio nascitur" (OS 3:43.33–44.3).

6. "[C]ertas gloriae suae notas insculpsit, et quidem adeo claras et insignes ut sublata sit quanlibet rudibus et stupidis ignorantiae excusatio" (OS 3:45.6–8).

7. One finds references to the "sense of divinity" throughout Augustine's corpus; see, e.g., *City of God* 11.27: "for we have another and far superior sense, belonging to the inner man, by which we perceive what things are just and what unjust" (trans. Marcus Dods, in *Select Library of Nicene and Post-Nicene Fathers*, series 1, vol. 2 [Grand Rapids: Wm. B. Eerdmans Publishing Co., 1979], 221); "Habemus enim alium interioris hominis sensum isto longe praestantiorem, quo justa et injusta sentimus" (J.-P. Migne, ed., *Patrologia Latina*, vol. 41 [Paris, 1845], col. 341). See also Augustine's *Confessions*, trans. J. G. Pilkington, in *Select Library of Nicene and Post-Nicene Fathers*, series 1, vol. 1 (Grand Rapids: Wm. B. Eerdmans Publishing Co., 1979), book 10, chap. 6. Augustine is not Calvin's only patristic source. See

Lactantius (*Divine Institutes* 3.10, in *Ante-Nicene Fathers*, vol. 7 [Grand Rapids: Wm. B. Eerdmans Publishing Co., 1979], 78). Here, Lactantius agrees with Cicero, whom he quotes on the divine sense. See Cicero, *De legibus* 1.8.24, a passage very similar to chapter 3 of Calvin's *Institutes*, 1.3. In addition, see Justin Martyr, *De monarchia* 1: "Although human nature at first received a union of intelligence and safety to discern the truth, and the worship due to the one Lord of all, yet envy, insinuating the excellence of human greatness, turned men away to the making of idols. . . . For the truth is of itself sufficient to show forth, by means of those things contained under the pole of heaven, the order [instituted by] Him who has created them" (trans. G. Reith, *Ante-Nicene Fathers*, vol. 1 [Grand Rapids: Wm. B. Eerdmans Publishing Co., 1979], 290).

8. In contrast to Augustine, who deploys the notion in much the same manner as Calvin, Thomas puts it to quite a different use. See his *Summa Theologia*, 1a, art. 12, questions 2–5: "That divine presence is instantly perceived by the mind on the sight of and through bodily things comes from two causes, from its own penetrating clearness and from the gleaming of divine brightness in our renewed bodies" (*S.T.* 1a.12, 4 ad 2, trans. Herbert McCabe, O.P., in *Summa Theologia*, vol. 3 [New York: McGraw-Hill Book Co., 1964], 13); "Quod autem statim visis illis corporibus divina praesentia ex eis cognoscatum per intellectum ex duobus contingit, scilicet ex perspicuitate intellectus, et ex refulgentia divinae claritatis in corporibus innovatis" (ibid., p. 12). My reference is not meant to imply that Calvin was familiar with Thomas's position on the *divinitatis sensus*. I wish simply to point to the fact that even Scholastic theologians familiar with Thomas would not have found Calvin's position on the matter problematic. See Arvin Vos, *Aquinas, Calvin, and Contemporary Protestant Thought: A Critique of Protestant Views of the Thought of Thomas Aquinas* (Grand Rapids: Wm. B. Eerdmans Publishing Co., 1985).

9. Epicurus "alone perceived, first, that the gods exist, because nature herself has imprinted a conception of them on the minds of all mankind. . . . For the belief in the gods has not been established by authority, custom or law, but rests on the unanimous and abiding consensus of mankind"; "Solus enim vidit primum esse deos, quod in omnium animis eorum notionem inpressisset ipsa natura. . . . Cum enim non instituto aliquo aut more aut lege sit opinio constituta maneatque ad unum omnium firma consensio" (*De natura deorum* 1.16.43 and 17.44; pp. 44–45).

10. For the most developed defense of the influence of Cicero, see Grislis, "Calvin's Use of Cicero in the *Institutes*," 1:1–5, 5–37.

11. Cicero, *De natura deorum* 3.3.8, pp. 292–93.

12. Inst. 1.3.1 and 1.3.3; 1.3.44 and 1.3.46; OS 3:38.39.

13. According to Calvin's view of redemption, he most likely would have supported the claim that once the human creature is restored through grace to right relation with God, the divine seed is also restored to an original, productive state; and in this sense, it continues to be an active part of our knowledge of God. However, it is notable that this type of argument does not constitute an explicit part of his theological anthropology or his discussion of justification and sanctification.

14. For the distinction between the two terms see Otto Gründler, "The Problem of *Semen fidei* in the Teaching of Calvin," in *Calvinus servus Christi* (Budapest: Presseabteilung des Raday-Kollegiums, 1988), 205–7.

15. One of the clearest examples of a Reformed epistemologist who argues for the foundational status of the *divinitatis sensus* is Cornelius Van Til, *A Christian Theory of Knowledge* (Grand Rapids: Baker Book House, 1969). Also see John Leith, *An*

Introduction to the Reformed Tradition: A Way of Being the Christian Community (Atlanta: John Knox Press, 1977).

16. See also Cicero, *De natura deorum* 2.4.12, p. 135.

17. On a more speculative note, it is possible that these descriptions of barbarians and savages would have found new meanings in the sixteenth-century context of the discovery of "the new world." This is a subject on which little work has been done in the area of Calvin studies but which promises to raise important critical questions about the rhetorical function of an emerging racist ideology in early modern Europe. See Margaret Trabue Hodgen, *Early Anthropology in the Sixteenth and Seventeenth Centuries* (Philadelphia: University of Pennsylvania Press, 1964). Also see David Brion Davis, *The Problem of Slavery in Western Culture* (Ithaca, N.Y.: Cornell University Press, 1966).

18. For a discussion of Aristotle's depiction of the "atheist" and the role this depiction played in Renaissance Europe, see Nauert, *Agrippa and the Crisis of Renaissance Thought*, 153.

19. See Cicero, *De natura deorum* 1.23, pp. 62–63, 60–61; 3.3,7, pp. 192–93.

20. It should be noted that within the constraints of Calvin's theology, it often appears that belief in a God who does not actively engage in the lives of the human creature is tantamount to not believing in God at all or to questioning the existence of God. In this regard, see Calvin's discussion of the Epicureans in chapter 2 of the *Institutes*.

21. François Berriot, *Athéismes et athéistes au XVIe siècle en France*, vol. 2 (Lille: Thesis arf, 1984), 593–613, 847–67; Jean Wirth, " 'Libertines' et 'Epicuriens': Aspects de l'irréligion au 16e siècle." On Gruet and Caroli, see *Letters of John Calvin*, vol. 4, ed. Jules Bonnet, trans. David Constable and M. R. Gilchrist (Philadelphia: Presbyterian Board of Publication, 1858), 125–28, 268–70.

22. John Calvin, *Concerning Scandals*, trans. John W. Fraser (Grand Rapids: Wm. B. Eerdmans Publishing Co., 1978).

23. *Ibid.*, 2.

24. *Ibid.*, 59–62.

25. On Agrippa's "atheism," see Nauert, *Agrippa and the Crisis of Renaissance Thought*, and Yates, *The Occult Philosophy in the Elizabethan Age*. On Dolet, see Christie, *Etienne Dolet*, and Dawson, *Toulouse in the Renaissance*. On Bonaventure Des Periers, see Christie, *Etienne Dolet*, 228–29. On Rabelais, see Screech, *Rabelais*.

26. One could speculate on several reasons Calvin might have had for caricaturing in this particular manner. For example, as I discussed briefly in the preceding chapter, Calvin was engaged in an ideological battle with this group of humanists as he competed for financial support from the court of Marguerite Navarre. Such a rhetoric would have most assuredly served his polemical agenda with respect to this community. On an even more speculative note, it could be because Lyon, a city where many of these "Epicureans" had spent a considerable amount of time, was emerging as Geneva's principal economic competitor in the areas of publishing and commercial trade. In this context, rhetorically identifying its commercial successes with the immoral excesses of "atheism" would have been to Calvin's advantage. Hence, polemically marginalizing this community could have served to advance Geneva's political and economic interests while simultaneously feeding Calvin's pedagogical and apologetic appetite. On the political and economic relations between Geneva and Lyon, see J.H.M. Salmon, *Society in Crisis*, and Donald Kelley, *The Beginning of Ideology*. On the role of rhetoric,

economics, and early modern conceptions of property, see the work of Patricia Parker, *Literary Fat Ladies: Rhetoric, Gender, Property* (New York: Methuen Press, 1987).

27. Ross William Collins, *Calvin and the Libertines of Geneva*, 109–11 and 153–200. For a brief discussion of the conflict between Bolsec and Calvin, see McGrath, *A Life of John Calvin*, 16–17.

28. With regard to their relation to the term "Epicurean," it may be significant that both Gruet and Caroli spent time amongst the ranks of humanists in the court of Marguerite Navarre, although again at different periods in the life of the court. On the famous "Meaux Circle" and its relation to Geneva, see Henry Heller, *The Conquest of Poverty*, 27–69.

29. In 1547, Gruet was summoned by the Consistory, tried, and executed for the crime of "unbelief." Although in 1537 Caroli was tried for the same crime, his sentence was exile. See Collins, *Calvin and the Libertines of Geneva*, 109–11 and 153–200.

30. On Calvin's opinion of Gruet, see his letter to Falais, 14 July 1547, *Letters of John Calvin*, 125–28; and his letter to the Siegneury of Geneva, May 1550, *ibid.*, 268–70. Also see Walker, *John Calvin*, 304–7.

31. See Wirth, "'Libertines' et 'Epicuriens,'" and Berriot, *Athéismes et athéistes*. For the origin of the debate on this point, see Henri Busson, "Les Noms des incrédules au XVIe siècle," *Bibliothèque d'Humanisme et de Renaissance* 16 (1954): 273–83; Lucien Febvre, *Le problème de l'incroyance au XVIe siècle: La religion de Rabelais* (Paris: Albin Michel, 1942); and P. O. Kristeller, "Atheism and the French Tradition of Free Thought," *Journal of the History of Philosophy* 6 (1968): 233–43.

32. For a developed discussion of Calvin's rhetorical depiction of the atheists see Berriot, *Athéismes et athéistes*, 593ff.

33. On atheism among the Italian humanists, see P. O. Kristeller, "Atheism," 233–43, and Busson, "Les Noms," 273–83.

34. On this point, the Annales school is of little assistance because their investigations of Calvin were limited to his shorter treatises, and the *Institutes* was completely neglected.

35. One of the most fascinating aspects of Calvin's textual generation of this "modern atheist" is the possibility that, if the Annales debate is correct and no historical referent actually existed, then the identity of the European atheist was being forged in the space of discursive rhetoric for purely polemical purposes. This is a rather startling possibility given that the term "atheist" acquired so much historical and intellectual capital in the decades and centuries that followed.

36. Margaret Ferguson discusses this dynamic in the introduction to *Trials of Desire: Renaissance Defense of Poetry* (New Haven, Conn.: Yale University Press, 1983). She argues that for marginal communities, the task of generating a constructive identity cannot be separated from the task of apologetics and polemics precisely because the relations of power that constitute a marginal community demand that their identity be forged in the context of a battle for discursive space that the marginal community is not permitted to occupy.

37. T. Min-Ha Trinh discusses the rhetorical process whereby identity is formed by the positing of an other in *Woman, Native, Other: Writing, Postcoloniality, and Feminism* (Bloomington: Indiana University Press, 1989). Although she does not apply her analysis to texts such as Calvin's, she does argue that this kind of strategy is found throughout the canons of Western literature. For a similar discussion, see Michel de Certeau, *Heterologies: Discourses on the Other*, trans. Brian Massumi (Minneapolis: University of Minnesota Press, 1986).

6

CALVIN AND THE RHETORICS OF CONTEMPORARY THEOLOGY

Nothing frustrates a rhetorician more than an interruption that breaks the flow of an eloquent speech, cuts off the course of language, and leaves it immobilized from its goal of persuasion. But as orators have known for centuries, interruptions are to be expected if one speaks or writes in the public arena, for audiences are hardly ever passive and often prove quite unruly. John Calvin would no doubt find the conclusion of this book to be one such interruption. After all, I am cutting off Calvin's rhetoric by abruptly stopping my analysis of the *Institutes* at the very moment he is ready to begin an important part, his doctrine of Creation. But it is also true that the test of truly skillful orators lies in their ability to turn an interruption to their own advantage and quickly integrate it into their larger rhetorical project. If Calvin were present, he would assuredly turn my conclusion to his own advantage and continue to move eloquently toward the broader theological goals he pursues.

In Calvin's absence, however, the task of integration is left to the present author. Still, the example of Calvin bids one ask: Can it be done? Can this book's intervention in the rhetorical development of the *Institutes* be turned to some greater advantage? Can it be integrated into a broader project? If so, what might that broader project look like? What is the significance of this book? And what broader theological goals do my readings of Calvin seek to accomplish? These are the questions this conclusion aims to address. Because they are questions that would be foremost in the mind of an orator, they are also questions that Calvin probably would most gladly bequeath to any theologian who seriously studies the legacy of the vast rhetorical tradition in which he stands.

If the overarching purpose of this book were solely to offer a comprehensive rhetorical analysis of Calvin's theology, then my efforts would obviously be far from complete. Indeed, I have examined only three of the shortest chapters in the *Institutes* and have left the doctrines that constitute the rest of his theology virtually untouched. I say "virtually" untouched because each part of the *Institutes* anticipates and depends on all its other parts, and in my readings, I have anticipated directions in which

Calvin will move in later sections of the text. Still, it is clear that until the rhetorical expressions of doctrines such as Providence, Law and Gospel, Justification and Sanctification, and the Church are explored, an account of Calvin's theology must remain dramatically incomplete. Does this then mean that the analysis of this book is incomplete? I think not.

As Calvin's own introductory chapters illustrate, beginnings are important. They provide a space for defining the conceptual ground upon which the text's argument will develop. They introduce, arrange, and order the types of questions and issues that the text will either deal with or ignore. They also help to situate the audience by defining the role the readers should play in the activity of reading. Beginnings seek to capture the audience's attention by convincing them that the project at hand is important and promises to be interesting. And, most significantly, if the beginning is effective, it cultivates in the reader a sense of anticipation, an eager hope that one's reading will bring with it certain rewards—perhaps a shift of insight, a new perspective, or maybe just a more nuanced appreciation of the subject matter. I hope that this book constitutes, in its present scope, one such beginning.

As an introduction to Calvin and rhetoric, this book is designed to help readers start to imagine the directions in which further rhetorical readings of Calvin's *Institutes* might move. The field is promising and rewarding results of study await the diligent interpreter. But this reward will not come easily. This book does not provide a precise formula for reading that, once applied to the text, automatically produces expected conclusions. As my own readings have demonstrated, rhetorical analyses can move in many directions, generate a variety of interpretive angles, and at times, yield quite unexpected insights into the linguistic play of discourse. Indeed, the nuances and ambiguities of a rhetorical reading are what makes it such an exciting new way to approach a text that has been encrusted with the interpretive layers of almost five centuries.

Given the indeterminacy of rhetorical analysis—along with my claim that "the field is promising"—it may be tempting to assume that "reading rhetorically" means reading the text in any way that strikes the reader's fancy. While it is true that no reader can approach the *Institutes* without bringing to it a number of cultural or more immediately personal preconceptions, rhetorical interpretation need not lend itself to endlessly subjective readings. In fact, one function of the preceding chapters has been to try to define what constitutes a respectful rhetorical reading of Calvin. I use the term "respectful" because it highlights the reality that the *Institutes*, as a literary artifact, has its own integrity: it has a range of appropriate interpretations, with a texture and a structure that are capable of resisting irrelevant readings or ideas. The work is also the product of a particular historical era, a fact that reinforces the text's resistance to facile and anachronistic appraisals. Similarly, as a theological work, the text situates itself within both a genre of writing and a religious tradition that further mark the limits of its goals. Respecting these limits does not mean that only a certain number of readings will be considered "correct"; there remains ample room for multiple assessments. It does mean, however, that the possibility of a theological and/or historical misreading does exist, and this possibility alone suggests that the text's meanings are not infinitely subject to relativized interpretations.

Apart from these general comments about the limits to interpretations of the text, what actual parameters have been offered in the course of this book? Are there more specific guidelines that might assist in further theological probings of Calvin's rhetoric? There are many, some of which have emerged in my readings of Calvin's first three chapters, some of which have not yet been identified. For the purpose of this conclusion, however, I want to focus on one particular set of parameters, ones that stand out with distinctive clarity in the opening sections of the *Institutes*. These are the parameters that mark Calvin's understanding of the task and function of theological discourse.

THE DOUBLE PURPOSE OF
THEOLOGICAL DISCOURSE

For Calvin, theological discourse is marked by a double purpose: it seeks to witness to the revelation of God in scripture, and it seeks to do so in a language capable of moving the hearts, minds, and wills of its audience toward an ever-deepening life of faith. It is important to note, however, that these two goals are interrelated. Theologians are required to write eloquently and to move their audiences to faith precisely because God's revelation, as spoken through the prophets and apostles, has as its own goal the creation of a faithful covenant between God and human persons. In other words, the rhetoric of theology must be persuasive and hence accommodating because God's own word is inherently persuasive and accommodative. Thus, theologians are called to use the persuasive tools of rhetoric to build Christian piety because God's revelation itself seeks to establish and nurture this piety.

For Calvin, the practice of constructing rhetorically eloquent theology mirrors the persuasive character of God's word. Analogously, rhetoric can help to illuminate the complexities of Calvin's doctrine of revelation. According to Calvin, human persons come to know God through the revelatory oration that God, as the Grand Rhetorician, speaks to them, and this revelatory word or language consists of God's will for obedient response (true piety) and promise of the "benefits" of salvation for those who are called. This word is not ephemeral or abstract but material and historical; in the case of revelation, that material substance resides in the language of scripture, the splendor of creation, and the person of Jesus Christ. Calvin further argues that this revelatory speech constitutes the entire scope of what human persons know of the divine. Beyond this, all knowledge of

God is speculative and must be avoided lest one, in deluded arrogance, pretend to grasp the hidden mind or being of God.

In terms of the doctrine of revelation, Calvin's rejection of such speculative moves implies that one cannot get behind the act of God's speaking and discover or infer the prior idea or essence of God's truth, which, resting in the mind of God, serves as the revelatory content that is then dressed in a persuasive form in order to be heard by humanity.[1] Having cut off this avenue for conceptualizing behind the structure of revelation, Calvin leaves one with a doctrine of revelation that focuses on the accommodated materiality of God's enunciated word in scripture, creation, and Jesus Christ. And how is this divinely enunciated word to be understood? According to Calvin, it is understood in terms of its ability to persuade, to build covenant, and to bestow the benefits of salvation. In short, it is assessed in terms of its action or function.

Calvin also hesitates to use a simplistic version of the form/content distinction to typify the theologian's endeavor to construct true and faithful doctrines. Instead, he more often describes the work of theology in terms of its persuasive effectiveness. According to Calvin, doctrinal formulations that fail to nurture the piety of the audience to whom they are written are "empty" and "merely flit in the brain."[2] While they may appear to conform to the content of scripture, they will nonetheless flounder about aimlessly in the realm of practice if they lack the rhetorical eloquence necessary to evoke the appropriate response. In such an instance, when form fails to persuade, true doctrine is neither preached nor taught, and these doctrinal formulations cannot be salvaged by virtue of their correspondence to some abstracted notion of true content. In contrast, doctrines that exploit a full range of persuasive maneuvers and hence effectively move the audience to faith are doctrines that can lay claim to the title "true doctrine" insofar as they conform to the rule and measure of revelation itself. They are, in short, doctrines that actually work within the communities to whom they are addressed, and they work to the degree that through the materiality of language, they create and sustain the covenant relation between God and humanity.

How does Calvin's approach assist the theologian concerned in constructing doctrines that work in this way? Several answers emerge from his own practice. To construct persuasive theological discourse, Calvin suggests, a theologian must be attentive to the specificity of the audiences she or he addresses. This specificity includes many things, things such as a community's needs, linguistic expectations, cultural practices, religious orientation, and the material conditions of daily life. Once a theologian becomes sensitized to these conditions, then the language of his or her theological discourse can be rhetorically accommodated to speak in a manner capable of moving and persuading the audience to know, obey, and render praise to God and subsequently, to better love and care for one's neighbors. It should be stressed that for Calvin, these accommodative gestures are never deployed simply to increase the writer's popularity or political power. They are deployed in order to build up the community of faith. In other words, these accommodative gestures are designed to stand solely in service of nurturing Christian piety.

It is also clear that Calvin understands the task of theology to be one in which the community of faith is strengthened not only because its members are told what to do or believe; the rhetoric of theology also works at a more subtle and often indeterminate level where lives are dispositionally reshaped and reoriented. As I have suggested in my analysis of the appeals that structure Calvin's discussion of piety in chapter 2, the rhetoric of theology seeks to nurture its audience by taking it on a linguistic adventure in which, if the rhetoric works, the audience experiences its life as being drawn into and normatively shaped by the word of God. As his readers move through these appeals, the doxological rhetoric of Calvin's discussion works to dispositionally place them where their hearts and minds are directed to the divine and they enjoy the "benefits of faith." A similarly subtle project structures the rhetoric of chapter 3. Here, the faithful are strengthened not only because they are told that the "seed of divinity" is implanted within them, but also because Calvin develops the identity of a faithless, atheistic community over and against which the identity of the pious community is constructed. In this way, Calvin's rhetoric orients the disposition of its readers by defining the linguistic and hence cultural space within which to locate their self-understanding. In light of these examples, Calvin's approach aims at crafting doctrinal formulations capable of both constituting and reinforcing a Christian character. This character, because of the cultural space it inhabits, is deeper than mere intellectual assent and more enduring than flashes of momentary insight.

Calvin also believes that this process of shaping his audience's disposition requires him to take seriously the political relations that mark the cultural space inhabited by his readers. As the polemics, the apologies, and the sermonic interludes in these chapters suggest, his theology is designed to be received by different groups of readers, many of whom will be foes rather than friends and skeptics rather than believers. The textual complexities of these chapters also suggest that their multiple audiences are intimately tied to one another through a variety of power relations. For example, one reader, the king of France, had the power to issue orders upon which hung the life of many evangelical French Reformers. Likewise, the Roman clerics whom Calvin attacks had the authority and resources to turn public opinion against the reforming communities Calvin was struggling to strengthen. Another audience, the French humanists and their aristocratic supporters, controlled political and economic resources on which these fragile communities depended to survive. In the city of Geneva, complex power relations structured the ongoing battles between Calvin's own political party and the Libertines as well as the

Anabaptists. Similarly, relations of power structured the continual struggle between the old Genevan citizens and the surging influx of French immigrants. Influencing the balance of power were growing tensions between Geneva's desire for civil autonomy and its increasing need for military support from stronger Swiss cantons.

While it is not unusual for a theologian to write in the midst of immense social conflict, it is quite striking that Calvin so readily and openly uses his major theological work to respond to the political tensions of his day. As he builds theological arguments in the *Institutes*, he is continually waging rhetorical wars against opponents, teasing forth the sympathies of wealthy skeptics, and reinforcing the resolve of the persecuted. What is additionally striking about the way his theology negotiates these complex relations is that addressing questions of politics and power forms an integral part of his theological project and not just an afterthought or an optional addendum. The centrality of political questions is evidenced by the likelihood that no single doctrine in the *Institutes* exists that does not engage in these rhetorical maneuvers while simultaneously struggling to bear witness to the revelation of God in scripture. One can imagine why Calvin relentlessly pursues these varied political agendas if one remembers that the final goal of doctrine is to nurture a disposition of piety by accommodating the rhetoric of divine wisdom to the cultural specificity of its audiences. As a Renaissance humanist and lawyer, Calvin recognizes that cultural specificity includes the material conditions and hence the relations of power constituting the ever-fluctuating boundaries of a given social space. In light of this, it seems obvious that if theological discourse is to cultivate dispositions and character, then it must also cultivate, contest, reinforce, or create the political relations that mark the limits of the very communities whose dispositional orientation is at stake. Thus, one may say that when rhetoric is brought into the service of Christian piety, it must confront the political spaces that piety inhabits.

As my readings of the *Institutes* have suggested, the presence of multiple political agendas complicates the task of interpreting Calvin's theology. While it is clear that Calvin's primary agenda lies in nurturing the piety of those whom he believes to be the faithful, he often uses his rhetorical skills to twist and manipulate the dispositions of his enemies in ways that can hardly be described as edifying. At times, he uses the language of doctrine to break down and demoralize his opponents, and he does so by invoking a rhetoric of divine judgment designed to fracture the confidence of his enemies by cultivating dispositions of fear and guilt. At other times, he seeks to manipulate the sympathies of potential supporters by deploying rhetorical strategies that are more aptly defined as seductive rather than nurturing. There are places in the *Institutes* where one can easily discern which disposition Calvin is strategically attempting to inculcate, but more often, Calvin's rhetorical dexterity allows him to encourage simultaneously all these dispositions in the space of a single image, phrase, sentence, or paragraph.

In order to capture the rhetorical complexity of doctrines shaped by such maneuvers, it is useful to keep in mind the historical contexts that influence the text because these contexts help determine which audience should be regarded as the recipient of nurture and encouragement and which audience might require more defensive or apologetic moves. If one loses sight of these contexts, then it is not only difficult to discern the play of the text's interwoven purposes, but it is also possible to misinterpret seriously the rhetorical force of a given doctrine. For example, if these contexts are ignored, one might take a set of images whose primary target is Calvin's enemy and mistakenly read Calvin as if he were harshly scolding or denouncing the struggles of his friends. Or one might take a litany of phrases designed to uplift the spirits of the persecuted and mistakenly assume that Calvin is according divine sanction to the claims of the dominant culture. In his three prefaces to the *Institutes,* Calvin openly worries about the possibility that such errors will occur—that his doctrines will be misread and misused—and he attempts to forestall this by explicitly identifying his audiences and his varied purposes with regard to each. In this manner, Calvin links his doctrinal formulations to cultural contexts of power relations and social conflicts.

If one wishes to give a historically respectful account of Calvin's theology, then the presence of these contexts must not be overlooked, for without them, it is impossible to give an account of the rhetorical aim of his doctrines. This is not to say, however, that these contexts represent a set of static historical facts that can firmly ground one's understanding of Calvin's doctrines. The contexts Calvin lays out in his prefaces are clearly a product of Calvin's own interpretive processes and, as such, they represent his contextually biased view of the communities he engages. It is also the case that there are audiences whom his text does not address directly but who nonetheless might be discerned in its cracks and margins. Similarly, there are no doubt many audiences that Calvin never names in his prefaces, audiences that never surface in the course of his discourse, but ones that he consciously envisions as readers of his text. Once these dimensions of the social contexts that initially influenced Calvin's theology are acknowledged, it is evident that they must remain indeterminate and perhaps even disparate. However, this observation need not result in a wholesale rejection of using such contexts to understand the rhetorical force of his discourse. Noting these ambiguities simply gives caution and adds a critical edge to the ways in which textual contexts are studied.

The fact that Calvin links his doctrinal formulations to cultural contexts marked by power relations should not go unnoticed by contemporary readers who seek to make constructive use of the *Institutes* by allowing its rhetoric to speak in present-day contexts where social relations are quite different from Calvin's original situation. This is particularly important for Christians in the Reformed tradition, who may appeal to the authority of Calvin when evaluating the adequacy of their churches' theology. The history of Reformed Protestantism offers repeated examples of Calvin's doctrines being used in contexts where no analysis of audience or power relations is given, and where Calvin's doctrines are used as if they were not rhetorically crafted to serve the interests of particular communities. When the text is abstracted from its rhetorical framework and carried into new applications where the lines of power are differently configured, one can misconstrue the meaning and force of Calvin's doctrines, especially if no attempt is made to assess its new rhetorical functions and to measure these functions against Calvin's original contexts and purposes.

While it is obvious that Calvin's original context will never be repeated in history, a rhetorical reading of the *Institutes* as well as a rhetorical assessment of the text's ever-changing audiences allows one to ask critical questions about the character of subsequent uses of Calvin's doctrines. Do new applications of Calvin's doctrines merely serve to support the status quo or do they speak to the exiled, the persecuted, and the besieged? Do these new renderings inadvertently prevent the church from hearing a word of comfort and grace by promoting a rhetoric of relentless judgment, or do they nurture a pious disposition where the covenant between God and humanity is honored and the love of neighbor encouraged? And most important, as Calvin's doctrines travel through history and rhetorically engage new communities, one must continuously ask, whom are they seeking to empower and whom are they judging as arrogant or ungodly? These are the types of questions Calvin himself appears to ask, and they are questions that the rhetoric of divine revelation requires every generation of theological readers to ask as well.

This concludes my summary of the basic rhetorical insights that structure Calvin's expressed understanding of the task of theology. I hope that they mark a path that can be followed in the process of exploring the rhetorical play of additional chapters and sections in the *Institutes*. Again, these insights do not constitute something like a "rhetorical calculus" into which one can simply insert Calvin's discursive maneuvers in order to determine correct answers or precisely formed rhetorical interpretations. Rather, such insights are best utilized when treated as guideposts that may not necessarily mark out the precise terrain of Calvin's text but nonetheless indicate a path that both respects the structure of the *Institutes* and permits the exploration of some of its most complex features. If this path is chosen, then the reader is sure to return with interpretations of Calvin's discursive landscape that will be very different from many previous interpretations of the *Institutes* that ignore its rhetorical contexts. Indeed, this rhetorical path is one that has long been neglected and even ignored by the ahistorical and often idealist course that succeeding generations of Enlightenment theologians carved out for the field of Calvin studies. Yet traces of this older Renaissance path still remain, and if it is followed, it may well take one across and beyond those Enlightenment forms of interpretation and into a present-day world where language is once again rich with rhetorical possibilities.

THE NATURE AND FUNCTION OF DOCTRINE

If one's interests are primarily those of a historical theologian who specializes in Calvin and the Reformation, then the aims of this book should be quite apparent. I have tried to clear the neglected path of the rhetorical tradition in the hope that it will continue to lead to productive new (and also very old) interpretations of Calvin's theology. However, I undertook this project with another set of interests in mind as well. These interests are shared by a broad range of contemporary constructive theologians, many of whom have no specific interest in Calvin or the Reformation tradition but are nonetheless occupied with questions concerning the relation between language, culture, power, and the distinctive character of Christian discourse. If one lends a careful ear to my accounts of the procedures that guide Calvin's doctrinal formulations, one will have already heard some surprising echoes of present-day conversations on these topics, topics that are typically discussed under the rubric of "the character of Christian claims" or "the nature and function of doctrine." These echoes are particularly strong in conversations in which the Enlightenment's influence on Western theology is being carefully assessed and the modern project of liberal theology is being tested and debated.

While the presence of such echoes between Calvin and contemporary discussions of language may be surprising, they are not completely unexpected. The works of William Bouwsma, Quentin Skinner, Michael Walzer, Max Weber, and Robert Kingdon, to name only a few, have highlighted the peculiar position Calvin occupies with respect to modern Western thought. As an early modern figure, he anticipates—indeed, he helps to construct—many of the conceptual pillars upon which modernity stands, pillars whose meanings range from an understanding of persons as subjects to a scientific and objectivist assessment of nature and culture. Yet Calvin also remains immersed in a worldview that is distinctly premodern in character, a worldview that sees the cosmos as ruled by divine and demonic forces and in which communal notions of identity are still stronger than an ideology of isolated individualism. It is also a worldview with language that is still dominated by the rhythms of decorous rhetoric and thus resists being too easily squeezed into the carefully honed categories of either an empiricist or idealist epistemology.

Standing as he does between these two worlds—one distinctly premodern, the other leaning toward the Enlightenment—Calvin offers contemporary theologians a unique vantage point from which to assess the character of theological language. He is close enough to the present to facilitate conversation insofar as he shares some modern preoccupations, but he is distant enough to offer a perspective on language that is radically different from present-day views. Given its unique vantage point, Calvin's model of theological discourse has the capacity to make a significant contribution to contemporary systematics at a variety of levels. However, these contributions cannot be easily charted, partly because it is difficult to systematize Calvin, and partly because the framework out of which he operates does not find its precise parallel in the frameworks of present-day discussions. In light of these limitations, the most one can hope to do is highlight those places where Calvin's view of theology intersects with questions and issues that presently occupy discussions related to theological discourse, power, culture, and theories of representation.[3]

Before I highlight these points of intersection, I must offer a word of caution. Anyone familiar with the field of contemporary systematic theology will no doubt agree that questions concerning method often rule the day. Given this obsession with method, it is tempting to make constructive use of Calvin by trying to define his own "theological methodology"; this is a temptation that should be approached with caution. In most instances, discussions of method presuppose that the theologian being analyzed has constructed a conceptually tight—some would say "totalizing"—theological system. The tightness of this system is usually predicated on the presence of underlying philosophical and/or theological principles that can be investigated and, if they prove to be internally coherent, laid out with a certain degree of analytic precision.

If one approaches Calvin's text with this understanding of theological method, then efforts to extract such a method will be extremely frustrating and ultimately destined to failure. As a Renaissance humanist, Calvin rejected the philosophical speculations of the Scholastics. He did not construct a philosophically tight or analytically rigorous system. Yet this does not mean that his theology is incoherent. His doctrines seek coherence through being a faithful witness to scripture while also unleashing potential social forces by their rhetorical functioning. Furthermore, the lack of a precise theological method does not mean that Calvin's theology stands completely devoid of epistemological presuppositions. Such presuppositions abound, but it would be impossible to pull them into a rigorously philosophical scheme because they continuously shift. Like any other piece of insight or linguistic play of image—indeed, like any other rhetorical game—the gestures that Calvin uses come from several different epistemological frameworks whose principal similarity lies in their being brought into the service of nurturing piety. Thus, what one finds in the *Institutes* is not the presence of a particular theological methodology but rather an ad hoc collection of many methods and systems, all of which are used to buttress Calvin's central and clearly practical goal: the persuasive aim of teaching sound doctrine and thereby building up the community of faith.

Yet the absence of a unified theological methodology in the *Institutes* need not be viewed as an obstacle to assessing the relevance of a rhetorical reading of Calvin for contemporary theology. There are many other aspects of his understanding of religious discourse worth considering. These include specific reflections on method. One example is Calvin's eminently practical view of the function of theological language, which shows the inadequacy of a strictly pictorial or propositionalist account of doctrinal language. According to the pictorial model, words are linguistic signs that convey meaning by virtue of their ability to point or refer to extralinguistic realities, each of which constitutes the "real object" that language seeks to name. When this model of language is applied to Christian doctrine, doctrine is described as a set of linguistic propositions whose adequacy resides in their ability to point appropriately to extralinguistic "facts" about God and the world. According to this model, then, a statement like "knowledge of God and knowledge of self are interrelated" is taken as a propositional truth claim about a state of affairs concerning God and human persons.

It is evident in the *Institutes* that Calvin intends to make truth claims about God's will for humanity and often does so in the form of propositions. But if one focuses solely on this dimension of his theology, one may overlook the other ways in which Calvin uses language to open up the truths of revelation. For example, in chapter 1, Calvin's proposition concerning the relation between self and divine knowledge is worked over with a rhetorical rigor that eventually undercuts and fractures what appears to be the original "state of affairs" to which the proposition points. As I have illustrated in my rhetorical reading of this chapter, Calvin's initial proposition serves as an invitation to his humanist colleagues, but it is a proposition that, in the course of the chapter, he subtly dismantles and then reconstructs in order to both attract and reorient the sympathies of this particular audience. In this instance, the central point of his discourse is not carried in its propositional form but rather is embedded in a rhetorical play of disrupted claims and displaced images.

A similar dynamic is at work in chapter 3, where the central proposition of Calvin's argument is that a sense of divinity is implanted in all persons and therefore no one can claim not to know God. However, having made this assertion, Calvin then proposes in the next chapter that this sense in fact never produces a recognition of God. If one's analysis of theological discourse remains limited to its propositional character, then it appears that Calvin has made two contradictory assertions. However, if one attends to the rhetorical play of the text, a different picture emerges. It becomes increasingly evident that his discussion of the divine sense serves to do more than describe a state of affairs to which his audience must assent. It establishes the terms of a discursive gesture out of which Calvin will describe the identity of the pious. To do this rhetorically, Calvin subverts and fractures his central propositions.

As these two examples suggest, theological discourse can open up the truths of revelation by means other than the asserted truth claims of a tight theological system. For Calvin, truth is made known if the discourse of theology succeeds in persuading its audience to conform to a life of piety, and this persuasion can be predicated on the play of images, metaphors, rhythms, and discursive breaks that are far from propositional or formally systematic in character. In fact, Calvin often brings his audience to knowledge of God through rhetorical gestures where signs slip, where double meanings are exploited, and where propositional stability is broken and meaning is left to emerge in its cracks. Given this dynamic, Calvin scholars should hesitate to interpret his theology by analytically distilling it into propositionally tight truth claims. If their interpretive project follows this course, then it may require them to distill out the logically imprecise but nonetheless crucial rhetorical gestures through which Calvin opens up the truth of divine wisdom.

These examples also suggest that Calvin may be an interesting conversation partner for both theorists and theologians who describe their own projects as poststructuralist. While it would be an exaggeration to argue that Calvin completely dismisses the importance of making theological truth claims that are propositional in character, he does deploy linguistic gestures that not only defy propositional logic but may at times be driven by the desire to subvert the logical play of his initial assertions. As a poststructuralist would no doubt point out, Calvin continually builds sets of binary differences, such as self-knowledge and divine knowledge, or piety and ungodliness. Through these he establishes a certain set of definitions. However, these definitions are never as final as they may initially appear. In the course of his discussion, he often inverts the relation between his binarisms—eclipsing primary terms while putting in the foreground the repressed second terms. This functions to disorient or cleverly reorient the assumptions of referential order brought to the text by his readers. Likewise, these binarisms often become so fractured and displaced that their ability to refer in any straightforward manner is lost. But because Calvin does not always seek referential closure or a tightly logical structure of terms, the chaotic play induced by his inversions does not finally count as a loss but as a gain. It is a play that, if rhetorically effective, opens up the possibility of readers' being grasped by a divine wisdom that can only speak to them in the fractured remains of their linguistic frameworks. When this occurs, one discovers that Calvin has brought the reader not to the end of theology but to its beginning—a beginning filled with enormously constructive possibilities.

This conversation between Calvin, poststructuralists, and propositionalists raises a number of intriguing questions about which modern theory (or theories) of representation one might choose to describe Calvin's discursive practices. Admittedly, the whole notion of a "theory of representation" would have been foreign to Calvin, at least the understanding of "theories of representation" that is common in current academic discussions. For this reason, it is important to acknowledge that Calvin's theology will always resist the conceptual constraints of modern theory. Nevertheless, when contemporary theologians evaluate traditional doctrines in order to determine their meaning, their usefulness, and their faithfulness to the witness and mission of the present-day church, they inevitably raise questions about representation. And because of the complexity of Calvin's discursive practices, his doctrines offer interesting grist for this particular modern mill.

At one level, Calvin is quite willing to make statements that appear to refer in a straightforwardly pictorial manner. When he asserts that "God has implanted in all a certain understanding of his divine majesty," he is not speaking analogically or metaphorically. Rather, he is describing a "state of affairs" that can be evaluated following the logic of a strict correspondence theory of truth—what is said conforms exactly to reality. At another level, however, Calvin is a master of metaphor. This allows him to slip constantly into analogical language. Here there is not a dependence on a strict ontological correspondence between sign and the thing signified since it is the analogical play that conveys truth. This is particularly apparent in chapter 3, where Calvin collects a whole host of metaphors to illustrate the function and power of God's divine seed. When Calvin uses language in this manner, one needs to make looser judgments about the meaning of his terms and the way they "represent" because the terms themselves are not firmly anchored.

The notion of "analogical language," however, does not completely capture the force of some of Calvin's most provocative discussions. There are clearly instances in which Calvin constructs doctrines by invoking descriptions of divine/human interactions that are best understood not as "facts" or "analogies" but as realist narratives drawn from the scriptural story. This kind of language is evident in the closing sentences of chapter 1, when biblical references begin to carry the weight of Calvin's argument. Here, it seems that Calvin invokes the plain or literal sense of the text to narratively shape the identity of the reader who takes the biblical story as "the straightedge against which they are shaped."[4] In addition to the narrative gestures, Calvin also deploys a deconstructive rhetoric that depends on the subversion of his readers' narrative expectation as well as their anticipation of either propositional or analogical correspondence and closure. In these instances, it may be that the only correspondence one can hope to construct in the process of interpreting Calvin's doctrines is a correspondence of silence and gaps. In addition to using gestures that can be roughly described in terms of four tropological models, Calvin's discourse also seeks coherence in its persuasive power and the disposition it affects. When one considers this dimension of his discursive practices, it appears that one's interpretive judgments need to shift from a metaphysics of signs or narrative form to a set of more pragmatic judgments about rhetorical adequacy and dispositional productivity.

In light of this last observation about the dispositional productivity of Calvin's theology, it is tempting to make him into a modern-day functionalist, and pursuing this possibility is not without its merits. Calvin's predilection for viewing doctrine in terms of its social use-value comes very close, at times, to a functionalist approach to theology, in which the truth of doctrine resides in its ability to actually do something, to persuade the hearts of the audience to pursue a life of piety. If it accomplishes this "function," then it is true and good; if it fails, then doctrine no longer witnesses to the truth and goodness of divine wisdom, no matter how "correct" its propositional pointing may be. While this does not imply that an unpersuasive propositional account of revelation is unequivocally false, it does imply that such a doctrinal formulation may be pastorally and ecclesially useless. And as Calvin repeatedly tells his readers, there is nothing worse than "useless doctrine"—or doctrine that does not properly "function" to serve the ends of true piety.

A further indication of Calvin's functionalist leanings lies in his understanding of how doctrines acquire meaning. According to Calvin's textual practices, it appears that the meaning of a doctrine is to be measured by the quality and character of the social disposition it encourages. Thus, one can only assess its meaning in light of the context in which it is deployed, for it is in the reception of doctrine that its meaning happens and dispositions are formed. This received meaning, furthermore, does not consist of purely intellectual grasping. While it includes such grasping, the fullness of meaning is born out in the life practices it helps to shape. Therefore, when assessing the meaning of doctrine, theologians need to pause and consider how it operates in the social context of its deployment and what kinds of social action it encourages. In short, they must consider the inexorable bond between the linguistic act and its social function.

Should Calvin, then, be read as a thoroughgoing functionalist? It may well be. But if so, his is a Christianly tempered functionalism, one tempered by the authoritative role that scripture and revelation play in determining the limits of doctrinal truth and meaning. Insofar as revelation constrains and informs Calvin's rhetoric, he clearly does not embrace a functionalism that takes its bearings only from changing communal needs and desires. In this regard, revelation serves to ground his reflections and thereby restrain a functional relativism. However, one could argue that even with the witness of scripture as his guide, Calvin could still be placed within the functionalist camp, given that he often describes both revelation and scripture in starkly functional terms as well. When God is positioned as the Grand Orator, the quality and character of God's word are assessed primarily in terms of their persuasive action. As Calvin suggests, God speaks to the world for the purpose of persuading the creature's heart and mind to serve and praise God.

If one wants to protect this view of revelation from a strictly functionalist interpretation, then one must ask Calvin if there is a truth that is God, or is about God, which can be used to describe "who" this God is who speaks to the world in the accommodated language of redemption and grace. Does this God have an identity that is more than the sum of God's speech-acts? Can this God be named in the language of "essence" or "eternal reality"? Unfortunately, Calvin's answers to such questions remain ambiguous. It seems that he would like to answer strongly yes, there is such an essence. But for Calvin, the dangers of speculating about God's immanent reality are so enormous that he avoids the task of giving specific content to God's eternal identity and being. And in this avoidance, he often shrouds his "hidden God" in a theological silence that is quite profound. Given this silence, one could argue that a perplexingly functional doctrine of God is all that is left. That Calvin would be uneasy with such a conclusion is clear. That his theology can avoid it, however, is far from obvious.

CALVIN AND CONTEMPORARY
DISCUSSIONS OF DOCTRINE

Where does this leave one, then, in terms of assessing Calvin's relation to contemporary discussions of doctrine? As far as Calvin's challenge to a pictorial or strictly propositional view of theology is concerned, I have already discussed the ways in which his doctrinal formulations might intrigue theologians with poststructuralist inclinations. His challenge to a strictly propositional account of doctrine would also find obvious and deep resonances among theologians whose understanding of theological discourse has been influenced by the work of the later Wittgenstein and his students in the British analytic tradition.[5] Here, the insight that language is constructed to do things—to help one get around in the world—echoes sentiments found in the discussion carried on by Calvin and other Renaissance humanists. In terms of the views of doctrine produced by this modern train of thought, Calvin promises to be a fascinating interlocutor, negotiating a familiar terrain but arriving at some unexpected conclusions.

For example, the notion that doctrine can be elucidated by its effects on one's attitudes and actions raises issues from which a Wittgensteinian consideration of the limits of translation would profit. Furthermore, Calvin works in this manner without stumbling into a fideistic isolationism that separates faith claims from the rest of life.[6] Although he deeply appreciates the internal logic of discursive fields of meaning—for example, a phrase or an argument may only serve to strengthen the piety of those persons whose linguistic practices are already structured by a similar discourse of piety—he recognizes that doctrines that function in this manner can never do so in a completely enclosed cultural arena. Rather, his own doctrines use rhetorical procedures that continually address complicated public arenas where persons other than the "pious" speak, where meanings constantly shift, and where linguistic gestures can be interpreted in multiple ways. In this arena, apologetics clearly has a place and depends on the workings of public discourses.[7] And for Calvin, this apologetic enterprise need not depend on philosophy to make it publicly accessible; it can draw upon a vast reservoir of cultural images and metaphors in its deployment of rhetoric. Similarly, apologetics may even be based on more strictly dogmatic discussions because the language of dogmatics is as open to rhetorical nuance as its apologetic sister. This does not imply, however, that the two are the same; it merely points to the fluid functions that theological discourse can serve. Again, this latter point emerges with particular clarity in my reading of Calvin's opening chapter.

It is also interesting to compare Calvin's view of doctrine with contemporary theological assessments of North American pragmatism. As I discussed in earlier chapters, the humanist movement in early modern Europe had its own deeply pragmatic streak. The young Calvin's *Commentary on Seneca's "De clementia"* offers evidence that this streak left its mark on Calvin. In this text, he argues that a proper translation of Seneca's work into the language of the sixteenth century respects both Seneca's own cultural context and the cultural complexities of Calvin's own day. He states that one must understand not only how Seneca used words but also what kind of use-value Seneca's arguments served in the social world of Rome. Similarly, Calvin asks about both the usage and cultural value of the contemporary terms that he intended to employ as he translated Seneca. In making these evaluations about Seneca's usage and his own cultural usage, Calvin's judgments are not grounded only in a metaphysics of language; they are ordered also by a set of pragmatic distinctions that indicate a profound appreciation for the social production of meaning. Here, one discerns the resonance between Calvin's position and current North American pragmatists.

However, as Calvin begins the task of constructing Christian doctrines, these earlier sentiments undergo a subtle transformation. He continues to make judgments about the meaning of doctrine based on its social function and use, and he continues to respect the complexity of the ways by which doctrines must be accommodated to the capacities and contexts of their audiences. But Calvin also develops a more solid and lucid sense of the end toward which his scholarly endeavors should move. His discursive practices are no longer designed to simply reproduce the variant cultural meanings of a text that may have accumulated a high level of academic authority but nonetheless wields only an ambiguous degree of moral or religious force. When he takes up the task of formulating Christian doctrine, his judgments concerning its discursive propriety are measured against a rule with a very different normative authority. The adequacy of his discursive gestures is judged by the authority of revelation witnessed to in scripture and by the tangible effects that discourse has on the community of faith to whom he speaks. Thus, his pragmatic assessments of meaning are limited both by the character of a historical community and by the revelatory truth of God's word. And for Calvin, these limits are not finally negotiable or dispensable.

For this reason, Calvin would most likely not come to public discourse with the skeptical agenda of a thoroughgoing pragmatist. He would come with extremely firm views about the ways in which communities should be structured and the privileged status of a "pious disposition." Furthermore, he would most likely refute the notion that his position is the product of highly particularized interests that, being culturally variant, stand on historically shifting sands. He would argue, instead, that they rest upon the firm reality of God's will for creation as written in the law and made manifest in the gospel. However, he would prove an interesting conversation partner for other pragmatists because he would not try to argue his position the way a traditional foundationalist might. If he tried to defend his position by deploying a specific theory of "being," he would get tied up in the philosophical knots he struggles so hard to avoid in the *Institutes*. And his ability to defend his position on the basis of the empirical realities of this world would be as shaky as the empirical arguments he subverts in his doctrine of Creation. Failing these strategies, Calvin would finally be pushed to discuss the nature and character of God's revealed will. At this point, he would surely baffle his interlocutors with his description of a Grand Rhetorician whose word is deeply accommodating, functionally determined, and immersed in the vicissitudes of history while at the same time being a word that stands against history as its normative measure and judge—a peculiar combination, to say the least.[8]

This picture of Calvin's conversation with North American pragmatists, as well as his conversations with poststructuralists, analytic language theorists, and functionalists, is admittedly sketchy. However, to develop fully all the implications of Calvin's view of both normative truth claims and the role of community as the measure of discursive effectiveness, it is necessary to say much more about his understanding of doctrine and the truth status of revelation, and unfortunately Calvin does not make this task an easy one for several of the reasons I have already mentioned. First, as a pre-Enlightenment figure, he does not share a modern interest in establishing normative criteria for assessing truth claims: he simply believes that God's word is true. And because most of his interlocutors, both supporters and opponents, agreed with this simple claim, the majority of Calvin's energy in the *Institutes* is poured into arguments about what doctrine and the scriptures do, not just whether they are true or false. Second, the veil Calvin has secured around God's divine being leads to a doctrine of revelation that features a word of God focused on encouraging certain communal practices through rhetoric rather than on demanding simple assent to propositional truths about God that can be detached from the practices that constitute a life of faith. In this way, Calvin's doctrine of revelation resists facile attempts to glean from it a static notion of truth and its structure.

These interesting twists and ambiguities in Calvin's understanding of doctrine and the nature of truth claims, however, need not finally lead to a dead end when one endeavors to assess Calvin's relevance for contemporary theology. Instead, if one follows the paths that lead to these unsettling ambiguities, one finds oneself in the middle of yet another modern conversation about the nature and function of doctrine. The conversation I now refer to is the one initiated by theologians who, for lack of a better term, have been called postliberal theologians. Like Calvin, these theologians find a purely propositional account of doctrine inadequate for describing the work that doctrines do; and again, like Calvin, they avoid—or at least try to avoid—getting mired in questions concerning the truth status of theological claims about God. They approach the process of analyzing doctrine by first looking at the Christian religion in the same way an anthropologist examines any set of cultural-linguistic rules structuring a community's beliefs, actions, and attitudes.[9] According to contemporary anthropologists, who have inspired the postliberal perspective, religions function as "comprehensive interpretive schemes, usually embodied in myths or narrative and heavily ritualized, which structure human experience and understanding of self and world";[10] in other words, these interpretive schemes provide the linguistic framework within which the lives and thoughts of a community are shaped.

Within this framework, doctrines play a significant role: they serve as regulative rules that determine the types of speech that are considered meaningful while simultaneously setting boundaries that exclude other forms of speaking and acting. In this way, doctrines provide the grounding grammar in and through which persons view the world around them and understand their own identity and actions in that world. This view of doctrine also carries with it an assumption about the relationship between language, doctrine, and experience. According to this model, doctrine works like language, understood in the broadest anthropological sense of the term, insofar as doctrines serve as the conceptual apparatus that makes religious experience possible. The assertion that language precedes experience also leads theologians who view doctrine from a cultural-linguistic perspective to be highly suspicious of theologians who reverse the relation between language and experience in order to argue that doctrine merely serves to express or name a prelinguistic religious feeling or existential orientation.

Although postliberal theologians frequently acknowledge that pre-Enlightenment thinkers had a much deeper appreciation for the cultural shaping accomplished by doctrine than did their Enlightenment successors, they have yet to explore the full extent to which Calvin's view of doctrine resonates with their own. In fact, if my reading of Calvin's rhetorical understanding of theology is correct, it may be that Calvin stands as the best—or most explicit—example of a Reformation figure who self-consciously composed doctrine with an eye toward its creative cultural function.[11] Beginning in chapter 1, Calvin rhetorically situates his readers in such a way that their "knowledge of the self" is pulled into and narrated by the language of scripture, the source of "knowledge of God." He accomplishes this by setting up a textual dynamic that models the role doctrine plays in the mind of the readers: doctrine is to be the "rule by which they [the readers] are measured," the regulative framework within which their understanding of self, world, and God is to unfold. In chapter 2, Calvin develops this textual dynamic further as he takes his readers through a discursive composition designed to evoke a disposition, in both its emotional and intellectual dimensions, of praise and obedience to God. Again, through his rhetorical maneuvers, he uses the language of doctrine to cultivate a discursive environment where the reader acquires the linguistic and dispositional skills that Calvin believes are necessary for a life of faith, and these skills consist of much more than a simple capacity to assent to certain propositional statements about God. Rather, these skills reorient the readers' actions and attitudes and refocus the conceptual lens through which they perceive themselves, their opponents, their neighbors, and their communal responsibilities.

Calvin continues to construct this regulative framework in chapter 3 when he textually creates an "other" as the foil against whom he defines the identity of "the pious." Here, it appears that Calvin is not simply giving linguistic expression to the already constructed subjectivities of his readers. Rather, he creates a historically unprecedented "other" that, because of its uniqueness, sets the terms through which a new form of subjectivity can emerge. In this way, he perhaps sets in motion a discursive play of oppositions that will have tremendous impact upon the communal identity and actions of Reformed Christians for years to come. This is not to say that Calvin created the "we-they" distinctions that have dominated Christian discourse for centuries. It only points to the particular twist Calvin gives this dynamic (through his creation of the atheist) and the privileged position he gives it as the focus of one of the first three chapters of the *Institutes*. For postliberal theologians who try to be anthropologically sensitive to the cultural work that doctrines perform, this insight into Calvin's doctrines cannot be overlooked.

Although Calvin would not have been familiar with the contemporary terms of the debate on the relation between religious experience and doctrinal language, his position in chapter 3 offers some provocative insights on this topic, insights that should certainly capture the attention of the postliberal camp. At first glance, it appears that Calvin is describing something like an innate, prelinguistic religious experience that is universally present in all persons by virtue of the divinely implanted "seed of religion." It is possible that having asserted the presence of this seed, Calvin could then go on to discuss how the language of scripture and doctrine simply expresses or names this innate but prelinguistic knowledge. However, this is not the path he chooses. Instead, Calvin harshly announces that this innate knowledge is useless because sin has made it impossible for even the faithful to know God intuitively. Thus, Calvin argues, human beings are dependent on the word or language of God as given in scripture to set the terms through which knowledge of God is communicated. Although Calvin does not state this as directly as one might hope, the implication of his discussion is that scripture and its interpretation in doctrine together form the linguistic preconditions necessary for an experience of the divine. And although he also affirms that this experience depends on the work of the Spirit, even the Spirit must move through the word and not alone, as the Anabaptists would have it, to create the cultural-linguistic framework within which the grace and judgment of

God—which are all the creature can grasp of God—are felt, experienced, and thereby known.

A crucial dimension of the postliberals' approach to doctrine is their respect for the ways in which doctrines, as regulative rules that shape beliefs and dispositions, recommend certain actions and produce particular institutional forms. As mentioned earlier, it is not unusual for theological discussions of Calvin's doctrines to highlight discrete passages in the third and fourth books of the *Institutes* as the foundation of his social ethics and his practical advice on questions related to ecclesial and civil institutions. Unfortunately, this desire to divide up the *Institutes* into either purely theological sections or sections of a more practical and directly ethical nature completely overlooks the degree to which "purely theological" doctrines also dispose the readers toward particular kinds of social action. For a theologian who is cognizant of the subtle ways in which doctrines shape lives and therefore implicitly shape action, this kind of distinction is unproductive, for it leads to a truncated understanding of the roots of Reformed ethics. As I have demonstrated in my rhetorical readings, Calvin is constantly deploying discursive gestures that encourage or restrict certain forms of communal action. For example, in chapter 2, Calvin's highly legalist and militaristic imagery of God as "protector of the pious" may have had enormous impact on the types of actions the evangelical community took to defend itself against attacks launched by the French state. And throughout all three chapters that I discuss, Calvin sets up a discursive stage upon which he places a variety of actors, each of whom is given a role and script. As the play unfolds, the reader learns how all these actors are to be perceived and how their actions are to be interpreted—as neighborly, potentially friendly, or outrightly offensive and dangerous. In this manner, Calvin actively constitutes the subjective identity of his actors and sets the temper of their social interactions. What could possibly be more ethically determinative than staging the conceptual world through which persons identify and communicate (or do not communicate) with one another?

This last point suggests that Calvin's understanding of doctrine may be a useful model for contemporary theologians who share the basic perspective of the postliberals but who wish to raise additional questions concerning the roles that power, culture, and politics play in the formation and function of doctrine.[12] While the postliberal approach recognizes the degree to which doctrines influence the character of a community's social practices, the critical link between social and political practices and specific doctrines is frequently overlooked or reductively dismissed on the grounds that the political import of doctrine is determined by cultural-linguistic factors that fall outside the regulative power of theological discourse.[13] However, if one takes Calvin's doctrines as an example of culturally regulative rules, it is clear that this issue cannot be so easily ignored. It must be taken seriously because, as I stated earlier, the regulative functions of Calvin's doctrines are inextricably linked to and determined by the social contexts within which those doctrines are deployed. This is illustrated by Calvin's use of doctrine to create theological identities that play off one another in patterns marked according to relations of power. While this patterning is most obvious in his introductory "Prefatory Address to King Francis I of France," where the politically weak but piously righteous evangelical Christians are pitted against the earthly strength of idolatrous clerics from Rome, this same dynamic occurs in virtually every sentence in the first three chapters of the *Institutes* as well. Thus, if one wants to make a critical assessment of the cultural-linguistic world created by Calvin's doctrines, one must look directly at the political configurations his discourse evokes and the kinds of social action it thereby encourages.

Confronting the continuous presence of the political agendas that drive Calvin's doctrinal formulations promises not only to enrich present interpretations of Calvin's theology; it is also an exercise that, if applied to contemporary doctrinal formulations, may help one to identify the often hidden or unacknowledged, but nonetheless decisive, political functions that doctrine serves as it shapes and rules the linguistic contours of a community's beliefs, actions, and dispositions. In the past several decades, feminist, liberation, political, mujerista, womanist, black, and African-American theologians—to name only a few—have struggled to do precisely this, to expose both the politically oppressive and liberative ways in which many of the church's traditional doctrines have been used. As they attempt to reconstruct Christian doctrines whose rhetoric and concomitant social function serve progressive political agendas, these theologians have tried to illustrate the varied ways in which one and the same doctrine may construct radically different worldviews depending on the social identity of the community within which a given doctrine is deployed.

For example, recent North American feminist assessments of the "doctrine of election" have argued that an ecclesiology that divides the world into the righteous and the reprobate may serve, at times, to bolster the confidence and strengthen the resolve of the marginalized if they occupy the position of the righteous. However, when the same binary logic is deployed by a dominant culture in order to justify genocidal social programs against marginal communities that are identified as reprobate, this doctrine is clearly operating in a pernicious regulative capacity.[14] Similarly, South African liberation theologians have overturned traditional readings of the doctrines of reconciliation, justification, and sanctification as they have struggled to reconceive the meaning of Christian forgiveness in the context of apartheid's legacy. Using theological arguments that draw heavily upon a functional notion of doctrine, they have described how "forgiveness" can serve both oppressive and empowering ends depending on the social locations of the community that is called to forgive and the community that is required to repent and be forgiven. For theologians who are engaged in exposing and critiquing the shifting uses of doctrine, it may be a welcome surprise to learn that John Calvin, the supposed architect of so many of the Reformed churches' most oppressive doctrines, was himself highly cognizant of the potential uses and political misuses of his theology.[15] This dimension of Calvin's thought may also surprise more conservative theologians who are suspicious of theologies that explicitly link their doctrinal formulations to specific political agendas. Although Calvin did not call his text a "political theology," it is quite apparent that this culturally astute and socially committed reformer situated his own discourse in the midst of a highly politicized context. By doing so, Calvin took a position and carved out a space for ideas whose relations to the power structures of his day were both complex and conflictual.

CALVIN AS A COMMUNAL RHETORICIAN

When one writes about a "great man" in European history, it is tempting to cast him as either villain or hero, and contemporary readings of Calvin have contained both images. When cast as villain, he appears as the austere and oppressive tyrant of Geneva who bequeathed to future generations of Christians a rhetoric of severe self-control and discipline as well as a propensity to view the world as a battle between the righteous and the reprobate. When he is cast as hero, he appears either as the valiant protector of orthodox doctrine or as the ideological backbone of a revolutionary Christianity. If my own reading has leaned in any direction, it has been the latter, more positive assessment. I have admittedly struggled to show a side of Calvin's doctrines that might prevent him from being prematurely dismissed as an unsalvageable patriarch or forestall his being too easily lauded as the conservative founder of "correct" Calvinist doctrine.

The problem with talk about heroes and villains, however, is its tendency to obscure the communal character of a person's actions, whether those actions consist in writing books on Christian doctrine or organizing revolutionary cells in small country villages and towns. By focusing on Calvin's rhetoric and continually raising questions about the effects his language would have had on his reading audience, I hope that I have made at least initial steps toward showing the deeply communal processes that structured the writing of the *Institutes*. Calvin wrote with, for, and to communities marked by both the conflicts and hopes of his age. He not only sought to shape them but was himself shaped by the practices of the various communities through which he passed during his life. In some of these communities he found acceptance, taught the faith, and grew in power and fame; in others, he experienced the intellectual challenge of the most highly educated persons of his day and sharpened his skills as a scholar and orator; in yet others, he met with resistance, faced exile, and saw his closest friends tortured and killed. In all these contexts, his emerging identity and theological vision were marked, molded, and tempered by the people he knew and with whom he struggled.

When one reads his texts now, almost five centuries later, these same communities leave their marks on every page. If one listens closely, one can hear their voices echoing in the rhetorical gestures, arguments, and images that Calvin places before the reader, for one cannot read rhetorically without imagining an audience. They are there: the Genevan merchants, the despised Scholastics, the erudite humanists, the eager students, the evangelical French parishioners. In the gaps, silences, and unintended excesses of Calvin's language, one can also sense the eclipsed presence of persons he constructs to attack: the "Epicureans," the "atheists," the immoral and crafty "men," and the many other faces who are not welcomed into the text even as adversaries. If my readings of Calvin's doctrines have been compelling, then his text should bear witness not only to the identity of the man who wrote it but also, and perhaps most crucially, to the complex identities of the communities that produced it and to whom it is addressed.

When one reads the *Institutes* in the present, its historical and communal meanings for a contemporary audience should also not be overlooked. As it has been interpreted and deployed as an authoritative summary of doctrine throughout the past centuries, it too has traveled through various communities, served different functions, and accrued a variety of meanings. As a contemporary reader, one cannot ignore this history; both its glory and its pain must be recognized because when it is read by the church, it is read by institutions that have themselves been formed by these histories and renderings of the text. Through its rhetorical gestures, the *Institutes* has empowered communities like the new world Puritans while it has also eclipsed the presence of the native communities they colonized and often destroyed. It has laid the theological groundwork for revolution in South Africa just as it has participated in the construction of apartheid ideology. And all these voices, speaking in varied tongues are still heard if present-day readers imagine the text's many rhetorical audiences over the years.

Insofar as its doctrines continue to regulate the cultural worldview of readers who call themselves Reformed, the *Institutes* continues to make this community of readers its active, faithful audience as well. It continues to pull this community into its rhetorical milieu, to dispose its Reformed readers to action, and to position those it defines as "pious" in the politically complex terrain of the world. The "church," in this sense, is still there, in the text, in its complex center or its silent but erupting margins. And, in an interesting way, the *Institutes* itself becomes audience to the text history has passed on. As audience, will the text revolt or will it comply with the interpretations history has laid upon it? Will the text rebound or will it resist even the interruption of my own interpretive renderings? While neither language nor the Spirit is predictable enough to predetermine the answer to these questions, Calvin would remind his reader that the word of God stands constant. So one reads, one acts, and one moves through the world of rhetoric in constant expectation.

NOTES

1. For a discussion of Calvin's view of God's hidden essence, see Brian Gerrish, "To the Unknown God: Luther and Calvin on the Hiddenness of God," *Journal of Religion* 53 (1973): 263–92.

2. *Inst.* 1.5.9, p. 61.

3. In the discussion that follows, I mention a number of theological "schools of thought," which include references to propositionalists, poststructuralists, functionalists, Wittengensteinians, British language analysts, North American pragmatists, postliberals, and "liberation" theologians. These references are used to construct a map whose sole function is to highlight points at which Calvin's theology intersects with contemporary concerns. The map itself is very rough and its contours are often exaggerated for the purpose of comparison. I realize that very few theologians actually "fit" (in a pure form) the descriptions I offer, and for this reason, I hope the reader will try to avoid "filling in the gaps" with names of particular theologians. With regard to the postliberal and liberation perspectives, however, my references become more explicit because these perspectives come closest to my own and, I believe, they hold the most promise for future work on Calvin.

4. Despite the ambiguities inherent in the notion of the "plain," "literal," or "narrative" sense, I find it a useful way to describe discursive practices that are obviously neither "factual" nor "analogical" in character. See Hans W. Frei's discussion of Reformation understandings of narrative in *The Eclipse of the Biblical Narrative* (New Haven, Conn.: Yale University Press, 1974), 1–50.

5. Although he would not place himself within the British analytic tradition, the work of Paul Holmer moves in a direction that shares some affinities with the reading I give of Calvin. These affinities are most evident in his "Wittgensteinian-like" discussions of the life practices and grammars that shape the actions as well as beliefs of Christians. See Holmer, "Wittgenstein and Theology," in D. M. High, ed., *New Essays in Religious Language* (New York: Oxford University Press, 1969); and *The Grammar of Faith* (San Francisco: Harper & Row, 1978).

6. For example, Calvin's position differs significantly from the fideistic perspective defended in the work of D. Z. Phillips. See Phillips, *Religion without Explanation* (Oxford: Basil Blackwell Publisher, 1976).

7. William Werpehowski, "Ad Hoc Apologetics," *Journal of Religion* 66, no. 3 (1986): 282–301. Although Werpehowski does not develop a case for Calvin's apologetic gestures, he describes the fluidity of discursive functions in a manner that resonates with Calvin's theological practices.

8. For a useful discussion of the interplay between these seemingly incommensurable positions, see Ronald Thiemann, *Revelation and Theology: The Gospel as Narrated Promise* (Notre Dame, Ind.: Notre Dame Press, 1985).

9. The model of anthropological analysis that has been most influential among postliberal theologians is the model described by Clifford Geertz in *The Interpretation of Cultures* (New York: Basic Books, 1973).

10. George Lindbeck, *The Nature of Doctrine: Religion and Theology in a Postliberal Age* (Philadelphia: Westminster Press, 1984), 32.

11. Hans Frei develops this point in the opening chapter of *The Eclipse of the Biblical Narrative* (New Haven, Conn.: Yale University Press, 1974), 1–50.

12. For an example of a postliberal theologian who integrates political social theory into a postliberal agenda, see Kathryn Tanner, *The Politics of God* (Minneapolis: Fortress Press, 1992).

13. In a recent essay, Amy Plantinga Pauw engages in an insightful feminist conversation with the postliberal position represented by Lindbeck. She raises critical questions concerning the relationship between power, position, and the grammar of Christian doctrines. Pauw, "The Word Is Near You: A Feminist Conversation with Lindbeck," *Theology Today* 50 (1993): 45–55.

14. This critique of the relation among power, audience, text, and doctrine is developed with respect to election in the work of Letty Russell, *Church in the Round: Feminist Interpretation of the Church* (Louisville, Ky.: Westminster/John Knox Press, 1993), 151–81. Judith Plaskow also offers a compelling Jewish feminist assessment of the language of "the chosen" in *Standing Again at Sinai: Judaism from a Feminist Perspective* (New York: Harper & Row, 1990).

15. See John W. De Gruchy, *Liberating Reformed Theology: A South African Contribution to an Ecumenical Debate* (Grand Rapids: Wm. B. Eerdmans Publishing Co., 1991); and Richard Shaull, *The Reformation and Liberation Theology: Insights for the Challenges of Today* (Louisville, Ky.: Westminster/John Knox Press, 1991).

APPENDIX

CALVIN: INSTITUTES
(Book 1, chaps. 1–3)

BOOK ONE

The Knowledge of God the Creator

CHAPTER I

THE KNOWLEDGE OF GOD AND THAT OF OURSELVES ARE
CONNECTED. HOW THEY ARE INTERRELATED

I. Without knowledge of self there is no knowledge of God

Nearly all the wisdom we possess, that is to say, true and sound wisdom, consists of two parts: the knowledge of God and of ourselves. But, while joined by many bonds, which one precedes and brings forth the other is not easy to discern. In the first place, no one can look upon himself without immediately turning his thoughts to the contemplation of God, in whom he "lives and moves" [Acts 17:28]. For, quite clearly the mighty gifts with which we are endowed are hardly from ourselves; indeed, our very being is nothing but subsistence in the one God. Then, by these benefits shed like dew from heaven upon us, we are led as by rivulets to the spring itself. Indeed, our very poverty better discloses the infinitude of benefits reposing in God. The miserable ruin, into which the rebellion of the first man cast us, especially compels us to look upward. Thus, not only will we, in fasting and hungering, seek thence what we lack; but, in being aroused by fear, we shall learn humility. For, as a veritable world of miseries is to be found in mankind, and we are thereby despoiled of divine raiment, our shameful nakedness exposes a teeming horde of infamies. Each of us must, then, be so stung by the consciousness of his own unhappiness as to attain at least some knowledge of God. Thus, from the feeling of our own ignorance, vanity, poverty, infirmity, and—what is more—depravity and corruption, we recognize that the true light of wisdom, sound virtue, full abundance of every good, and purity of righteousness rest in the Lord alone. To this extent we are prompted by our own ills to contemplate the good things of God; and we cannot seriously aspire to him before we begin to become displeased with ourselves. For what man in all the world would not gladly remain as he is—what man does not remain as he is—so long as he does not know himself, that is, while content with his own gifts, and either ignorant or unmindful of his own misery? Accordingly, the knowledge of ourselves not only arouses us to seek God, but also, as it were, leads us by the hand to find him.

2. Without knowledge of God there is no knowledge of self

Again, it is certain that man never achieves a clear knowledge of himself unless he has first looked upon God's face, and then descends from contemplating him to scrutinize himself. For we always seem to ourselves righteous and upright and wise and holy—this pride is innate in all of us—unless by clear proofs we stand convinced of our own unrighteousness, foulness, folly, and impurity. Moreover, we are not thus convinced if we look merely to ourselves and not also to the Lord, who is the sole standard by which this judgment must be measured. For, because all of us are inclined by nature to hypocrisy, a kind of empty image of righteousness in place of righteousness itself abundantly satisfies us. And because nothing appears within or around us that has not been contaminated by great immorality, what is a little less vile pleases us as a thing most pure—so long as we confine our minds within the limits of human corruption. Just so, an eye to which nothing is shown but black objects judges something dirty white or even rather darkly mottled to be whiteness itself. Indeed, we can discern still more clearly from the bodily senses how much we are deluded in estimating the powers of the soul. For if in broad daylight we either look down upon the ground or survey whatever meets our view round about, we seem to ourselves endowed with the strongest and keenest sight; yet when we look up to the sun and gaze straight at it, that power of sight which was particularly strong on earth is at once blunted and confused by a great brilliance, and thus we are compelled to admit that our keenness in looking upon things earthly is sheer dullness when it comes to the sun. So it happens in estimating our spiritual goods. As long as we do not look beyond the earth, being quite content with our own righteousness, wisdom, and virtue, we flatter ourselves most sweetly, and fancy ourselves all but demigods. Suppose we but once begin to raise our thoughts to God, and to ponder his nature, and how completely perfect are his righteousness, wisdom, and power—the straightedge to which we must be shaped. Then, what masquerading earlier as righteousness was pleasing in us will soon grow filthy in its consummate wickedness. What wonderfully impressed us under the name of wisdom will stink in its very foolishness. What wore the face of power will prove itself the most miserable weakness. That is, what in us seems perfection itself corresponds ill to the purity of God.

3. Man before God's majesty

Hence that dread and wonder with which Scripture commonly represents the saints as stricken and overcome whenever they felt the presence of God. Thus it comes about that we see men who in his absence normally remained firm and constant, but who, when he manifests his glory, are so shaken and struck dumb as to be laid low by the dread of death—are in fact overwhelmed by it and almost annihilated. As a consequence, we must infer that man is never sufficiently touched and affected by the awareness of his lowly state until he has compared himself with God's majesty. Moreover, we have numerous examples of this consternation both in The Book of Judges and in the Prophets. So frequent was it that this expression was common among God's people: "We shall die, for the Lord has appeared to us" [Judg. 13:22; Isa. 6:5; Ezek. 2:1; 1:28; Judg. 6:22–23; and elsewhere]. The story of Job, in its description of God's wisdom, power, and purity, always expresses a powerful argument that overwhelms men with the realization of their own stupidity, impotence, and corruption [cf. Job 38:1ff.]. And not without cause: for we see how Abraham recognizes more clearly that he is earth and dust [Gen. 18:27] when once he had come nearer to beholding God's glory; and how Elijah, with uncovered face, cannot bear to await his approach, such is the awesomeness of his appearance [1 Kings 19:13]. And what can man do, who is rottenness itself [Job 13:28] and a worm [Job 7:5; Ps. 22:6], when even the very cherubim must veil their faces out of fear [Isa. 6:2]? It is this indeed of which the prophet Isaiah speaks: "The sun will blush and the moon be confounded when the Lord of Hosts shall reign" [Isa. 24:23]; that is, when he shall bring forth his splendor and cause it to draw nearer, the brightest thing will become darkness before it [Isa. 2:10, 19 p.].

Yet, however the knowledge of God and of ourselves may be mutually connected, the order of right teaching requires that we discuss the former first, then proceed afterward to treat the latter.

CHAPTER II

What It Is to Know God, and to What Purpose the Knowledge of Him Tends

1. Piety is requisite for the knowledge of God

Now, the knowledge of God, as I understand it, is that by which we not only conceive that there is a God but also grasp what befits us and is proper to his glory, in fine, what is to our advantage to know of him. Indeed, we shall not say that, properly speaking, God is known where there is no religion or piety. Here I do not yet touch upon the sort of knowledge with which men, in themselves lost and accursed, apprehend God the Redeemer in Christ the Mediator; but I speak only of the primal and simple knowledge to which the very order of nature would have led us if Adam had remained upright. In this ruin of mankind no one now experiences God either as Father or as Author of salvation, or favorable in any way, until Christ the Mediator comes forward to reconcile him to us. Nevertheless, it is one thing to feel that God as our Maker supports us by his power, governs us by his providence, nourishes us by his goodness, and attends us with all sorts of blessings—and another thing to embrace the grace of reconciliation offered to us in Christ. First, as much in the fashioning of the universe as in the general teaching of Scripture the Lord shows himself to be simply the Creator. Then in the face of Christ [cf. 2 Cor. 4:6] he shows himself the Redeemer. Of the resulting twofold knowledge of God we shall now discuss the first aspect; the second will be dealt with in its proper place.

Moreover, although our mind cannot apprehend God without rendering some honor to him, it will not suffice simply to hold that there is One whom all ought to honor and adore, unless we are also persuaded that he is the fountain of every good, and that we must seek nothing elsewhere than in him. This I take to mean that not only does he sustain this universe (as he once founded it) by his boundless might, regulate it by his wisdom, preserve it by his goodness, and especially rule mankind by his righteousness and judgment, bear with it in his mercy, watch over it by his protection; but also that no drop will be found either of wisdom and light, or of righteousness or power or rectitude, or of genuine truth, which does not flow from him, and of which he is not the cause. Thus we may learn to await and seek all these things from him, and thankfully to ascribe them, once received, to him. For this sense of the powers of God is for us a fit teacher of piety, from which religion is born. I call "piety" that reverence joined with love of God which the knowledge of his benefits induces. For until men recognize that they owe everything to God, that they are nourished by his fatherly care, that he is the Author of their every good, that they should seek nothing beyond him—they will never yield him willing service. Nay, unless they establish their complete happiness in him, they will never give themselves truly and sincerely to him.

2. Knowledge of God involves trust and reverence
    What is God? Men who pose this question are merely toying with idle speculations. It is more important for us to know of what sort he is and what is consistent with his nature. What good is it to profess with Epicurus some sort of God who has cast aside the care of the world only to amuse himself in idleness? What help is it, in short, to know a God with whom we have nothing to do? Rather, our knowledge should serve first to teach us fear and reverence; secondly, with it as our guide and teacher, we should learn to seek every good from him, and, having received it, to credit it to his account. For how can the thought of God penetrate your mind without your realizing immediately that, since you are his handiwork, you have been made over and bound to his command by right of creation, that you owe your life to him?—that whatever you undertake, whatever you do, ought to be ascribed to him? If this be so, it now assuredly follows that your life is wickedly corrupt unless it be disposed to his service, seeing that his will ought for us to be the law by which we live. Again, you cannot behold him clearly unless you acknowledge him to be the fountainhead and source of every good. From this too would arise the desire to cleave to him and trust in him, but for the fact that man's depravity seduces his mind from rightly seeking him.

    For, to begin with, the pious mind does not dream up for itself any god it pleases, but contemplates the one and only true God. And it does not attach to him whatever it pleases, but is content to hold him to be as he manifests himself; furthermore, the mind always exercises the utmost diligence and care not to wander astray, or rashly and boldly to go beyond his will. It thus recognizes God because it knows that he governs all things; and trusts that he is its guide and protector, therefore giving itself over completely to trust in him. Because it understands him to be the Author of every good, if anything oppresses, if anything is lacking, immediately it betakes itself to his protection, waiting for help from him. Because it is persuaded that he is good and merciful, it reposes in him with perfect trust, and doubts not that in his loving-kindness a remedy will be provided for all its ills. Because it acknowledges him as Lord and Father, the pious mind also deems it meet and right to observe his authority in all things, reverence his majesty, take care to advance his glory, and obey his commandments. Because it sees him to be a righteous judge, armed with severity to punish wickedness, it ever holds his judgment seat before its gaze, and through fear of him restrains itself from provoking his anger. And yet it is not so terrified by the awareness of his judgment as to wish to withdraw, even if some way of escape were open. But it embraces him no less as punisher of the wicked than as benefactor of the pious. For the pious mind realizes that the punishment of the impious and wicked and the reward of life eternal for the righteous equally pertain to God's glory. Besides, this mind restrains itself from sinning, not out of dread of punishment alone; but, because it loves and reveres God as Father, it worships and adores him as Lord. Even if there were no hell, it would still shudder at offending him alone.

Here indeed is pure and real religion: faith so joined with an earnest fear of God that this fear also embraces willing reverence, and carries with it such legitimate worship as is prescribed in the law. And we ought to note this fact even more diligently: all men have a vague general veneration for God, but very few really reverence him; and wherever there is great ostentation in ceremonies, sincerity of heart is rare indeed.

CHAPTER III

THE KNOWLEDGE OF GOD HAS BEEN NATURALLY IMPLANTED IN THE MINDS OF MEN

I. The character of this natural endowment
There is within the human mind, and indeed by natural instinct, an awareness of divinity. This we take to be beyond controversy. To prevent anyone from taking refuge in the pretense of ignorance, God himself has implanted in all men a certain understanding of his divine majesty. Ever renewing its memory, he repeatedly sheds fresh drops. Since, therefore, men one and all perceive that there is a God and that he is their Maker, they are condemned by their own testimony because they have failed to honor him and to consecrate their lives to his will. If ignorance of God is to be looked for anywhere, surely one is most likely to find an example of it among the more backward folk and those more remote from civilization. Yet there is, as the eminent pagan says, no nation so barbarous, no people so savage, that they have not a deep-seated conviction that there is a God. And they who in other aspects of life seem least to differ from brutes still continue to retain some seed of religion. So deeply does the common conception occupy the minds of all, so tenaciously does it inhere in the hearts of all! Therefore, since from the beginning of the world there has been no region, no city, in short, no household, that could do without religion, there lies in this a tacit confession of a sense of deity inscribed in the hearts of all.

Indeed, even idolatry is ample proof of this conception. We know how man does not willingly humble himself so as to place other creatures over himself. Since, then, he prefers to worship wood and stone rather than to be thought of as having no God, clearly this is a most vivid impression of a divine being. So impossible is it to blot this from man's mind that natural disposition would be more easily altered, as altered indeed it is when man voluntarily sinks from his natural haughtiness to the very depths in order to honor God!

2. Religion is no arbitrary invention
Therefore it is utterly vain for some men to say that religion was invented by the subtlety and craft of a few to hold the simple folk in thrall by this device and

that those very persons who originated the worship of God for others did not in the least believe that any God existed. I confess, indeed, that in order to hold men's minds in greater subjection, clever men have devised very many things in religion by which to inspire the common folk with reverence and to strike them with terror. But they would never have achieved this if men's minds had not already been imbued with a firm conviction about God, from which the inclination toward religion springs as from a seed. And indeed it is not credible that those who craftily imposed upon the ruder folk under pretense of religion were entirely devoid of the knowledge of God. If, indeed, there were some in the past, and today not a few appear, who deny that God exists, yet willy-nilly they from time to time feel an inkling of what they desire not to believe. One reads of no one who burst forth into bolder or more unbridled contempt of deity than Gaius Caligula; yet no one trembled more miserably when any sign of God's wrath manifested itself; thus—albeit unwillingly—he shuddered at the God whom he professedly sought to despise. You may see now and again how this also happens to those like him; how he who is the boldest despiser of God is of all men the most startled at the rustle of a falling leaf [cf. Lev. 26:36]. Whence does this arise but from the vengeance of divine majesty, which strikes their consciences all the more violently the more they try to flee from it? Indeed, they seek out every subterfuge to hide themselves from the Lord's presence, and to efface it again from their minds. But in spite of themselves they are always entrapped. Although it may sometimes seem to vanish for a moment, it returns at once and rushes in with new force. If for these there is any respite from anxiety of conscience, it is not much different from the sleep of drunken or frenzied persons, who do not rest peacefully even while sleeping because they are continually troubled with dire and dreadful dreams. The impious themselves therefore exemplify the fact that some conception of God is ever alive in all men's minds.

3. Actual godlessness is impossible

Men of sound judgment will always be sure that a sense of divinity which can never be effaced is engraved upon men's minds. Indeed, the perversity of the impious, who though they struggle furiously are unable to extricate themselves from the fear of God, is abundant testimony that this conviction, namely, that there is some God, is naturally inborn in all, and is fixed deep within, as it were in the very marrow. Although Diagoras and his like may jest at whatever has been believed in every age concerning religion, and Dionysius may mock the heavenly judgment, this is sardonic laughter, for the worm of conscience, sharper than any cauterizing iron, gnaws away within. I do not say, as Cicero did, that errors disappear with the lapse of time, and that religion grows and becomes better each day. For the world (something will have to be said of this a little later) tries as far as it is able to cast away all knowledge of God, and by every means to corrupt the worship of him. I only say that though the stupid hardness in their minds, which the impious eagerly conjure up to reject God, wastes away, yet the sense of divinity, which they greatly wished to have extinguished, thrives and presently burgeons. From this we conclude that it is not a doctrine that must first be learned in school, but one of which each of us is master from his mother's womb and which nature itself permits no one to forget, although many strive with every nerve to this end.

Besides, if all men are born and live to the end that they may know God, and yet if knowledge of God is unstable and fleeting unless it progresses to this degree, it is clear that all these who do not direct every thought and action in their lives to this goal degenerate from the law of their creation. This was not unknown to the philosophers. Plato meant nothing but this when he often taught that the highest good of the soul is likeness to God, where, when the soul has grasped the knowledge of God, it is wholly transformed into his likeness. In the same manner also Gryllus, in the writings of Plutarch, reasons very skillfully, affirming that, if once religion is absent from their life, men are in no wise superior to brute beasts, but are in many respects far more miserable. Subject, then, to so many forms of wickedness, they drag out their lives in ceaseless tumult and disquiet. Therefore, it is worship of God alone that renders men higher than the brutes, and through it alone they aspire to immortality.

BIBLIOGRAPHY

PRIMARY SOURCES

Calvin

De scandalis. Edited by P. Barth and W. Niesel. Vol. 2 of *Opera Selecta.* Munich: Kaiser Verlag, 1926–52.

Excuses des messieurs les Nicodemites (1545). In *Three French Treatises,* edited by Francis M. Higman. University of London: Athlone Press, 1970.

Institution de la Religion Chréstienne. Edited by Jacques Pannier. Paris: Société d'Edition "Les Belles Lettres," 1961.

Ioannis Calvini opera quae supersunt omnia. Edited by Wilhelm Baum, Edward Cunitz, and Edward Reuss. 59 vols. (Cited as OC) Also found in *Corpus Reformatorum:* vols. 29–87. Brunsvigae: C. A. Schwetschke, 1863–1900.

Ioannis Calvini Opera Selecta. Edited by Peter Barth and Wilhelm Niesel. 5 vols. Munich: Kaiser Verlag, 1926–52. (Cited as OS)

Translations

"Against the Libertines." Translated by Robert G. Wilkie and Allen D. Verhey, with an introduction by Allen D. Verhey. *Calvin Theological Journal* 15 (1980): 190–219.

Calvin's Commentary on Seneca's "De clementia." Edited and translated by Ford Lewis Battles and André Malan Hugo. Leiden: E. J. Brill, 1969.

Concerning Scandals. Translated by John W. Fraser. Grand Rapids: Wm. B. Eerdmans Publishing Co., 1978.

Institutes of the Christian Religion. Edited by J. T. McNeill. Translated by Ford Lewis Battles. 2 vols. Library of Christian Classics, vols. 20 and 21. Philadelphia: Westminster Press, 1960. (Cited as *Inst.*)

Institutes of the Christian Religion, Embracing almost the whole sum of piety, & whatever is necessary to know concerning the doctrine of salvation: A work most worthy to be read by all persons zealous for piety, and recently published. 1536 edition. Translated and annotated by Ford Lewis Battles. Grand Rapids: Wm. B. Eerdmans Publishing Co., 1989.

Introduction to the Commentary on the Psalms. In *Calvin's Commentaries and Letters,* edited by Joseph Haroutunian. Library of Christian Classics, vol. 23. Philadelphia: Westminster Press, 1958.

218

Letters of John Calvin. Edited by Jules Bonnet. Translated by David Constable and M. R. Gilchrist. Philadelphia: Presbyterian Board of Publication, 1858.

The Mystery of Godliness and Other Selected Sermons. Grand Rapids: Wm. B. Eerdmans Publishing Co., 1950.

Psychopannychia: Tracts and Treatises. Edited by T. F. Torrance. Translated by Henry Beveridge, with an introduction by Walter Zimmerli. Grand Rapids: Wm. B. Eerdmans Publishing Co., 1958.

Miscellaneous

Augustine. *City of God.* Translated by Marcus Dods. A Select Library of the Nicene and Post-Nicene Fathers of the Christian Church, edited by Philip Schaff. Grand Rapids: Wm. B. Eerdmans Publishing Co., 1978–79.

————. *Confessions.* Translated by J. G. Pilkington. A Select Library of the Nicene and Post-Nicene Fathers, edited by Philip Schaff. Grand Rapids: Wm. B. Eerdmans Publishing Co., 1979.

————. *Soliloquies I.* Translated by Charles Starbuch. A Select Library of the Nicene and Post-Nicene Fathers of the Christian Church. Grand Rapids: Wm. B. Eerdmans Publishing Co., 1978. (The Latin text used in chapter 3 is found in *Patrologia Latina,* 32, col. 872d. Edited by J.-P. Migne. Paris: 1877.)

Bucer, Martin. *Enarrationes perpetuae in sacra quatuor evangelia, recognitae nuper et locis compluribus auctae.* Strasbourg, 1530.

Budé, Guillaume. *De transitu Hellenismi ad Christianismum.* Book 3 in *Omnia Opera Gulielmi Budaei.* 1557 ed. Reprint, Farnborough: Gregg, 1963.

Cicero. *De finibus bonorum et malorum.* Translated by H. Rackham. Edited by E. H. Warmington. Loeb Classical Library. Cambridge: Harvard University Press, 1971.

————. *De inventione.* Translated by H. M. Hubbell. Loeb Classical Library. Cambridge, Mass.: Harvard University Press, 1976.

————. *De legibus.* Translated by Clinton Walker Keyes. Edited by E. H. Warmington. Loeb Classical Library. Cambridge: Harvard University Press, 1970.

————. *De natura deorum.* Translated by H. Rackham. Edited by E. H. Warmington. Loeb Classical Library. Cambridge: Harvard University Press, 1967.

————. *Orator.* Translated by H. M. Hubbell. Loeb Classical Library. Cambridge, Mass.: Harvard University Press, 1971.

————. *De oratore.* Books 1 and 2 translated by E. W. Sutton. Book 3, translated by H. Rackham. Loeb Classical Library. 2 vols. Cambridge, Mass.: Harvard University Press, 1967–68.

Clement. *Instructor.* Vol. 2 in A Select Library of the Nicene and Post-Nicene Fathers of the Christian Church, edited by Philip Schaff. Grand Rapids: Wm. B. Eerdmans Publishing Co., 1978–79. (The Latin text used in chapter 3 is found in *Patrologia Graeca,* 8, col. 536a. Edited by J.-P. Migne. Paris: 1891.)

Dolet. *L'Erasmianus sive Ciceronianus d'Etienne Dolet,* 1535. Facsimile of the *De imitatione ciceroniana.* Edited by E. V. Telle. Geneva: Droz, 1974.

Erasmus. *Adagiorum chiliades tres.* In *Opera,* vol. 2, edited by J. Leclerc. Leiden: 1703, and Louvain: 1704. (For the English I have used *Adages.* 4 vols. Translated by M. M. Phillips. Toronto: University of Toronto Press, 1982–92.)

————. *The Ciceronian, a Dialogue on the Ideal Latin Style: Dialogus Ciceronianus.* In *The Collected Works of Erasmus,* vol. 28, translated and annotated by Betty I. Knott. Toronto: University of Toronto Press, 1974–94.

————. *On Copia of Words and Ideas (De utraque verborum ac rerum copia).* Edited and translated by D. B. King and H. D. Rix. Milwaukee: Marquette University Press, 1963.

————. *On the Two-Fold Abundance of Words and Ideas (De duplici copia verborum ac rerum commentarii duo).* In *The Collected Works of Erasmus,* vol. 24, translated and annotated by Betty I. Knott. Toronto: University of Toronto Press, 1974–94.

Lactantius. *The Divine Institutes.* Books 1–7. Translated by William Fletcher and edited by Alex Roberts. In *The Ante-Nicene Fathers,* vol. 7. Grand Rapids: Wm. B. Eerdmans Publishing Co., 1979.

Martyr, Justin. *De monarchia.* Translated by G. Reith and edited by Alex Roberts. In *The Ante-Nicence Fathers,* vol. 1. Grand Rapids: Wm. B. Eerdmans Publishing Co., 1979.

Petrarch, Francesco. *Le Familiare XXIV, 2. (Familiarium rerum libri).* Edited by Vittorio Rossi. Florence: Sansoni, 1933–42.

————. *"De sui ipsius et multorum ignorantia."* In *Prose: Francesco Petrarcha,* edited by G. Martellotti et al., Milan and Naples: R. Riccardi, 1955. (I have used an English translation of this text: "On His Own Ignorance," by Hans Nachod, in *Renaissance Philosophy of Man,* edited by Ernst Cassirer, Paul Oskar Kristeller, and John Herman Randall, Jr., Chicago: University of Chicago Press, 1948.)

————. *"De vita solitaria."* In *Prose: Francesco Petrarcha,* edited by G. Martellotti et al., Milan and Naples: R. Riccardi, 1955. (I have used an English translation of this text by Jerrold Seigel in *Rhetoric and Philosophy in Renaissance Humanism,* 46–47. Princeton, N.J.: Princeton University Press, 1968.)

Plato. *Alcibiadaes Major.* Translated by W.R.M. Lamb. Cambridge, Mass.: Harvard University Press, 1964.

————. *The Republic.* Translated by Paul Shore and edited by E. H. Warmington. Loeb Classical Library. Cambridge, Mass.: Harvard University Press, 1969.

Quintillian. *The Institutio Oratoria of Quintillian, Book X, Vol IV.* Translated by H. E. Butler. Loeb Classical Library. Cambridge, Mass.: Harvard University Press, 1966.

Salutati, Coluccio. *Epistolario di Coluccio Salutati.* 4 vols. Edited by Francesco Novati. Rome: 1891–1911. (I have relied on the English translations by Jerrold Seigel in *Rhetoric and Philosophy in Renaissance Humanism.* Princeton, N.J.: Princeton University Press, 1968, 63–98.)

Seneca. *Ad Lucilium epistulae morales.* Translated by Richard M. Gummere. Loeb Classical Library. Cambridge, Mass.: Harvard University Press, 1967.

Thomas, Aquinas. *Summa Theologia, Vol. 1.* New York: McGraw-Hill Book Co., 1964.

de Valla, Lorenza. *Elegantiae linguae latinae, IV, Opera, Vol I of Monumenta Politica et Philosophica Rariora.* Turin, 1962. (I have used an English translation of a portion of this text by Jerrold Seigel in *Rhetoric and Philosophy in Renaissance Humanism,* 154–55. Princeton, N.J.: Princeton University Press, 1968.)

————. *"On the True Good."* In *Scritti Filosofici e Religiose,* edited by Giorgio Radetti. Florence, 1953. (I have used an English translation of this text by Jerrold Seigel in *Rhetoric and Philosophy in Renaissance Humanism,* 142. Princeton, N.J.: Princeton University Press, 1968.)

Zwingli, Huldreich. *Commentary on True and False Religion.* Edited by S. M. Jackson and C. N. Heller. Durham: Labyrinth, 1981, © 1929. In *Opera,* by Huldrici

Zuinglii, vol. 3, edited by M. Schuler and J. Schulthess. Zürich: Officina
Schulthessiana, 1832.

SECONDARY SOURCES

Allen, Percy Stafford. *The Age of Erasmus: Lectures Delivered in the Universities of Oxford and London.* Oxford: Clarendon Press, 1914.
Altman, Joel B. *The Tudor Play of Mind: Rhetorical Inquiry and the Development of Elizabethan Drama.* Berkeley: University of California Press,1978.
d'Amico, John. *Renaissance Humanism in Papal Rome.* Baltimore: Johns Hopkins
University Press, 1983.
Armstrong, Brian G. "The Nature and Structure of Calvin's Thought according to
The Institutes: Another Look." In *John Calvin's Institutes: His Opus Magnum,*
55–81. Proceedings of the Second South African Congress for Calvin Research,
31 July–3 August 1984. Potchefstroom, Transvaal, Republic of South Africa:
Potchefstroom University for Christian Higher Education Press, 1986.
Ayers, Robert H. "Language, Logic, and Reason in Calvin's *Institutes.*" *Religious
Studies* 16 (1980): 283–97.
Balke, Willen. *Calvin and the Anabaptist Radicals.* Translated by William Heynen.
Grand Rapids: Wm. B. Eerdmans Publishing Co., 1981.
Barth, Karl. *Church Dogmatics.* Translated by G. W. Bromiley and edited by G. W.
Bromiley and T. F. Torrance. Edinburgh: T. & T. Clark, 1977.
Barth, Peter. *Das Problem der naturliche Theologie bei Calvin, Theologische Existenz
Heute.* Vol. 18. Munich: Kaiser Verlag, 1935.
Barton, F. Whitfield. *Calvin and the Duchess.* Louisville, Ky.: John Knox Press, 1989.
Battenhouse, Roy W. "The Doctrine of Man in Calvin and Renaissance Platonism."
Journal of the History of Ideas 9 (1948): 447–71.
Battles, Ford Lewis. "God Was Accommodating Himself to Human Capacity." *In-
terpretation* 31 (1977): 19–38.
————. "The Sources of Calvin's Seneca Commentary." In *Courtney Studies in Re-
formation Theology I: John Calvin,* 38–66. Edited by G. E. Duffield. Appleford: Sut-
ton Courtenay Press, 1966.
Benoit, Jean Daniel. *Calvin, Directeur d'âmes.* Strasbourg: Oberlin Press, 1947.
Bergier, Jean-François and Robert M. Kingdon, eds. *Registres de la Compagnie des
pasteurs de Genève au temps de Calvin.* Geneva: Droz, 1962–1964.
Berriot, François. *Athéismes et athéistes au XVIe siècle en France.* 2 vols. Lille: Thesis
arf, 1984.
Bieler, André. *The Social Humanism of Calvin.* Translated by Paul T. Fuhrmann.
Richmond: John Knox Press, 1964.
Blaisdell, Charmarie. "Calvin's Letters to Women: The Courting of Ladies in High
Places." *Sixteenth Century Journal* 12, no. 3 (1982): 67–84.
————. "Renée de France: Between Reform and Counter-Reform." *Archiv für
Reformationsgeschichte* 63 (1972): 196–226.
Bloom, Harold. "The Necessity of Misreadings." In *Kabbalah and Criticism,* New
York: Seabury Press, 1974.
Bohatec, Josef. *Budé und Calvin: Studien zur Gedankenwelt des französischen Frühhu-
manismus.* Graz: Böhlaus, 1950.

Bolgar, R. R. *The Classical Heritage and Its Beneficiaries*. London: Cambridge University Press, 1954.

Borgeaud, Charles. *L'Académie de Calvin*. Vol. 1 in *Historie de l'Université de Genève*. Geneva, 1900–1934.

Bourrilly, E., ed. *Calvin et la Réforme en France*. Aix-en-Provence: Faculté Libre de Théologie Protestante, 1959.

Bouwsma, William. "Anxiety and the Formation of Early Modern Culture." In *After the Reformation: Essays in Honor of J. H. Hexter*, edited by Barbara Malament, Philadelphia: University of Pennsylvania Press, 1980.

―――. "Calvin and the Renaissance Crisis of Knowing." *Calvin Theological Journal* 17 (November 1982): 190–211.

―――. *Calvinism as Theologia Rhetorica*. Edited by William Bouwsma and William Wuellner. Protocol of the Fifty-fourth Colloquy, 28 September 1986. Center for Hermeneutical Studies in Hellenistic and Modern Culture. Berkeley: General Theological Union and University of California Press, 1987.

―――. "Changing Assumptions in Later Renaissance Culture." *Viator* 7 (1976): 421–40.

―――. *The Interpretation of Renaissance Humanism*. Washington, D.C.: Service Center for Teachers of History, 1966.

―――. *John Calvin: A Sixteenth-Century Portrait*. New York: Oxford University Press, 1988.

―――. "Lawyers in Early Modern Culture." *American Historical Review* 78 (1973): 303–37.

―――. "The Peculiarity of the Reformation in Geneva." In *Religion and Culture in the Renaissance and Reformation: Sixteenth-Century Essays and Studies*. Edited by Stephen Ozment. Kirksville, Mo.: Sixteenth Century Journal Publishers, 1989.

―――. "The Two Faces of Humanism: Stoicism and Augustinianism in Renaissance Thought." In *Itinerarium Italicum: The Profile of the Italian Renaissance in the Mirror of Its European Transformations* (dedicated to Paul Oskar Kristeller on the occasion of his seventieth birthday), edited by Heiko A. Oberman, with Thomas A. Brady, Jr., Leiden: E. J. Brill, 1975.

Bouyer, Louis. *Autour d'Erasme: Études sur le christianisme des humanistes catholiques*. Paris: Editions du Cerf, 1955.

Boyle, Marjorie O'Rourke. *Erasmus on Language and Method in Theology*. Buffalo: University of Toronto Press, 1977.

Brady, Thomas A., Jr. *Ruling Class, Regime, and Reformation in Strasbourg, 1520–1555*. Leiden: E. J. Brill, 1978.

―――. *Turning Swiss: Cities and Empires, 1450–1550*. Cambridge and New York: Cambridge University Press, 1985.

Breen, Quirinius. *Christianity and Humanism: Studies in the History of Ideas*. Grand Rapids: Wm. B. Eerdmans Publishing Co., 1968.

―――. *John Calvin: A Study in French Humanism*. Grand Rapids: Wm. B. Eerdmans Publishing Co., 1931.

―――. "John Calvin and the Rhetorical Tradition." *Church History* 26 (1957): 3–21.

Broeyer, Fritz. "A Pure City: Calvin's Geneva." In *The Quest for Purity: Dynamics of Puritan Movements*, edited by Walker E. A. van Beek, New York: Mouton de Gruyter, 1988.

Burke, Kenneth. *A Grammar of Motives.* New York: Prentice Hall Press, 1945.
————. *The Rhetoric of Religion: Studies in Logology.* Berkeley: University of California Press, 1970.
Burnyeat, Myles, ed. *The Skeptical Tradition.* Berkeley: University of California Press, 1983.
Busser, Fritz. "Elements of Zwingli's Thought in Calvin's *Institutes.*" In *In Honor of John Calvin, 1509–1564: Papers from the 1986 International Calvin Symposium, McGill University,* edited by E. J. Furcha, 1–27. ARC Supplement, 3. Montreal: Faculty of Religious Studies, McGill University, 1987.
Busson, Henri. "Les Noms des incrédules au XVIe siècle." *Bibliothèque d'Humanisme et de Renaissance* 16 (1954): 273–83.
Cassirer, Ernst. *The Individual and the Cosmos in Renaissance Philosophy.* Translated by Mario Domandi. Philadelphia: University of Pennsylvania Press, 1963.
Cassirer, Ernst, Paul Oskar Kristeller, and John Herman Randall, Jr., eds. *Renaissance Philosophy of Man: Selections in Translation.* Chicago: University of Chicago Press, 1969.
Cave, Terrence. *The Cornucopian Text: Problems of Writing in the French Renaissance.* Oxford: Clarendon Press, 1979.
————. "Problems of Writing in Sixteenth-Century France." Manuscript, New Haven: Yale University, 1989.
Certeau, Michel de. *Heterologies: Discourses on the Other.* Translated by Brian Massumi. Minneapolis: University of Minnesota Press, 1986.
Chrisman, Miriam Usher. *Lay Culture, Learned Culture: Books and Social Change in Strasbourg, 1480–1599.* New Haven, Conn.: Yale University Press, 1982.
————. *Strasbourg and the Reform: A Study in the Process of Change, 1520–1555.* New Haven, Conn.: Yale University Press, 1967.
Christie, Richard Copley. *Etienne Dolet, the Martyr of the Renaissance, 1508–1546: A Biography.* London: Macmillan & Co., 1899.
Clasen, Claus Peter. *Anabaptism: A Social History, 1525–1618. Switzerland, Austria, Moravia, South and Central Germany.* Ithaca, N.Y.: Cornell University Press, 1972.
————. "Medieval Heresies in the Reformation." *Church History* 32 (1963): 392–414.
Colish, Maria. *The Mirror of Language: A Study in the Medieval Theory of Knowledge.* Lincoln: University of Nebraska Press, 1983.
Collins, Ross Williams. *Calvin and the Libertines of Geneva.* Toronto: Clarke, Irwin and Co., 1968.
Davis, David Brion. *The Problem of Slavery in Western Culture.* Ithaca, N.Y.: Cornell University Press, 1966.
Davis, Natalie Zemon. *Society and Culture in Early Modern France.* Stanford: Stanford University Press, 1975.
Dawson, John Charles. *Toulouse in the Renaissance: The Floral Games; University and Student Life; Etienne Dolet.* New York: Columbia University Press, 1923.
De Gruchy, John W. *Liberating Reformed Theology: A South African Contribution to an Ecumenical Debate.* Grand Rapids: Wm. B. Eerdmans Publishing Co., 1991.
Dixon, Peter. *Rhetoric: The Critical Medium.* London: Methuen, 1971.
Douglass, Jane Dempsey. *Women, Freedom, and Calvin.* Philadelphia: Westminster Press, 1985.
Doumergue, Emile. *Jean Calvin: Les hommes et les choses de son temps.* 7 vols. Lausanne: Georg Bridel, 1899–1927.

Dowey, Edward A., Jr. *The Knowledge of God in Calvin's Theology*. 2d ed. New York: Columbia University Press, 1952.

Engel, Mary Potter. *John Calvin's Perspectival Anthropology*. Atlanta: Scholars Press, 1988.

Febvre, Lucien. *Life in Renaissance France*. Edited and translated by Marion Rothstein. Cambridge, Mass.: Harvard University Press, 1977.

———. *Le problème de l'incroyance au XVIe siècle: La religion de Rabelais*. Evolution de l'Humanite, 53. Paris: Albin Michel, 1942.

Ferguson, Margaret, Maureen Quilligan, and Nancy J. Vickers. *Rewriting the Renaissance: The Discourses of Sexual Difference in Early Modern Europe*. Chicago: University of Chicago Press, 1986.

Ferguson, Margaret, Maureen Quilligan, and Nancy Vickers, eds. *Trials of Desire: Renaissance Defenses of Poetry*. New Haven: Yale University Press, 1983.

Fish, Stanley. *Self-Consuming Artifacts: The Experience of Seventeenth Century Literature*. Berkeley: University of California Press, 1972.

Forstman, Henry Jackson. *Word and Spirit: Calvin's Doctrine of Biblical Authority*. Stanford, Calif.: Stanford University Press, 1962.

Foucault, Michel. *Power/Knowledge: Selected Interviews and Other Writings, 1972–1977*. Edited and translated by Colin Gordon. New York: Pantheon Books, 1980.

Frei, Hans. *The Eclipse of Biblical Narrative*. New Haven: Yale University Press, 1974.

Furcha, E. J., ed. *In Honor of John Calvin, 1509–1564: Papers from the 1986 International Calvin Symposium, McGill University*, ARC Supplement. Montreal: Faculty of Religious Studies, McGill University, 1987.

Ganoczy, Alexandre. *La bibliothèque de l'Académie de Calvin*. Geneva: Droz, 1969.

———. *The Young Calvin*. Translated by David Foxgrover and Wade Provo. Philadelphia: Westminster Press, 1987.

Geertz, Clifford. *The Interpretation of Cultures*. New York: Basic Books, 1973.

Gerrish, Brian A. *The Old Protestantism and the New: Essays on the Reformation Heritage*. Chicago: University of Chicago Press, 1982.

———. "To the Unknown God: Luther and Calvin on the Hiddenness of God." *Journal of Religion* 53 (1973): 263–92.

Giamatti, A. Bartlet. *Exile and Change in Renaissance Literature*. New Haven, Conn.: Yale University Press, 1984.

Gill, Katherine. "Open Monasteries for Women in Late Medieval and Early Modern Italy: Two Roman Examples." In *The Crannied Wall: Women, Religion, and the Arts in Early Modern Europe*, edited by Craig A. Monson, Ann Arbor: University of Michigan Press, 1992.

Gilmore, Myron Piper. *Humanists and Jurists: Six Studies in the Renaissance*. Cambridge, Mass.: Belknap Press of Harvard University, 1963.

Girardin, Benoît. *Rhétorique et théologique: Calvin, le Commentaire de l'Epitre aux Romans*. Théologique Historique, 54. Paris: Editions Beauchesne, 1979.

Gloede, Gunter. *Theologia Naturalis bei Calvin*. Stuttgart: Kohlhammer, 1935.

Gray, Hannah H. "Renaissance Humanism: The Pursuit of Eloquence." *Journal of the History of Ideas* 24 (1963): 497–514.

Greenblatt, Stephen. *Renaissance Self-Fashioning: From More to Shakespeare*. Chicago: University of Chicago Press, 1980.

Grislis, Egil. "Calvin's Use of Cicero in the Institutes I:1–5: A Case Study in Theological Method." *Archiv für Reformationsgeschichte* 62 (1971): 5–37.

————. "Seneca and Cicero as Possible Sources of John Calvin's View of Double-Predestination." In *In Honor of John Calvin, 1509–1564: Papers from the 1986 International Calvin Symposium, McGill University,* edited by E. J. Furcha. ARC Supplement. Montreal: Faculty of Religious Studies, McGill University, 1987.

Grundersheimer, Werner L., ed. *French Humanism: 1470–1600.* London: Macmillan & Co., 1969.

Gründler, Otto. "The Problem of *Semen fidei* in the Teaching of Calvin." In *Calvinus servus Christi.* Die Referate des Congres International des recherches Calviniennes vom 25. bis 28. August 1986 in Debrecen. Hrsg. Von Wilhelm Neuser. Budapest: Presseabteilung des Raday-Kollegiums, 1988.

Hall, Basil. *John Calvin: Humanist and Theologian.* 2d ed., revised. London: London Historical Society, 1967.

Harbison, Elmore Harris. *The Christian Scholar in the Age of Reformation.* New York: Charles Scribner's Sons, 1956.

Harkness, Georgia. *John Calvin: The Man and His Ethics.* New York: Henry Holt & Co., 1931.

Haroutunian, Joseph. "General Introduction to Calvin's Commentary and Letters." In *Calvin: Commentaries.* Library of Christian Classics. Philadelphia: Westminster Press, 1958.

Heller, Henry. *The Conquest of Poverty: The Calvinist Revolt in Sixteenth-Century France.* Leiden: E. J. Brill, 1986.

Higman, Francis. "Calvin the Writer." (Manuscript, New Haven: Yale University, 1989).

————. *Censorship and the Sorbonne: A Bibliographical Study of Books in French Censored by the Faculty of Theology, 1520–1551.* Geneva: Librairie E. Droz, 1979.

————. "De Calvin à Descartes: La création de la langue classique." *Revue d'Humanisme et de Renaissance* 15 (1986): 5–18.

————. "The Reformation and the French Language." *L'Esprit créateur* 16 (1976): 20–36.

————. *The Style of John Calvin in His French Polemical Treatises.* Cambridge: Oxford University Press, 1967.

————. "Theology in French: Religious Pamphlets from the Counter-Reformation." *Renaissance and Modern Studies* 23 (1979): 128–46.

Hillerbrand, Hans Joachim. *The World of the Reformation.* New York: Charles Scribner's Sons, 1973.

Hodgen, Margaret Trabue. *Early Anthropology in the Sixteenth and Seventeenth Centuries.* Philadelphia: University of Pennsylvania Press, 1964.

Holmer, Paul. *The Grammar of Faith.* San Francisco: Harper & Row, 1978.

————. "Wittgenstein and Theology." In *New Essays in Religious Language,* edited by D. M. High. New York: Oxford University Press, 1969.

Hopfl, H. M. "The Training of a Lawgiver." In *The Christian Polity of John Calvin,* 5–18. Cambridge and New York: Cambridge University Press, 1982.

Huizinga, Johan. *Erasmus and the Age of Reformation.* Translated by F. Hopman. New York: Harper, 1957.

Jameson, Fredric. *The Political Unconscious: Narrative as Socially Symbolic Act.* Ithaca, N.Y.: Cornell University Press, 1981.

Kahn, Victoria A. *Rhetoric, Prudence, and Skepticism in the Renaissance.* Ithaca, N.Y.: Cornell University Press, 1985.

Kelley, Donald. *The Beginning of Ideology: Consciousness and Society in the French Reformation.* Cambridge: Cambridge University Press, 1981.

————. "Civil Science in the Renaissance: Jurisprudence in the French Manner." In *Foundations of Modern Historical Scholarship: Language, Law, and History in the French Renaissance*. New York: Columbia University Press, 1970.

Kelsay, John. "Prayer and Ethics: Reflections on Calvin and Barth." *Harvard Theological Review* 82:2 (1989): 169–84.

Kelso, Ruth. *Doctrine for the Lady of the Renaissance*. Urbana: University of Illinois Press, 1956.

Kennedy, George A. *The Art of Rhetoric in the Roman World: 300 B.C.–A.D. 300*. Princeton, N.J.: Princeton University Press, 1972.

————. *Classical Rhetoric and Its Christian and Secular Traditions from Ancient to Modern Times*. Chapel Hill: University of North Carolina Press, 1980.

————. *Greek Rhetoric Under Christian Emperors*. Princeton, N.J.: Princeton University Press, 1983.

Kennedy, William J. *Rhetorical Norms in Renaissance Literature*. New Haven, Conn.: Yale University Press, 1978.

Kingdon, Robert M. "Calvin and the Government of Geneva." In *Calvinus ecclesiae Genevensis custos*, edited by W. Neuser. International Congress on Calvin Research. Frankfurt am Main and New York: Lang, 1984.

————. *Geneva and the Coming of the Wars of Religion in France: 1555–1563*. Geneva: Librairie E. Droz, 1956.

Kristeller, Paul O. "Atheism and the French Tradition of Free Thought." *Journal of the History of Philosophy* 6 (1968): 233–43.

————. *Renaissance Concepts of Man*. New York: Harper & Row, 1972.

————. *Renaissance Thought: The Classic, Scholastic, and Humanist Strains*. New York: Harper & Row, 1961.

————. "Rhetoric in Medieval and Renaissance Culture." In *Renaissance Eloquence: Studies in the Theory and Practice of Renaissance Rhetoric*, edited by James Murphy. Berkeley: University of California Press, 1983.

————. *Studies in Renaissance Thought and Letters*. Rome: Edizioni di storia e letteratura, 1956–1985.

La Capra, Dominick. "Rethinking Intellectual History and Reading Texts." In *Modern Euorpean Intellectual History: Reappraisals and New Perspectives*, edited by Dominick La Capra and Steven L. Kaplan. Ithaca, N.Y.: Cornell University Press, 1982.

La Garanderie, Marie Madeline de. "Guillaume Budé: A Philosopher of Culture." *Sixteenth Century Journal* 19, no. 3 (1988): 379–87.

Lang, A. "The Sources of Calvin's *Institutes* of 1536." *Evangelical Quarterly* 8 (1936): 130–41.

Lanham, Richard A. *The Motives of Eloquence: Literary Rhetoric in the Renaissance*. New Haven, Conn.: Yale University Press, 1976.

La Russo, Dominic A. "Rhetoric in the Italian Renaissance." In *Renaissance Eloquence: Studies in the Theory and Practice of Renaissance Rhetoric*, edited by James Murphy. Berkeley: University of California Press, 1983.

Lavao, Ronald. *Renaissance Minds and Their Fictions: Cusanus, Sidney, and Shakespeare*. Berkeley: University of California Press, 1985.

Le Franc, Abel. *Calvin et l'éloquence française*. Paris: Librairie Fischbacher, 1934.

————. *La jeunesse de Calvin*. Paris: Librairie Fischbacher, 1888.

Leith, John. *An Introduction to the Reformed Tradition: A Way of Being the Christian Community*. Atlanta: John Knox Press, 1977.

Levi, Anthony. *Pagan Virtue and the Humanism of the Northern Renaissance*. London: Society for Renaissance Studies, 1974.

Lindbeck, George. *The Nature of Doctrine: Religion and Theology in a Postliberal Age*. Philadelphia: Westminster Press, 1984.

Linder, Robert D. "Calvinism and Humanism: The First Generation." *Church History* 44 (1975): 167–81.

Lobstein, P. "La connaissance religieuse d'après Calvin." *Revue de théologie et de philosophie* 42 (1909): 53–110.

Mackintosh, Hugh Ross. *Types of Modern Theology: Schleiermacher to Barth*. New York: Scribner, 1937.

McGrath, Alister E. *A Life of John Calvin: A Study in the Shaping of Western Culture*. Oxford: Basil Blackwell Publisher, 1990.

McNeil, David. *Guillaume Budé and Humanism in the Reign of Francis I*. Geneva: Librairie Droz S. A., 1975.

McNeill, John T. *The History and Character of Calvinism*. New York: Oxford University Press, 1954.

Manley, Lawrence. *Convention: 1500–1750*. Cambridge, Mass.: Harvard University Press, 1980.

Marmelstein, J. W. *Etude comparative des textes latins et français de l'Institution de la Religion chrestienne par Jean Calvin*. Paris, Groningen, and The Hague, 1921.

Martines, Lauro. *The Social World of the Florentine Humanists: 1390–1460*. Princeton, N.J.: Princeton University Press, 1963.

Monter, E. William. *Calvin's Geneva*. New York: John Wiley & Sons, 1967.

Mullett, Michael A. *Radical Religious Movements in Early Modern Europe*. London: Allen & Unwin, 1980.

Murphy, James. *Rhetoric in the Middle Ages: A History of Rhetorical Theory from Saint Augustine to the Renaissance*. Berkeley: University of California Press, 1974.

Murphy, James, ed. *Renaissance Eloquence: Studies in the Theory and Practice of Renaissance Rhetoric*. Berkeley: University of California Press, 1983.

Natural Theology: Comprising "Nature and Grace" by Dr. Emil Brunner and the Reply "No!" by Dr. Karl Barth. Translated by Peter Fraenkel. London: Centenary Press, 1946.

Nauert, Charles G., Jr. *Agrippa and the Crisis of Renaissance Thought*. Urbana: University of Illinois Press, 1965.

Niesel, Wilhelm. *Theology of Calvin*. Translated by Harold Knight. Philadelphia: Westminster Press, 1956.

Nolhac, Pierre de. *Petrarch and the Ancient World*. Boston: Merrymount Press, 1907.

Oberman, Heiko A. "The Shape of Late Medieval Thought." In *The Pursuit of Holiness in Late Medieval and Renaissance Religion: Papers from the University of Michigan Conference*, edited by Charles Trinkhaus and Heiko A. Oberman. Leiden: E. J. Brill, 1974.

Oberman, Heiko A., ed., with Thomas A. Brady, Jr. *Itinerarium Italicum: The Profile of the Italian Renaissance in the Mirror of Its European Transformations*. Dedicated to Paul Oskar Kristeller on the occasion of his seventieth birthday. Leiden: E. J. Brill, 1975.

Ong, Walter Jackson. *Ramus, Method, and the Decay of Dialogue: From the Art of Discourse to the Art of Reason*. New York: Octagon Books, 1979.

Ozment, Steven. *The Age of Reform, 1250–1550: An Intellectual and Religious History of Late Medieval and Reformation Europe.* New Haven, Conn.: Yale University Press, 1980.

———. *Reformation in the Cities: The Appeal of Protestantism to Sixteenth-Century Germany and Switzerland.* New Haven, Conn.: Yale University Press, 1975.

Parker, Patricia. *Literary Fat Ladies: Rhetoric, Gender, Property.* New York: Methuen, 1987.

Parker, T.H.L. *John Calvin: A Biography.* Philadelphia: Westminster Press, 1975.

———. *Calvin's Doctrine of the Knowledge of God.* Rev. ed. Edinburgh: Oliver & Boyd, 1969.

Partee, Charles. *Calvin and Classical Philosophy.* Studies in the History of Christian Thought, 14. Leiden: E. J. Brill, 1977.

———. "Calvin and Experience." *Scottish Journal of Theology* 26:2 (1973): 169–81.

Pauw, Amy Plantinga. "The Word Is Near You: A Feminist Conversation with Lindbeck." *Theology Today* 50 (April 1993): 45–55.

Peter, R. "Geneva in the Preaching of John Calvin." In *Calvinus servus Christi: International Congress on Calvin Research,* edited by Wilhem H. Neuser, Budapest: Presseabteilung des Ráday-Kolleguims, 1988.

Phillips, D. Z. *Religion without Explanation.* Oxford: Basil Blackwell Publisher, 1976.

Plaskow, Judith. *Standing Again at Sinai: Judaism from a Feminist Perspective.* New York: Harper & Row, 1990.

Regosin, Richard L. "Recent Trends in Montaigne Scholarship: A Post-Structuralist Perspective." *Renaissance Quarterly* 37 (Spring 1984): 34–54.

Reulos, Michel. "L'importance des practiciens dans l'humanisme juridique." In *Pédagogues et Juristes,* 119–33. Congrès du Centre d'Etudes supérieures de la Renaissance de Tours, Etc. Paris: J. Vrin, 1963.

Roelker, Nancy Lyman. "The Appeal of Calvinism to French Noblewomen in the Sixteenth Century." *The Journal of Interdisciplinary History* 2 (Spring 1972): 391–418.

Roget, Amédée. *Histoire du peuple de Genève depuis la Réforme jusqu'à l'escalade.* 7 vols. Geneva: J. Jullien, 1870–1883.

Rousselle, Aline. *Porneia: On Desire and the Body in Antiquity.* Translated by Felicia Pheasant. London: Basil Blackwell Publisher, 1988.

Russell, Letty. *Church in the Round: Feminist Interpretation of the Church.* Louisville, Ky.: Westminster/John Knox Press, 1993.

Said, Edward. *The World, the Text, and the Critic.* Cambridge, Mass.: Harvard University Press, 1983.

Salmon, John A. H. "Cicero and Tacitus in Renaissance France." In *Renaissance and Revolt: Essays in the Intellectual and Social History of Early Modern France.* New York: Cambridge University Press, 1987.

———. *The French Wars of Religion: How Important Were Religious Factors?* Edited by J.H.M. Salmon. Boston: Heath, 1967.

———. *Renaissance and Revolt: Essays in the Intellectual and Social History of Early Modern France.* London: Cambridge University Press, 1987.

———. *Society in Crisis: France in the Sixteenth Century.* New York: St. Martin's Press, 1975.

Screech, Michael. *Rabelais.* Ithaca, N.Y.: Cornell University Press, 1979.

Searle, John R. *Speech Acts: An Essay in the Philosophy of Language*. New York: Cambridge University Press, 1969.

Seigel, Jerrold E. *Rhetoric and Philosophy in Renaissance Humanism: The Union of Eloquence and Wisdom*. Princeton, N.J.: Princeton University Press, 1968.

Selinger, Suzanne. *Calvin against Himself: An Inquiry in Intellectual History*. Hamden, Conn.: Archon Books, 1984.

Shaull, Richard. *The Reformation and Liberation Theology: Insight for the Challenges Today*. Louisville, Ky.: Westminster/John Knox Press, 1991.

Shoeck, Richard J. "Lawyers and Rhetoric in Sixteenth-Century England." In *Renaissance Eloquence: Studies in the Theory and Practice of Renaissance Rhetoric*, edited by James Murphy, Berkeley: University of California Press, 1983.

Shumaker, Wayne. *The Occult Sciences in the Renaissance: A Study in Intellectual Patterns*. Berkeley: University of California Press, 1972.

Skinner, Quentin. "The Origins of the Calvinist Theory of Revolution." In *After the Reformation, Essays in Honor of J. H. Hexter*, edited by Barbara C. Malament, Philadelphia: University of Pennsylvania Press, 1980.

Smits, Luchesius. *Saint Augustin dans l'oeuvre de Jean Calvin*. 2 vols. Assen: Van Gorcum and Co., 1957.

Spitz, Lewis. *The Religious Renaissance of the German Humanists*. Cambridge, Mass.: Harvard University Press, 1963.

Starn, Randolph. *Contrary Commonwealth: The Theme of Exile in Medieval and Renaissance Italy*. Berkeley: University of California Press, 1982.

Stauffer, Richard. *Dieu, la création et la providence dans la prédication de Calvin*. Berne: Peter Lang, 1972.

Struever, Nancy. *The Language of History in the Renaissance: Rhetoric and Historical Consciousness in Florentine Humanism*. Princeton, N.J.: Princeton University Press, 1970.

———. "Lorenza Valla: Humanist Rhetoric and the Critique of the Classical Languages of Morality." In *Renaissance Eloquence: Studies in the Theory and Practice of Renaissance Rhetoric*, edited by James Murphy, Berkeley: University of California Press, 1983.

Tanner, Kathryn. *The Politics of God*. Minneapolis: Fortress Press, 1992.

———. "The Practical Force of Theological Ideas: The Case of Predestination." (Unpublished essay, 1985)

Thiemann, Ronald. *Revelation and Theology: The Gospel as Narrated Promise*. Notre Dame, Ind.: Notre Dame Press, 1985.

Thomas, John Newton. "The Place of Natural Theology in the Thought of John Calvin." *Journal of Religious Thought* 15 (1957–1958): 107–36.

Tillich, Paul. *Systematic Theology*. Vol. 1. Chicago: University of Chicago Press, 1951.

Tompkins, Jane P. *Reader Response Criticism: From Formalism to Post-Structuralism*. Baltimore: Johns Hopkins University Press, 1980.

Torrance, T. F. *Calvin's Doctrine of Man*. London: Lutterworth Press, 1952.

———. *The Hermeneutics of John Calvin*. Edinburgh: Scottish Academic Press, 1988.

Tracy, James. *The Politics of Erasmus: A Pacifist Intellectual and His Political Milieu*. Toronto: University of Toronto Press, 1978.

Trinh, T. Minh-Ha. *Woman, Native, Other: Writing, Postcoloniality, and Feminism*. Bloomington: Indiana University Press, 1989.

Trinkaus, Charles. *"In Our Image and Likeness"*: *Humanity and Dignity in Italian Humanist Thought*, Vol. 1. Chicago: University of Chicago Press, 1970.

———. "Renaissance Problems in Calvin's Theology." *Studies in the Renaissance* 1 (1954): 59–80.

———. *The Scope of Renaissance Humanism.* Ann Arbor: University of Michigan Press, 1983.

———. "Themes for a Renaissance Anthropology." In *The Renaissance: Essays in Interpretation*, 83–125. London and New York: Methuen, 1982.

Tuvé, Rosemond. *Elizabethan and Metaphysical Imagery.* Chicago: University of Chicago Press, 1947.

Ullmann, Berthold L. *The Humanism of Coluccio Salutati.* Padua: Editrice Antenore, 1963.

Ullmann, Walter. *Medieval Foundations of Renaissance Humanism.* Ithaca, N.Y.: Cornell University Press, 1977.

Valesio, Paolo. *Novantigua: Rhetorics as a Contemporary Theory.* Bloomington: Indiana University Press, 1980.

Van Til, Cornelius. *A Christian Theory of Knowledge.* Grand Rapids: Baker Book House, 1969.

Viard, P. Z. *André Alciat: 1492–1550.* Paris: Société anonyme du Recueil Sirey, 1926.

Vickers, Brian, and Nancy Struever. *Rhetoric and the Pursuit of Truth: Language Change in the Seventeenth and Eighteenth Centuries.* Papers read at Clark Library Seminar, 8 March 1980. Los Angeles: University of California Press, 1985.

Vos, Arvin. *Aquinas, Calvin, and Contemporary Protestant Thought: A Critique of Protestant Views on the Thought of Thomas Aquinas.* Grand Rapids: Wm. B. Eerdmans Publishing Co., 1985.

Walker, D. P. *The Ancient Theology: Studies in Christian Platonism from the Fifteenth to Eighteenth Century.* London: Duckworth, 1972.

Walker, Williston. *John Calvin: The Organizer of Reformed Protestantism, 1509–64.* Translated by N. Weiss. 3d ed. New York: Schocken Books, 1969.

Wallace, Ronald. *Calvin's Doctrine of the Christian Life.* Grand Rapids: Wm. B. Eerdmans Publishing Co., 1959.

———. *Calvin's Doctrine of the Word and Sacrament.* Edinburgh: Oliver & Boyd, 1953.

Walzer, Michael. *The Revolution of the Saints: A Study in the Origins of Radical Politics.* Cambridge, Mass.: Harvard University Press, 1965.

Wencelius, Léon. "Le classicisme de Calvin." *Humanisme et Renaissance* 5 (1938): 231–46.

Wendel, François. *Calvin et l'humanisme.* Paris: Presses Universitaires de France, 1976.

———. *Calvin: Origins and Development of His Religious Thought.* Translated by Philip Mairet. New York: Harper & Row, 1963.

Wernle, Paul. *Calvin.* Vol. 3 of *Der evangelische Glaube nach den Hauptschriften der Reformatoren.* Tübingen: J.C.B. Mohr, 1919.

Werpehowski, William. "Ad Hoc Apologetics." *Journal of Religion* 66, no. 3 (1986): 282–301.

Williams, George. *The Radical Reformation.* Philadelphia: Westminster Press, 1962.

Willis, E. David. *Calvin's Catholic Christology: The Function of the So-Called "Extra Calvinisticum."* Studies in Medieval and Reformation Thought, vol. 2. Leiden: E. J. Brill, 1966.

————. "Rhetoric and Responsibility in Calvin's Theology." In *The Context of Contemporary Theology*, edited by Alexander J. McKelway and E. David Willis, Atlanta: John Knox Press, 1974.

————. "The Social Context of the 1536 Edition of Calvin's *Institutes*." In *In Honor of John Calvin, 1509–1564*, edited by E. J. Furcha. Papers from the 1986 International Calvin Symposium, McGill University. ARC Supplement. Montreal: Faculty of Religious Studies, McGill University, 1987.

Wirth, Jean. " 'Libertines' et 'Epicuriens': Aspects de l'irréligion au 16e siècle." *Bibliothèque d'Humanisme et de Renaissance* 39 (1977): 601–27.

Yates, Frances. *The Occult Philosophy in the Elizabethan Age*. London: Routledge & Kegan Paul, 1979.

Zanta, Léontine. *La Renaissance du Stoïcisme au 16e siècle*. Geneva: Slatkine Reprints, 1975.

INDEX